Pre-Industrial Societies

NEW PERSPECTIVES ON THE PAST

General Editor
R. I. Moore

Advisory Editors
Gerald Aylmer
Tanya Luhrmann
David Turley
Patrick Wormald

PUBLISHED

IN PREPARATION

PRE-INDUSTRIAL SOCIETIES

Patricia Crone

Basil Blackwell

Copyright © Patricia Crone, 1989
First published 1989

Basil Blackwell Ltd
108 Cowley Road, Oxford, OX4 1JF, UK

Basil Blackwell Inc.
3 Cambridge Center
Cambridge, MA 02142, USA

British Library Cataloguing in Publication Data

A CIP catalogue record for this book is available from the British Library.

Library of Congress Cataloging in Publication Data

Crone, Patricia, 1945–
    Pre-industrial societies / Patricia Crone.
        p.   cm. – (New perspectives on the past)
    Bibliography: p.
    Includes index.
    ISBN 0-631-15661-5 – ISBN 0-631-15662-3 (pbk.)
    1. Economic history.   2. Social history.   3. Political science.
    4. Europe – Economic conditions.   5. Europe – Social conditions.
    6. Europe – Politics and government.   I. Title.   II. Series: New
    perspectives on the past (Basil Blackwell Publisher)
    HC21.C76   1989
    330.9 – dc19

Typeset in 10 on 12 pt. Plantin
by Graphicraft Typsetters Limited, H.K.
Printed in Great Britain by
Billing & Sons Ltd., Worcester

Contents

For Martin,
who died on December 1, 1988

Editor's Preface

Ignorance has many forms, and all of them are dangerous. In the nineteenth and twentieth centuries our chief effort has been to free ourselves from tradition and superstition in large questions, and from the error in small ones upon which they rest, by redefining the fields of knowledge and evolving in each the distinctive method appropriate for its cultivation. The achievement has been incalculable, but not without cost. As each new subject has developed a specialist vocabulary to permit rapid and precise reference to its own common and rapidly growing stock of ideas and discoveries, and come to require a greater depth of expertise from its specialists, scholars have been cut off by their own erudition not only from mankind at large, but from the findings of workers in other fields, and even in other parts of their own. Isolation diminishes not only the usefulness but the soundness of their labours when energies are exclusively devoted to eliminating the small blemishes so embarrassingly obvious to the fellow-professional on the next patch, instead of avoiding others that may loom much larger from, as it were, a more distant vantage point. Marc Bloch observed a contradiction in the attitudes of many historians: 'when it is a question of ascertaining whether or not some human act has really taken place, they cannot be too painstaking. If they proceed to the reasons for that act, they are content with the merest appearance, ordinarily founded upon one of those maxims of common-place psychology which are neither more nor less true than their opposites.' When the historian peeps across the fence he sees his neighbours, in literature, perhaps, or sociology, just as complacent in relying on historical platitudes which are naive, simplistic or obsolete.

New Perspectives on the Past represents not a reaction against specialization, which would be a romantic absurdity, but an attempt to come to terms with it. The authors, of course, are specialists, and their thought and conclusions rest on the foundation of distinguished professional research in different periods and fields. Here they will free themselves, as far as it is possible, from the restraints of subject, region and period within which they ordinarily and necessarily work, to discuss problems simply as problems, and not as 'history' or 'politics' or 'economics'. They will write for specialists, because we are all specialists now, and for laymen, because we are all laymen.

'The World We Have Lost', before the universal transformation set in train during the last century or so by the advent of economies based on large-scale industrial production and global exchange, mass politics and culture and the human conquest of nature, is already almost beyond our grasp. The study of its history sets a more formidable challenge to the imagination of every successive generation of students as social and cultural conditions which their great-grandparents took for granted vanish into oblivion. We may evade the struggle with the obscure and forbidding ideologies, the bizarre behaviour and incomprehensible anxieties of existences organized quite differently from our own by reducing them to a tattle of pasteboard passions and ephemeral intrigues, or by dismissing them as "irrelevant", a domain of dusty antiquarians. Such trivialization grows daily more tempting, and daily more dangerous. The nature of pre-industrial society and the manner of its modernization – and the one can hardly be grasped if the other is misunderstood – are fundamental to every social science: it is not only our past but our present, the field upon which the most dangerous conflicts of the late twentieth century are being played out. There are, of course, many fine introductions to particular societies and civilizations and their histories, but they do not teach us how to think about pre-industrial societies as such, to recreate the context without which the event or conflict or triumph of which we read is incomprehensible. We all need a guidebook which combines the generality of social theory with the concreteness, the sense of reality, of good history. Patricia Crone has summoned an extraordinary combination of broad learning and bold reasoning to provide it. It will help new visitors to the pre-industrial world to make sense of much that looks at first like nonsense. Those who thought they knew their way around it will have to think again.

R. I. Moore

Preface

The aim of this book is to give students of complex pre-industrial societies an understanding of the constraints under which such societies have operated and the uniformities to which the constraints have given rise. No attempt is made to analyse the specific organization of any one society, let alone all of them, and history is reduced to the role of providing examples. The book endeavours to tell its readers what sort of patterns they should expect to find in the past, not what sort of patterns they will actually find in their particular fields. It is motivated by the consideration that pre-industrial societies evidently should not be approached in the light of modern presuppositions, but that modern students cannot be expected to know which of their own usually unconscious presuppositions they ought to forget. The book thinks away some essential features of industrial civilization and spells out the implications of their absence. The essential features are exceedingly simple, but the implications go far beyond what, in my experience, the average student can work out for himself.

All generalizations are simplifications, and a book which seeks to generalize about societies from the Sumerians to the Manchus must positively oversimplify. I make no apology for this: oversimplifications are precisely what beginners need. If you have no notion what a forest is, it helps to learn that it is a large area covered with trees which make it green, cool and good hiding in, though such a definition would be useless to a forester. It is generally assumed that students of history at university level do know what a forest is, so that they can be plunged straight into the study of this or that particular variety. But mostly they do not, and students of societies which are both pre-industrial and non-European are at a particular disadvantage: they cannot distinguish pre-industrial features of the most common kind from those peculiar to the civilizations with which they are concerned; their sense of what is normal and what unusual (and thus in need of further exploration) is deficient. The book attempts to remedy this deficiency by sketching a picture of what one might call pre-industrial normality; but I must stress that it does so without intellectual pretentions: it offers no stringent model or ideal type, merely a rough-and-ready guide.

I should like to thank Mark Elvin, Ernest Gellner, John Hall, Martin Hinds, Bob Moore and Fritz Zimmermann for extremely helpful comments on earlier drafts; I am particularly indebted to Bob Moore, whose assistance went far beyond that normally volunteered by series editors and several of whose points I have incorporated wholesale. If the result is faulty, it is not for lack of good advice.

PC

1

Introduction: What is a Complex Society?

Industry is a mode of production which first appeared in late eighteenth-century England and which proceeded utterly to transform the word at large. Most human societies today are either industrial or engaged in the process of industrializing; such wholly non-industrial societies as still exist are archaic pockets doomed to disappear in so far as they have not been placed under preservation order. Most people, and certainly all members of Western civilization, are thus born into a world which differs radically from that of their ancestors, with the result that most of human history is a closed book to them. Human history is not very long: the species to which we belong (*Homo sapiens*) has only existed for some 50,000 or, according to some recent finds, 100,000 years. But of those 50,000 or 100,000 years only some 200 years in one part of the world, elsewhere far fewer, have been lived under industrial conditions. We all take the world in which we were born for granted and think of the human condition as ours. This is a mistake. The vast mass of human experience had been made under quite different conditions.

The present work is an attempt to summarize those conditions, or rather some of them. It does not deal with the entire pre-industrial past, partly because there is too much of it and more particularly because primitive (or simple) and civilized (or complex) societies are too different to be treated together. This book is about the latter, and I shall henceforth use the word 'pre-industrial' as a shorthand for 'pre-industrial of the civilized kind'. (Economic historians sometimes distinguish societies on the eve of industrialization from other societies without industry by labelling the former pre-industrial and the latter agrarian; in this book, however, the terms pre-industrial and agrarian will be used synonymously.)

The civilized societies of the past resemble those of modern times, but in some ways the similarity is deceptive. One cannot come to grips with them without thinking away modernity and working out the consequences of its absence. This is precisely what we shall be doing in the following chapters, but before we start, we need to know what a 'civilized' society is. I should like to answer this question by inviting the reader to participate in a simple thought experiment.

Imagine that you and some friends and relatives of yours are ship-wrecked on an uninhabited island with no hope of ever getting back. What would you do? Obviously, you would have to start by finding something to eat. The ecology of the island might be such that you could feed yourselves by gathering fruit, berries and other edible plant material, supplementing your diet by hunting or fishing. But if you could, you would start growing things, for agriculture makes for a more dependable food supply than hunting and gathering: cereals such as grain, rice and millet can be stored; and your sedentary mode of life would enable to you to store both these and other things on a scale impossible to those who have to move to wherever prey and plants happen to be available in a particular season. (You might of course still engage in some hunting or fishing from time to time.)

Having solved the problem of food, what sort of organization would you need? Given that you would be both few (indeed friends and relatives) and devoid of external enemies, you obviously would not need much organization at all. You might have to meet from time to time for decisions on issues affecting all of you (such as whether or not to set up a granary for use in years of shortage) and also for the settlement of disputes threatening to disrupt the general peace (such as your claim that your neighbour had stolen part of your harvest); and no doubt the opinions of some would carry greater weight than those of others: some would be leaders and others would be led. But you would hardly need a *formal* leader. Your society would be stateless, or indeed acephalous, 'headless'. It would also be extremely primitive, that is to say lacking in social, economic, political and other differentiation on the one hand and poor in culture, both material and intellectual, on the other.

But now imagine that a very large number of you are shipwrecked on that island, or that the island is not uninhabited, but on the contrary full of hostile natives. If there were thousands of you, you might split up into several small acephalous societies, but then you might start quarreling over land, boundaries, noise or whatever. If so, you would need more in the way of political organization. You might also find that some societies had access to commodities that others lacked (such as salt, precious stones or metals), in which case you would start exchanging goods with each other, or in other words trading; some might then get very much richer than others, both within each community and between them, and some people might stop growing food altogether, earning enough by trade to buy it from others. Your internal homogeneity would be lost, meaning that disagreements between you would intensify; and the balance of power between the various communities would also be affected, meaning that some might try to dominate others. Under such circumstances, too, you would need much more in the way of organization. One the other hand, if the island were full of hostile natives, you would not be able to split up: you would have to stick together and coordinate your activities. And this would also force you to become more organized.

Let us assume that you have retained your internal homogeneity, but need a formal leader to coordinate your activities vis-à-vis dangerous outsiders: you elect a chief. Your chief might be able to go on producing his own food. (In fact, one would scarcely call him a chief, as opposed to a king or the like, if the did not.) But if his official duties were too time-consuming for him to engage in food production, how would he be able to live? Obviously, you would have to grow his food for him. But your chief might also need some people to help him on a full-time basis. For example, the natives might be so dangerous that it would be a good idea for some of you to form a standing army. If so, the rest of you would have to grow food for these soldiers too. But how much extra food should each of you produce, how should it be collected, how much should the recipients receive, and who should keep accounts of what is due and what has been handed over? Some of you would have to become administrators, and the rest of you would have to produce food on their behalf on top of everything else. But then you might find that you needed buildings for the quartering of the soldiers, the filing of administrative records, the storage of grain handed over, and so on; and the soldiers would need arms, clothes and cooking pots, while the administrators would need their pens and writing paper. So some of you would start producing buildings, pots, pans, clothes, arms, writing material and so on over and above your own needs, or indeed specialize in such production in return for some of that food which the soldiers and administrators have received from the rest of you; some would start trading in all these goods, and no doubt others would start specializing in the transmission of skills (e.g. teaching the administrators to read and write). The burden of feeding the artisans, traders and teachers would ultimately also fall on those of you who have remained cultivators. By this stage it is unlikely that you would still be thinking in terms of food and goods rather than a symbolic notation for such things, that is money. And since the ruler (the former chief) and his top military and civil servants would ultimately dispose of all the produce and/or money you hand over (that is, your taxes), they would also have acquired the habit of spending a great deal of it on all those goods and services which, though not directly required by their official functions, nonetheless enhance their status as well as sweeten their lives: sumptuous palaces, beautifully crafted furniture, utensils and instruments, pretty pictures, sculpture, music, poetry and other literature, medical attention and so forth. So some of you would have become artists, poets, musicians, dancers, doctors and other kinds of professionals, and the rest of you would indirectly have to pay for their detachment from the food production too. By now few of you would remember what primitive conditions were like. You would have acquired a state, and political organization would have caused your society to change beyond recognition. By now it would indeed be characterized by social, political, economic and institutional differentiation; and both material and intellectual culture would have become highly developed too. In short, your society would now be described as civilized.

You may well ask at precisely what point your society would be described as civilized rather than primitive, but this is a question to which there can be no one answer: different scholars will choose different cut-off points depending on the use to which they wish to put their definitions. As far as this book is concerned, the question can simply be ignored: the analysis will focus on societies so complex that they have passed the cut-off point by any definition. However, even the most complex version of your island society was an agrarian society rather than an industrial one: agriculture was the source of most of its wealth, manufacture supplying only a little and modern industry being completely absent. The end-product of your second shipwreck, in short, was a pre-industrial society of the civilized kind.

I had better emphasize that the thought experiment should *not* be taken as an account of how the first civilizations in history arose. For one thing, we landed on our island fully aware of such things as agriculture, writing, administration and government. We reconstituted them in our new setting, but we did not invent them from scratch, and it is by no means obvious that we *would* have invented them if we had not known about them. With hindsight it is easy to see what needs they fulfil, but needs can be met in different ways, or left unfulfilled, and it is clear from the historical record that special circumstances had to come together in order for the elements of complex organization to emerge. For another thing, the thought experiment completely fails to account for one element of fundamental importance in all human societies (and in the emergence of complex organization too), that is religion. No story in the style of *Robinson Crusoe* or *Lord of the Flies* can highlight the factors behind the emergence of religion because humans have religion (or at least a disposition for it) regardless of the type of society in which they live. Obviously, they do not have the same *kind* of religion in different societies, but there is no way in which we could have varied the conditions on our island so as to explain why they have religion at all: they had religion even before the present human species had evolved. Why this should be so is a fascinating question which cannot be properly discussed in this book, though I shall revert to the subject in chapter 7.

Whatever the circumstances behind the emergence of the first civilizations, however, all primitive societies develop into complex ones by division of labour, and this is the point which the thought experiment is meant to illustrate. We assumed that you needed someone to co-ordinate your activities for purposes of defence against outsiders, no more and no less: so some of you undertook to go on cultivating and others undertook to become co-ordinators. This was your first division of labour and its consequences were immense; your society continued to change, and all the subsequent changes were further divisions of labour: more and more people went into special occupations.

In historical fact, some measure of internal differntiation has usually preceded the arrival of state structures, not just followed it; and the arrival of state structures has not always sufficed to push a society through the entire evolution from primitivity to civilization: many have stopped at intermediary points. But the fact remains that rulers are the outcome of specialization (they specialize in power) and that this specialization is a crucial ingredient in the development of complex organization. On the one hand, there is a limit to the amount of differentiation a society can undergo without either disintegrating or else arranging for overall co-ordination of its members. The more people differ from one another, the more they come to depend on formal rules for peaceful interaction; and the greater the importance of such rules, the greater the need for an agency capable of enforcing them. States are thus a precondition for all that social, cultural and institutional complexity that we are in the habit of calling civilization. On the other hand, the very fact that rulers are specialists in power means that they are apt utterly to transform the society in which they emerge: states are not just a precondition for, but also an active element in the evolution of civilization. Let us look a bit more closely, then, at precisely what their emergence entails.

The appearance of rulers or, in impersonal terms, the state, means that hitherto dispersed power is concentrated, be it in one man, several or a set of offices adding up to a ruling institution. There were no concentrations of power in our stateless society: we did not even have a chief. Nobody could coerce anyone else, or rather nobody could do so for long. Some might have more forceful personalities, or more relatives and friends, than others, and some might reap good harvests in years of general crop failure; but such advantages were too transitory to make for permanent accumulations of power.

By the same token, nobody had the ability to impose order on everyone else. Enforcement of the rules thus rested on *self-help*. If you had run away with my water-skin on that island, it would have been up to me to get it back, be it by running after you and beating you up or by persuading friends and relatives to do so. Actually, given that we were so few, it is unlikely that I would have used force: everybody would have tried to persuade the two of us to stop quarrelling, and we would have found it difficult to hold out against everyone else. But if our numbers had multiplied to the point where disputes ceased to be in the nature of family quarrels, I would undoubtedly have had recourse to violence. Naturally, there would have been rules regarding its use: otherwise our society would have collapsed. Primitive societies generally regulate the use of self-help with reference to kinship: who should help whom, under what circumstances and when, turns on how people are related. If we had multiplied on our acephalous island, we would probably have evolved some form of tribal organization too. But primitive societies are never against the use of self-help; on the contrary, they rely on it. They merely try to mitigate the disruptive effects of its use.

By contrast, states necessarily curtail the use of self-help. What we did on our island was essentially to pool our power in a special agency manned by our ruler. In other words, we renounced the use of self-help and empowered someone else to keep order among us: if we disagreed, or if action was needed against the natives, then he had the right to decide what should be done and to coerce us into doing it. If you run away with my computer now on our modern British island, I am neither expected nor allowed to beat you up, and the only people I may ask to use force against you are the police. In fact, the state has been defined as an agency for the maintenance of internal order and external defence distinguished by its monopoly on the right to use force; and this is a helpful definition even if it is not quite correct: feudal states, for example, did not claim such a monopoly, let alone possess the means to enforce it; and states of other kinds have also tolerated self-help on a considerable scale. Other definitions accordingly single out acceptance of a final authority as the essence of statehood: though self-help may persist, the state has the *ultimate* right to decide what should be done; and though it may not monopolize the use of force, it can mobilize *enough* means of violence to retain its position as ultimate arbiter. Most definitions specify other features too (notably territoriality: states are demarcated in territorial terms even though they may be, and indeed mostly have been, defined with reference to dynastic, personal or religious loyalties). But whatever the best definition of the state may be, rulers would usually prefer their subjects to be disarmed, except by special licence, and forbidden to use force, except in self-defence (narrowly defined).

The division of labour between producers and maintainers of order is thus one conducive to a highly unequal relationship. Specialization does not always have this effect. If I grow cotton and you grow wheat, the chances are that I will be no more dependent on you than you are on me: the relationship between us will be one of complementarity and interdependence, not simply dependence. And in principle, of course, the same is true if I produce food and you keep order: where would you be if I stopped paying taxes? Where would I be if you let the hostile natives in? But in practice I have specialized in the production of wealth and you in the exercise of power, so that if I stop paying taxes you will react by forcibly *extracting* them; and if you decide to let the natives in there is little I can do about it. In practice our relationship is thus one in which you are the boss and I am the dependant.

All we wanted, back on our primitive island, was to defend ourselves: we set up some of us as rulers to preserve all of us. But in so doing we have exposed ourselves to what one might call the dilemma of the golden goose: one cannot specialize in the production of wealth (or for that matter children) without becoming both highly desirable *and* defenceless; the very fact that labour is divided up dictates that gold-bearing creatures are weak. Industrialization greatly modifies this dilemma, and there were occasional societies in pre-industrial times in which food producers retained a measure of political power. To this must be added that there are many different types of power in all human societies (military, economic, political, ideological and many more), so that history never reduces to a simple story of food producers versus rulers; the thought experiment is highly simplistic in its disregard of this fact. But even so, the division of labour from which the state ensued almost invariably transformed the free agriculturalists of primitive society into miserable *peasants*, that is to say rural cultivators whose surplus was forcibly transferred to a dominant group of rulers. ('Surplus' should not be envisaged as something left over or going spare: whatever the state and/or landlords could extract from the peasants in the form of taxes and/or rent is defined as surplus as long as the transfer did not kill off the peasants altogether.)

The sheer emergence of rulers thus differentiates society in terms of power and wealth alike: some are forced to pay and others are empowered to receive in return for political services which may or may not be performed. Contrary to what our thought experiment may suggest, rulers have not commonly owed their existence to social contracts whereby some undertook to grow food for others in return for political services, as opposed to a combination of internal developments and external pressures which caused some to come up on top and the rest to have no choice but to pay. Either way, however, the rulers' control of the agricultural surplus was crucial for the institutionalization of their power. It was a regular supply of wealth (be it in cash or kind) which allowed them to buy all those military and administrative services which they needed to make their dominance permanent. And it was precisely because their dominance was permanent that society typically continued to be further differentiated after their emergence. They could force their subjects to render more and more services and payments for investment in the state apparatus (in the form of roads, arms factories, larger bureaucracies, better policing or whatever), as well as for the purchase of pomp, luxury, art and entertainment.

In short, once some have power and others have none, the former will force the latter to pay for all kinds of goods, institutions and developments which nobody had even thought about before the state emerged, but which the state, or rather those who man it, dream up in the course of mulling over how best to perform their duties and/or how best to hang on to such power as they have. (To those involved, the two desiderata will appear as synonymous.) Differently put, coercion has played a massive role in the development of civilization.

The reader may well wonder, as have some political scientists, why anyone ever consented to the formation of states: who would not rather be his own master on a par with members of primitive societies? The answer, of course, is that people do not normally foresee the long-term effects of their own actions, and that in so far as they do, circumstances limit their choice. The Sumerians, who developed the first state structures on earth some 5000 years ago, evidently did not know what sort of Frankenstein's monster they were creating; and once the state existed, it proved to be so powerful an organization that it was bound gradually to absorb mankind at large, however much mankind at large might deplore it.

The state is a powerful type of organization because it enables human activity to be co-ordinated on a scale impossible to achieve in societies devoid of coercive agencies. A state can co-ordinate the actions of its subjects for warfare, defence, internal policing, the settlement of disputes, the creation of means of communication, the improvement of the means of production, precautionary measures against famine and disease, and many other aims (including ugly ones). It also allows for material and cultural developments that most of us appreciate. In stateless societies, by contrast, nothing much can be done unless everybody agrees, which is rarely the case (attempts at coercion by the stronger parties will simply cause the dissenters to secede); and the undifferentiated nature of society also means that the level of material and intellectual culture remains low: computers are unlikely to be invented in a society in which everybody is a food producer. Naturally, many states have only been able to perform a fraction of the above-mentioned roles, and all pre-industrial states were weak by the standards of their modern counterparts, as we shall see. Nonetheless, stateless societies confronted by states have almost always had to imitate the political organization of their neighbours in order to survive.

But of course state structures are purchased at the cost of problems. How can a complex society be kept together? What ultimate aim should it pursue? Who should make what decisions, and with what powers of coercion? How should the rest be induced to obey? To these and other questions an immense variety of answers have been given in both theory and practice since the state emerged, but in practice pre-industrial conditions impose certain constraints on what can be done and tried out, so that there are striking uniformities behind the otherwise bewildering variety of organizations attested for pre-modern times. It is to these uniformities that we must now turn.

Part I
The Pre-Industrial Pattern

2
Socio-economic Organization

To think away modern industry is to think away an enormous amount of wealth. Industry generates immense amounts of wealth because mechanical devices driven by inanimate fuel under human supervision are far more productive than are humans on their own: a machine tended by twenty workers can produce more pots in a single year than can twenty potters in a lifetime, at a fraction of the cost of maintaining twenty potters from youth to death. The pre-industrial world was not of course unfamiliar with mechanical devices, and some of these devices were driven by inanimate energy too (water wheels, windmills, ships); but most of them depended on human or animal energy for their operation, and though they certainly increased the productivity of human labour, the industrial breakthrough freed production from its dependence on animal and human muscle on an unprecedented scale, generating the huge quantity and range of goods which we have come to take for granted. By our standards, the products of the pre-industrial world were both few and very expensive.

Given the absence of modern industry, agriculture was by far the most important source of wealth, sometimes the only one. But the output of agriculture before the arrival of industry was also low: without mechanization, mass produced fertilizer, scientific plant breeding and other know-how, it did not yield very much. In most parts of the world it yielded significantly more in the eighteenth century than it did in the eighth (though there were areas of the Middle East where the reverse was the case); and this growth was a precondition for the industrial revolution in that it enabled more food producers to leave the land in order to become factory workers. But the enormous output characteristic of modern agriculture in the West is the result of this revolution. The average world farmer is still incapable of feeding more than five people, but the average farmer of Western Europe feeds twenty while his counterpart in USA feeds almost sixty. USA is a net food exporter, but without mechanization it would not be able to feed more than a fraction of its own population.

However, it is not merely modern industry that we must think away: modern means of communication and transportation were also absent. The pre-industrial world had no radios, telephones, walkie-talkies, telegrams, telex, fax or other instruments for rapid exchange of information at a distance, no computers for its processing, storage and retrieval, and no cars, trains, or planes for rapid dispatch of people or goods. There were not even any bicycles. People, goods and news alike travelled slowly. They could not travel faster than the fastest animal unless they went by sea, but even wind-driven ships moved slowly by modern standards (60–90 miles per day in medieval Europe), and more slowly still when they had to be propelled by oars. Transport by land tended to be even slower. Since the ship was the only vehicle driven by inanimate energy, maritime transport was not just the fastest, but also the cheapest available: in third-century Rome it was cheaper to ship grain from Alexandria to Rome at a distance of some 1250 miles than to transport it 50 miles by land. But all forms of transportation were slow and expensive by our standards.

The fact that agriculture and manufacture alike produced little meant that all pre-industrial societies were dominated by scarcity. (I must ask the reader to remember that throughout this book the word pre-industrial is used as a shorthand for 'pre-industrial of the civilized kind': hunter-gatherers and primitive agriculturalists were not usually poor in the sense of barely capable of fulfilling their basic needs. Scarcity in this sense is the outcome of complex organization.) At the same time, the inadequate nature of the means of transportation and communication meant that most people lived in very local worlds. These are the two fundamental features to which we shall return time and again. We may start by considering their implications at the level of socio-economic organization.

Populations

Pre-industrial populations were small. The population of England in c.1500 is estimated at 3–5 million, as opposed to some 55 million today, while the population of Egypt, said to be 37 million in 1975, is assumed to have been no more than 2.5 million in 1789. The Roman empire is believed only to have accommodated some 50–60 million people at the beginning of the Christian era, and the population of China is assumed to have been of roughly the same size until the eleventh century, when it may have reached 140 million; there were still only about 430 million Chinese in the mid-nineteenth century, as against some 1000 million today.

In most parts of the pre-industrial world the birthrate was high, but so was the death rate, and gains made in good years were regularly wiped out by famine, disease, war and other disasters in bad ones. Primitive means of transportation, inadequate roads and deficient marketing systems meant that even local crop failures could be fatal, one locality suffering shortages while neighbouring ones had plenty. Irregular food supplies clearly played a greater role in keeping the numbers down than the absence of modern medicine (though the accidental absence or disapperance of deadly diseases certainly helped), for in most parts of the world the population explosion, or in other words the accelerating population growth which has continued until today, began long before medicine had acquired its modern efficacy: in India it is supposed to have started as early as the sixteenth century, in China in the eighteenth, and it was also in the eighteenth century that it started in Europe.

At all events, the pre-industrial world was one in which human beings were relatively thin on the ground. They shared the ground with numerous animals which they have since eradicated, relegated to marginal areas or confined to zoos. One could still hunt lions and cheetahs in Crusader Syria, and wolves were still a menace in several parts of western Europe in the early nineteenth century.

Peasants

The low output of agriculture meant that the vast majority of people had to be peasants. Peasants were not of course the only food producers: fishermen, hunters and pastoralists (that is rearers of sheep, cattle or other livestock) also contributed their share. But the contribution of the latter was neither stable nor substantial enough to keep a complex society going. It was on agriculture, and above all on cereals such as grain, rice, millet and maize, that civilization rested (whence the fact that the term 'agrarian' is frequently used as a synonym for 'pre-industrial').

In some societies practically everyone was a peasant apart from the ruling elite, typically less than 2 per cent of the population. More commonly, some 10 per cent of the population were able to leave the production of food. But western Europe is believed to have supported no less than 15 per cent of its population in occupations other than agriculture as early as c.1300, the proportion having risen to about 20 per cent by c.1500; and it is also said to have risen to some 20 per cent in sixteenth-century Japan. Statistics such as these are largely guesswork, and most societies have left so little relevant information that it is hazardous even to guess, but the contrast with industrialized societies is glaring. Only 2.2 per cent of the working population are engaged in agriculture in contemporary USA, barely 3 per cent in Britain, and no more than 4–10 per cent in western Europe. Over half the working population are still engaged in agriculture in many other parts of the world, but figures as high as 80 per cent are becoming few and far between. In fully industrial countries, very small numbers of food producers suffice to keep very large numbers in other occupations; indeed, very small numbers produce too much.

Cities

What with some 80–90 per cent of the population being made up of peasants, the pre-industrial world was a very rural one. Cities were either few or small, or both. Urban populations of several millions were unknown (though some believe Hang-chou of thirteenth-century China to have been an exception), and even cities accommodating just one million people were rare. Most of them owed their size to the fact that they were centres of vast empires: thus imperial Rome, Constantinople, Baghdad, Peking and other Chinese capitals are all believed to have reached the million mark, though this, as everything else to do with figures in the pre-modern world, is disputed. But even huge empires could rarely maintain more than one city of that size (China being once more believed to have been an exception). The first medium-sized country to rival empires in respect of urbanization was eighteenth-century Japan, the capital of which (Edo, now Tokyo) accommodated over one million inhabitants, while two provincial towns (Kyoto and Osaka) accommodated about half a million each. But in this respect Japan was unique. Eighteenth-century European capitals, for example, only had about half a million inhabitants at the most (thus London and Paris); provincial towns were much smaller, and only 3 per cent of Europe's population at the time lived in large towns as against 10 per cent of Japan's.

Urban growth was hampered by the fact that inadequate means of transportation made provisioning difficult. Bulky commodities such as foodstuffs were particularly slow and expensive to move unless they could be sent by sea. Hence cities tended to be located either on rivers or canals (which coped with their water supplies too) or on the coast, as were the above-mentioned Hang-chou, Rome, Constantinople, Baghdad and Peking, as well as most other famous cities of the pre-modern world (London, Paris, Florence, Venice, Athens, Alexandria, Cairo, Edo, Kyoto, Osaka, etc). But even so, the provisioning of a modern megalopolis would have been beyond the capacity of any pre-industrial society. Still, the decisive factor behind the size of the cities was undoubtedly the inefficiency of agriculture: as long as most people had to grow food in order to keep society going, cities had to remain small. In Europe an urban population of 50,000 was regarded as impressive; in other parts of the world, cities half that size counted as big. And many cities were semi-rural in character, with gardens inside the city walls.

Whether they were capitals or provincial towns, large cities commonly owed their size to the presence of members of the ruling elite. Though the elite dependend on land for its income, it usually resided in cities rather than on the land. Cities being congregations of many people, they offered greater opportunities for social, commercial, intellectual and other exchanges than did the countryside: city life was exciting. Hence it was only where the economy was too primitive to sustain cities or where cities developed after the elite itself had taken shape that rural residence among the latter prevailed; but even rural elites often spent part of the year at the court, in what was or became the capital (as in western Europe, Sasanid Iran and Tokugawa Japan). Usually, it was thus in the capital, and to a less extent in provincial towns, that the rent collected by landlords and the taxes collected by the state, or in other words the agricultural surplus *tout court*, was spent. Hence it was also here that traders, craftsmen, doctors, lawyers, astrologers, literati, poets, tricksters, beggars, robbers and others congregated for a share of the cake.

There have been times when it was more profitable to participate in international commerce (that is trade generated by elites in other countries) than to service local rulers, with the result that the political capital might be eclipsed by a trading centre: thus Udong, the inland capital of nineteenth-century Cambodia was less than half the size of coastal Phnom Penh (which had a population of about 25,000). But such a dissociation between political and commercial capital was uncommon, if only because the commercial capital would tend to become the political capital too in the end (as it eventually did in Cambodia as well). Nineteenth century Thailand (then Siam), exemplifies the normal pattern in that both political and commercial power were concentrated at Bangkok.

It should be noted, however, that cities were not necessarily centres of either production or economic exchange. They might be purely ceremonial centres with little in the way of permanent population, visited once a year by the court (as was Persepolis) or by participants in religious festivals (the pattern once postulated for the cities of pre-Columbian America). More commonly, they were residential associations for the elite as well as political and administrative centres where public decisions were made, taxes assessed, law-courts held and so forth. The countryside would supply them with food, and sometimes also with labour and goods of other kinds, through taxation, rents and sometimes trade as well; but the cities would not necessarily produce anything for the countryside: they might by pure centres of consumption.

Usually, of course, some productive activity would spring up, but not necessarily for the benefit of anyone other than the city-dwellers themselves. The villagers in the immediate neighbourhood of the town might benefit from its presence; and if there were pastoralists in the area, they too were likely to engage in trade with it, for pastoralists cannot be self-sufficient and they have animal products to sell. (They can however do without cities as long as there are villagers with whom to exchange goods.) But even so, the vast majority of rural dwellers generally had little or no economic need for towns. They might benefit from the administrative and military services they offered, though some villagers, notably mountaineers, generally preferred to manage such matters on their own (as indeed they often had to). They might also depend on the city for religious and educational services, though again there were those who could provide the services in question for themselves. In comparison with modern cities, which are sources of vast amounts of industrial goods and a wide range of political, administrative and cultural services to urban and rural inhabitants alike, those of the pre-industrial world often have a parasitical appearance.

Bourgeoisie

Given the rural rather than urban nature of the pre-industrial world, there was rarely much in the way of a bourgeoisie, or what we would now call 'middle classes', that is to say urban dwellers who made a living out of manufacturing, commercial or professional skills, as opposed to tilling the land or living off landed income. (It should be noted that the European *bourgeois* behind the term bourgeoisie was a townsman entitled to participation in urban government, not any urban dweller. The word has however long been used in the wider sense adopted here.) Admittedly, once a ruling elite had come into existence, a fair number of other cultivators were apt to leave the land (10–20 per cent of the population, as mentioned already); but the vast majority of those who did so ended up at the bottom of society in terms of income and prestige alike, not somewhere in between.

Thus scarcity everywhere made for a huge population of vagrants, beggars, robbers and criminals of other types: no less than 10 per cent of the population of seventeenth-century France (estimated at 20 million or less) is believed to have fallen into this category. Of the rest, the majority were servants (who constituted a further 10 per cent of the population of western Europe in the seventeenth century), and unskilled employees of public institutions: soldiers, runners, town criers, diggers, sweepers, door-keepers and so on.

Workers in the modern sense of the word, that is to say people who sell their labour to productive enterprises, were far less common. It is true that agricultural labourers, sailors, boatmen, weavers and other hirelings (typically paid by the day) sooner or later made their appearance in most societies. But the fact that manufacture depended heavily on animal and human energy meant that productive enterprises rarely exceeded household size (which is not, of course, to say that they never did so); and where the household was the basic unit of production, such additional labour as might be needed could often be found by methods other than simple hire (as will be seen).

All those who had to work with their hands were despised, pre-industrial elites all over the world being united in their contempt for the 'vile and mechanical world of labour'. (One Thalassius was refused entry to the Senate in fourth-century Constantinople on the grounds that he owned a knife factory and was suspected of having worked in it himself: the prejudice had far more intercultural intelligibility than did the institution from which he was excluded.) And those who laboured for others were further stigmatized by their servile position and miserable pay, their status being particularly depressed where they found themselves in competition with slaves.

But even purveyors of more specialized goods and services were not necessarily better off. Village smiths and potters, rural and urban peddlars, cuppers, healers, mimers, jugglers, story-tellers and popular preachers, all these and many others had to subsist on such tiny sums as agrarian society could afford to spend on what we now call consumer goods, medical services and entertainment. Because the sums in any one place were so small, such people were often itinerant, moving from place to place in search of their meagre income and sometimes trying to improve on it by combining several specialities, as did for example the gypsies (who were tinkers, fortune-tellers and purveyors of trinkets and other knick-knacks wherever they went). It was for the same reason that fairs were periodic.

Naturally there were also specialists who catered for the elite, and such people belonged in an altogether different category: highly skilled and extravagantly rewarded (when not extravagantly ill-treated), they supplied exquisite pieces of craftmanship, exotic luxury goods, and high-powered intellectual, artistic, medical and financial services to the courts of aristocrats and kings. Such specialists tended to belong to the top. There were not however very many of them. The elite for which they catered was very rich indeed and thus capable of commanding goods and services of a quality which makes the products of industrial society look distinctly shabby; but by the same token this elite was very small, and the number of skilled people in its service was accordingly limited too.

In so far as pre-industrial societies had a middle class, in the non-technical sense of people who were neither utterly poor nor enormously rich, neither utterly despised nor immensely respected, it tended to consist in the first instance of middling owners or holders of land (yeomen, squires, kulaks or whatever), rather than traders, artisans, craftsmen and professional men. It is true that those who left the land in order to service the ruling elite required others to service themselves, and that those who serviced the purveyors to the court acquired purchasing power in their turn, a process which could, and sometimes did, snowball. When this happened, modern historians speak of 'the rise of the bourgeoisie'. The bourgeoisie has risen from time to time in a number of places, usually with major effects on the social, political and intellectual order: its position in any one society is invariably a fascinating question. In western Europe it rose to the point of creating modern civilization, but neither here nor elsewhere should its existence be taken for granted: a great deal of pre-industrial history was enacted without it.

Market

The parasitical relationship between town and country on the one hand and the embryonic nature of the bourgeoisie on the other were functions of a weakly developed market. To understand this point, let us go back for a moment to our island of chapter 1.

When we were shipwrecked in our thought experiment, we took up agriculture in order to eat, not in order to set up a business; we grew food for our own use (and in due course also for the state), just as we made clothes, utensils and other necessities for ourselves (and perhaps the state); and we supplied our own labour, each member of the household contributing his share: we did not hire it. In short, ours was a *subsistence economy*, and this is how all economies must have begun. But in the modern West we have a fully-fledged *market economy*: all foodstuffs, goods and labour are destined to be sold so that others can be bought, or differently put, all pass through that network of exchanges which we call the market. (The distinction between subsistence and market economies is reflected in that between 'peasants' and 'farmers'. Peasants produce for their own needs, whereas farmers produce for the market. Peasants may sell some of their produce, while conversely farmers may consume some of theirs: peasants do not necessarily practise pure subsistence economy, but subsistence is their first concern; conversely, farmers may not practise pure market economy, but profit is their primary aim, the key difference between the two being that the former run households whereas the latter run business enterprises. The reader should however be warned that many scholars use the two terms synonymously.)

Market economy is simply another example of divided labour: if I specialize in growing cotton and you in making pots, we both have to buy our food from others, who will probably specialize in the production of one type of food to the exclusion of others and thus become dependent on the market in their turn. This arrangement increases productivity because the person who limits himself to one activity accumulates specialist knowledge and finds himself able to concentrate on one set of tools and to standardize the work process. But this type of division of labour developed far more slowly than did state structures because it required efficient means of transportation in order to be viable: the market for cotton or pots in a single village is not large enough to support such specialization on its own. The fully developed market economy that we have today requires both mass production and a mass market, that is to say it is unthinkable without industry.

Most agrarian civilizations had economies intermediate between the primitive subsistence economy characteristic of our island and the fully developed market economy which prevails today: the degree to which market relations prevailed in a particular society is one of the key questions the historian must ask himself. Commonly, however, the market was weakly developed in three major respects.

Agricultural produce

First, there was not necessarily much of a market in agricultural produce; and in so far as there was, it did not necessarily involve the peasants themselves, let alone to their advantage.

Most societies have passed through a stage in which the peasants engaged in subsistence agriculture and paid rent and/or taxes in kind to their landlords and/or state, occasionally bartering some of their produce for commodities which they could not produce themselves (notably salt and iron) at periodic fairs, or in exchanges with itinerant traders. The reader is probably familiar with this stage from early medieval Europe: every village or manor was more or less *autarkic* (self-sufficient); money was rare and trade extremely limited.

But even where money had appeared, cities grown up and trade developed, the countryside might still be dominated by autarkic peasants whose families constituted units of production and consumption alike and who geared their economies to the needs of their working hands rather than to profit.

For one thing, the first trade to develop (apart from that in salt and iron) was rarely an internal one, but rather a long-distance trade generated by the elite, the commodities involved being easily portable or self-propelling luxury goods which commanded sufficiently high prices to make the enterprise worth while: spices, fine fabrics, precious metals, jewels, slaves, horses and the like. ('Merchants who trade across the seas value pearls and jade or else rhinoceros horn or tortoise shell. Merchants who trade overland either value salt and iron or else tea', as an eleventh-century Chinese writer put it.) The demand for luxury goods might greatly affect the suppliers, as it did in Malaya and Indonesia, but it rarely had much repercussion on the society of the importers because the customers were so few: the majority of people continued to cultivate for subsistence, consuming their own produce instead of marketing it.

For another thing, such trade in agricultural products as developed might likewise bypass the peasants themselves. Regional diversity was apt to generate exchanges; bureaucracies and standing armies might have to be provisioned, and urbanization inevitably created a demand for agricultural produce. In fact, few societies remained so primitive as to develop no trade at all in foodstuffs (such as grain, oil, wine or tea) and fibres (such as wool, cotton or silk), as well as other articles for everyday use (such as clothing, pottery and utensils of various kinds). But a great deal of commodity movement took place by order of, or under the control of, the state, that is it did not amount to a genuine trade at all (as opposed to 'administered trade' or 'redistribution'). Even when it did, both landlords and tax-collectors might collect their dues in kind and convert them into cash in the urban market, thereby stimulating trade, but leaving the subsistence economy of their peasants intact. Landlords might also insist on marketing their peasants' produce on the latter's behalf so as to keep them dependent. Indeed, commercial agriculture might do best if the peasants were eliminated altogether: thus the Romans who ran large wheat, vine and olive plantations used slave labour, as did the planters in the New World, while the landlords of sixteenth-century Poland reduced their serfs to near-slavery for the sake of large-scale export farming of rye.

The peasants were hampered by the fact that they could not profitably carry their goods for sale or exchange for more than 4–5 miles or so because the costs of transport were too high (unless they could send them by sea, or, in some unusual cases, via frozen rivers or snow-packed roads). Hence such trade as they engaged in tended to be extremely local or, as some would term it, cellular; and this enabled it to remain a barter trade too. Even in nineteenth-century France there were autarkic villages in which peasants bought only iron and salt and paid for everything else in kind, hoarding their money for the payment of taxes in so far as they handled it at all.

From time to time peasants were forced into market relations when their governments required them to pay taxes in cash rather than kind. This could indeed stimulate commercialization, at least for those who were well off: thus the shift to rents and taxes in cash is said to have been behind the appearance, in fifteenth-century Japan, of village markets which eventually grew into market towns. But it could also lead to ruin for the many who lived on the breadline. Given that the poor had no reserves, they all had to sell their harvest as soon as it was in, with the result that the market was glutted; selling their harvest at abnormally low prices, they would fall into debt to money-lenders, grain-merchants or landlords, who would reduce them to tenants, sharecroppers, agricultural labourers or vagrants. Most peasants had too little to spare to profit from market relations. In Japan, where their problems were aggravated by shortage of money, payment in rice was eventually restored; and when taxes in cash were reintroduced in 1873, they once more proved disruptive of the rural order.

This is not to say that peasants never marketed agricultural products on a significant scale in the pre-industrial world. On the contrary, in China, for example, the so-called 'medieval economic revolution' (c. 900–1200) resulted in a peasantry heavily involved in commercial activities, a development further intensified from the sixteenth century onwards; and here it was typically the *poorest* peasants who profited from market relations (for example by subsisting on millet in order to sell their rice, by engaging in cottage industry, or even by selling their labour). But poverty nowhere makes for a good bargaining position: The peasants always entered the market at a disadvantage, in so far as they had dealings with it at all.

Land

Secondly, there might not be much of a market in land. Many peasants were tenants or serfs and thus unable to alienate their land, or at any rate to do so without their landlord's consent. But even when they disposed of their own land, they did not normally regard it as a commodity to be bought, sold, given away or otherwise alienated like any other; nor for that matter did their landlords. To both, land meant subsistence for themselves and their kin. Both, in fact, typically regarded land as a family asset under the temporary management, as opposed to outright ownership, of whoever happened to be the family head. Individual members of the household might be denied rights of ownership altogether, all property being held in trust and administered by the head of the household on behalf of all (as in the Roman system of *patria potestas*); but at the same time the patriarch might himself be forbidden to alienate land and other family property without the consent of his kin and/or neighbours or the headman of the village. At the very least, kinsmen and/or neighbours had to be given first option. In Vedic India even kings could not give away land without the agreement of all neighbours affected; and kinsmen still had the right to intervene in the sale of land between members of their family and third parties in many parts of sixteenth-century Europe. In short, land was typically seen as vested in a larger group, not simply in the individual who happened to possess or cultivate it. This did not prevent it from being alienable, but it did stand in the way of a purely commercial approach to it.

As far as the elite was concerned, land was also too closely associated with noble status and political power to be treated as a mere commodity. In societies characterized by autarkic peasantries, the wielders of public power were necessarily rewarded in grants of land and its produce, there being no other form of wealth. Land ownership thus came to be reserved for the servants of the state, with the result that unconditional ownership of land tended to disappear altogether: property rights were parcelled out in a variety of claims, by different persons and institutions, to land burdened with a variety of different obligations (as in feudal Europe), and/or the ultimate ownership of all land was declared to vest in the ruler (as at various times throughout the world from China to Peru). In principle, land thus ceased to be an object of trade. It was acquired through grant from the state or from nobles (who might themselves have it from the state), and for the rest it was inherited (or usurped), invariably in return for services of one kind or another to the grantor or original owner.

In practice, few rulers had the power to enforce state ownership of all land against the wishes of the political and religious elite; and wherever trade, cities and a monetarized economy developed, land sooner or later came to be bought and sold. (Besides, many assertions of royal ownership were meant metaphorically.) It is estimated that over 80 per cent of the land was commercially alienable in nineteenth-century China: here, as so often, late traditional China represents the highest degree of development possible under preindustrial conditions. Comparable figures for other societies are difficult to come by; but even where land could in principle be bought and sold, it was often withheld from the market, the peasants continuing to regard it as a source of subsistence and the elite continuing to see it as an emblem of lordship. Landownership was suggestive of authority and prestige long after it had ceased to be directly linked with political power: in some late medieval European countries it was actually decreed that only nobles could acquire landed estates. Land enabled a gentleman to pursue a lifestyle appropriate to his rank: he would collect rents from his tenants and engage in politics or learned pursuits. And since his honour was vested in the land, he was not likely to treat it as a simple ecomonic asset to be sold off whenever he might need cash to whoever might be able to raise it.

Indeed, his very management of it might be very un-businesslike. Aristocrats being typically warriors by origin, they tended to dislike financial affairs, regarding the penny-pinching attitude of merchants as disgraceful, preferring a lifestyle of ostentatious consumption, more often than not delegating estate management to their stewards, agents or wives and limiting their own contribution to borrowing. (Indebtedness was a universal aristocratic disease.) Thus wives managed the financial affairs of the lords of medieval Japan; and according to a fifteenth-century precursor of *Woman's Own*, wives in Europe ought likewise to be 'wise and sound administrators' on behalf of their husbands, for ever away on battlefields. 'There is absolutely no shame in living within your income, however small it may be', Christine de Pisan declares, adding that 'there is nothing dishonourable [for a woman] about making herself familiar with the accounts', voicing sentiments to which she clearly expected a good deal of resistance: the commercial attitude came no easier to either aristocrats or their wives than it did to their peasants.

Still, the aristocratic lifestyle was expensive, commercial profits were frequently desirable, and landlords often did get involved with trade, if only at arm's length. Even then, however, they were apt to retain a thoroughly aristocratic attitude to the use of the wealth thus made. In tenth-century Baghdad a civilian elite of judges, secretaries and other bureaucrats set the tone; all lived off landed income, consorted with traders (though only immensely wealthy ones), bought and sold land as a matter of course, marketed much of its produce (at the hands of agents) and displayed a considerable interest in profits. But the profits were spent on extravagant self-advertisement in the form of luxurious housing and clothing, reckless hospitality, ostentatious patronage of scholars, and so on; it was not husbanded or ploughed back into business. Indeed, one member of this elite explicitly denounced 'the miserliness which some call "caution" and others "management"'. Seventeenth-century English gentlemen had the same contempt for 'unworthy penurious saving'; and a seventeenth-century Venetian nobleman who went so far as to pride himself on his thrift only did so because it enabled him to buy a landed estate 'proper to the station and reputation of my future heirs'. Gentlemen all over the world agreed that only traders were interested in money for its own sake.

Labour

Thirdly, there might not be much of a market in labour. Scarcity meant that it was impossible to pay for all the labour required; in so far as work was not to be left undone, people thus had to be coerced into doing it. The carrot being small, the stick had to be large, or in other words, labour was more commonly forced than hired.

Forced labour took a number of forms. One was slavery. Slaves were typically foreigners, either prisoners-of-war or else the victims of slaving expeditions: either way, the fact that they were rootless aliens made it easy to deprive them of all rights. They were mostly used in heavy, dangerous, dreary or demeaning work now taken over or facilitated by machines. Thus they were extremely common in the home, where they did domestic tasks; they were also used in mining, rowing, building and agriculture, particularly on large plantations devoted to a single crop, such as the wheat and olive plantations of Roman Sicily or the sugar, tobacco and cotton plantations of the Americas. (Plantation slavery has not however been common in history.) When, as sometimes happened, people enslaved members of societies more developed than their own, slaves would also provide skilled services as teachers, scribes, managers and the like: Greek and Near Eastern slaves educated the Romans in the last centuries BC; after the Muslim conquest of the Near East in the seventh century AD they educated the Arabs too. From time to time slaves have also been used in public positions normally reserved for free men, most strikingly in the Islamic world where they came to serve as soldiers, governors and generals; but this was a phenomenon of a different nature from the one with which we are concerned.

Slave-using societies might also enslave some of their own members. Thus impoverished people might sell their children, their wives or themselves into slavery; debt-bondage (handing over oneself in lieu of collateral) existed in many societies; enslavement by way of punishment for crimes existed in some. Most slave-owning societies allowed for the manumission of slaves, but the institution of slavery as such was only abolished in the nineteenth century.

Another prominent form of forced labour was serfdom. Many societies placed the entire food-producing population, or a large proportion of it, in a state of hereditary unfreedom. Peasants were commonly tied to the land, that is forced to remain cultivators wherever they happened to be registered by the state (for purposes of taxation or military service) or, if they were subjected to landlords, on the estate on which they had been born. In some places they were only forbidden to move until they had paid their debts (a variant on the theme of debt-bondage). In others, severe restrictions were placed even on temporary departures (sometimes in conjuction with the use of passports). Peasants might also be forbidden to alienate land without permission or to marry outside their lord's estate; they might be deprived of all legal recourse beyond their landlord's juris-diction, forced to render endless labour service, sold with the land and practically, or indeed wholly, reduced to slavery: it is not easy to say where serfs give way to slaves, countless degrees of freedom and unfreedom being attested in history. Rural unfreedom was a com-mon response to labour shortage, as in the late Roman empire, eastern Europe and Muscovite Russia from the sixteenth century onwards, and South-East Asia throughout its history. On the other hand, excessive supply of agricultural labour might also depress the status of the peasants in that it enabled landlords to dictate their own terms. (Labour shortage did not enable peasants to dictate theirs unless the internal market in agricultural products and other com-modities had developed sufficiently to make forced labour unprofit-able.) Like slavery, serfdom was long-lived: in China it had largely disappeared by the seventeenth century; in western Europe it was abolished in the eighteenth century; in eastern Europe and elsewhere it survived into the nineteenth.

Even when the peasantry was free, however, it was often forced to render labour service (corvée) to the state. In Europe, corvée was associated with tenancy and rendered to landlords: tenants had to work for a specified amount of time on their lord's demesne (i.e. that part of his estate which had not been leased to them). Elsewhere, however, it was the state (or both landlords *and* the state) which extracted labour from the peasants for the building of roads, defen-sive walls and irrigation systems, the transport of tax grain and comparable tasks. Corvée was often part of the regular taxes, or indeed their only or most important form, especially where no cur-rency existed: taxes could be collected in either labour or kind, but collecting them in kind might not be worth the cost of transport, whereas peasants conscripted for labour transported themselves. Corvée was however also used in societies with highly monetarized economies, such as late traditional China. In addition to providing labour as part of their taxes, peasants might be conscripted for major building works on an ad hoc basis. Many of the most astounding monuments of the past, such as the pyramids or Angkor Wat, were built by peasants requisitioned by the state. Today, projects such as the construction, repair or rebuilding of the Great Wall of China would cause flurries in the labour market, with intense competition for the contracts and much boasting, on the part of the government, of the huge number of jobs it had created; instead they caused intense suffering and several revolts, the first of these enterprises giving rise to folk ballads about the cruel emperor which are sung to this day, over 2000 years later. Corvée disappeared from Europe in the seventeenth and eithteenth centuries, from the rest of the world in the nineteenth and twentieth. (The British and the French found themselves incapable of doing without it in colonies such as Burma and Vietnam.) One form of it survives, however: in most countries military service is still, or once more, based on conscription.

So much for forced labour. It was not however the only reason why the labour market was weakly developed.

All agrarian civilizations made heavy use of ascribed status, that is to say status attributed to a person on the basis of features over which he has no control, such as sex, colour or ancestry, as opposed to acquired characteristics such as education and skill. Women were usually ascribed a position inferior to men by virtue of their sex. More strikingly, everyone might be allocated his slot in society on the basis of ancestry: in such societies everyone belonged to the social stratum of his father, sometimes very narrowly defined (actual occupation was hereditary) and sometimes rather more broadly (one could move up and down within a certain range). The Indian caste system is an extreme example of a social order based on ascription. But heredity might also be used to govern membership of certain crucial groups while others remained open: thus entry into the ranks of the aristocracy was often closed to everyone except arrivals by birth in order to prevent dispersal of its privileges, while conversely exit from the ranks of serfs was typically closed to prevent dispersal of the labour force. In fact, ancestry usually played a major role even when all social groups were theoretically open.

What this means is that descent rather than market forces determined who should do what: work had been allocated in advance to the social group into which one was born. The advantage of this lay in the automatic manner in which people were recruited and trained for their jobs. There was no need for elaborate educational systems (people were taught by their parents), or for job centres and other forms of impersonal labour exchange; nor indeed was there any need to advertise for a new occupant of the throne when the ruler died. It solved the problem of job allocation with minimal organization, or in other words it was cheap. (By contrast, consider the costs of a presidential election, or even the fuss and bother of filling a university post: it would be a lot easier simply to appoint the son.) It also worked, after a fashion, because most work was unskilled and because such skills as were required changed very slowly: if anyone can do a job as well as anybody else, elaborate procedures for job allocation are superfluous; and if skills do not change from one generation to the next, parents can train their children as well as anyone else. It did produce inept rulers, though also some very impressive ones; and when even artists came to be recruited by heredity in fifteenth-century Korea, it produced inept painters too.

Despite the prevalence of forced labour and heredity, there was room for something of a labour market in most societies. But even when there was one, it tended to work very differently from today.

Once more, scarcity played a crucial role. If you cannot pay for labour in either cash or land, you can make reciprocal arrangements with relatives, neighbours, allies and friends: they help you with certain things and you help them with others. Such arrangements were common where the need for extra hands was seasonal (peasants unable to afford hired labour commonly made use of them). On the other hand, if you needed labour on a permanent basis, you could offer board, lodging and general care to whoever was willing to become a member of your household: instead of paying wages to a hireling, you could offer to take him in.

This is what a great many people did. Throughout pre-industrial history, from the very beginning until the very end, the labour market was heavily dominated by what amounted to contracts of adoption. Obviously, your hireling would have to submit to your authority on a par with other members of the household: being more than a simple lodger, he would have to behave as if he were your son. Just as you would take in the whole man, not just his labour, so he would switch social allegiance, becoming your follower rather than a neutral labourer. This solution was also dictated by the world outside your household. Given that (for reasons to which I shall come back in the next chapter), people were either enemies or friends in the political sense, there was little hope of hiring neutral labour anyway: the hireling could not be expected to leave behind his social background, political allegiance and religious persuasion for eight hours a day on a par with modern workers; he was either one of yours or he was not. Hence the concept of labour as a commodity distinct from the person offering it (wage labour) was weakly developed: you could not buy the labour without the man, just as the labourer could not sell it without thereby selling himself.

The hireling might be adopted as a son or daughter in the literal sense of the word on the understanding that he or she would supply the labour which children would have supplied if the adopter had not lost or failed to have them: adoption contracts of this kind are attested as early as the second millenium in Babylonia. Alternatively, he might be admitted into the household, preferably at a tender age, as an apprentice or indentured servant whose sheer powerlessness vis-à-vis the master guaranteed that he would be a pliable instrument. Where slaves existed, people preferred them to freeborn persons because slaves were not persons at all until they were manumitted, in which case they became persons bound to their master by an immense sense of gratitude (provided, of course, that the manumission was not simply a way of turning an aged dependant into the streets). They too might be adopted in the literal sense of the word or simply incorporated into the household. Both options are attested for the ancient Near East and Greece; and in the Muslim Middle East slaves and freedmen were widely used by craftsmen, manufacturers and traders in lieu of free apprentices.

Hirelings were also used in largescale enterprises (including the army), and here too they were typically admitted on condition of total submission, by indenturing themselves on terms which practically robbed them of their freedom. Usually they were people who had lost their social backing, be it because their parents were too poor to maintain them, their kinsfolk too poor, too few or too dispersed to help them, or because they had disgraced themselves: a Chinese iron-smelter of the twelfth or thirteenth century recruited five hundred furnace-workers from among absconded criminals. Whatever the reason, hirelings were people who were forced to sell themselves to others, like prostitutes. They were subject to their master's authority, which was unremarkable as long as they were children, but which rendered them servile as soon as they were adults. Where slaves existed, they were a bad alternative; and where they were absent, they performed their work. No wonder that hirelings were generally despised. 'A free man does not live under the constraint of another', as Aristotle put it. A tenth-century Muslim who jokingly referred to Muhammad as the hireling of Khadija (the woman who first employed and then married him) was being very risqué indeed.

The fact that neutral labour barely existed in the pre-industrial world had the further effect that you were unlikely to get very far without patronage. You had to know somebody who knew your employer and who could recommend you, guarantee your reliability and assure him that you were of the right social, political and religious background: who you were was far more important than what you could do, especially when labour was unskilled. In the modern world people likewise prefer to hire cleaning-ladies on the basis of recommentations from friends rather than unknown employers because the crucial question is not whether she can clean (anyone can), but whether she can be entrusted with your home. In the pre-industrial world, trust was always of overriding importance, with the result that such job market as existed was dominated by personal networks: I would recommend you and you would recommend my son; you would recommend my nephew and I would recommend your friend.

Many placements were made within small communities in which everyone knew everybody anyway; apprenticeships were generally arranged by parents, and even when they were not, the chances were that the employer would know all there was to know about the hireling before he took him in. But for positions in the bureaucracy and other forms of government service an extended network of relatives, friends and allies was highly desirable, if not indispensable. There is a Chinese story, set in the time of the Ming (1368–1644), in which a totally illiterate person passes the civil service examinations and gets promoted from one position to another because he unwittingly behaves in a fashion suggesting that he is the relative or protégé of a highly influential person. This is comic fiction (in reality the examination system was hard to bend), and patronage could not usually make up for utter ineptitude: in a tenth-century Muslim story a high-ranking bureaucrat regretfully finds the only son of a deceased friend to be so stupid that he cannot make him a judge ('the lad is such a fool that he would utterly disgrace my recommendation', as Macauley said of a cousin in 1833). But though a patron would disgrace himself by supporting a complete ignoramus for a skilled job, there was nothing shameful about patronage as such: it benefitted employer and employee alike. Wherever trust mattered as much as or more than skills, nepotism was a virtue, not a sign of corruption.

Lack of economic integration

The limited development of the market in respect of agricultural produce, land and labour meant that the pre-industrial world was characterized by a low degree of economic integration. Where subsistence economy prevailed, every household was more or less self-sufficient and every village largely or wholly independent of the next. In so far as the peasants traded at all, they would do so within an area infinitely smaller than the state, whereas the elite might be part of an economic network far wider than any political unit, obtaining its luxury goods from far-away and exotic lands: the state embraced no market of its own. Where the growth of cities, higher agricultural output and improvements in the means of transportation stimulated internal commerce, there might be close economic ties between a city and its hinterland, or between one province and another, or between the inhabitants of other kinds of marketing areas; but even so, it is only by way of exception that one can speak of national economies in pre-industrial times. Few commodities reached state-wide circulation; and in so far as they did, they were mostly beyond the purchasing power of the peasants who constituted the vast majority of the population. 'Brocade woven in Szechwan is prized the Empire over', a Chinese scholar of the Mongol period (1280–1368) observed; but though Chinese peasants were by then heavily involved with the market, selling foodstuffs, cash crops, handicraft and even labour, brocade was hardly a common item on their shopping lists. Regional specialities such as sugar and olive oil also travelled far within the tenth and eleventh-century Muslim caliphate, as did numerous equivalents of Szechwan brocade and even fresh fruit (transported in leaden containers packed with ice); but the costs were such that only members of the ruling elite and wealthy townsmen could afford them. Economic integration was usually limited in either geographical or social terms, and it was often limited in both respects.

By modern standards, pre-industrial economics were underdeveloped. Such surplus as the agricultural sector produced passed into the hands of a ruling elite given to spending every penny it had on consumption, not on investments in trade or manufacture; conversely, those who made money out of trade or manufacture were apt to convert it into membership of the ruling elite. Loans taken out by the elite were overwhelmingly meant to solve consumption crises, not to provide capital for productive enterprises; and the same was true of loans taken out by peasants because the latter were so impoverished: they borrowed simply in order to eat. Accordingly, lending money was extremely risky, a fact reflected in exorbitant interest rates. Interest rates being impossibly high, the capital for productive enterprises had to come from sources other than moneylenders, be it from the funds of families or guilds or from partnerships in which resources were pooled. Moreover, since the agricultural surplus ended up with the ruling elite, sensible businessmen concentrated their efforts on the production and/or provision of extremely expensive items for the very rich, not on everyday goods for sale to the masses: it was only here and there that catering for the masses, or some of them, paid off. The archetypal businessman traded in pearls. He traded in pearls because extravagant consumption was characteristic of the elite, whereas the masses rarely had much purchasing power. His activities thus reflected and reinforced the underdeveloped and non-integrated character of the economy.

This completes the socio-economic thumb-nail sketch. It goes without saying that there never was any such thing as a 'typical' pre-industrial society. Some were more primitive and many were more sophisticated than indicated here; all had identities of their own not considered, and none was as static as the sketch might seem to indicate. But whether we are aware of doing so or not, we all operate with identikits of one kind or another, and what this sketch is meant to do is simply to replace identikits based on modern conditions with one based on the past. The rest of the book should be read with the same qualification in mind.

3
The State

Where states emerged

In the thought experiment of the first chapter we generated a state on the assumption that our island could support agriculture and that we ourselves were familiar with state structures. Think away either assumption and the result would have been very different: we might have formed warring bands to cope with the hostile natives, or a confederacy. In real life many parts of the pre-industrial world remained stateless until modern times because one or the other feature presupposed by us was absent.

As regards the first presupposition, we have seen that an agricultural surplus was indispenable for the maintenance of states: states were thus incapable of surviving where agriculture was non-existent or marginal. Deserts, steppes, tundras and polar regions could be conquered by external powers, but they could not support complex societies on their own; and external powers generally found them too poor and unimportant to be worth the effort.

Admittedly, when such economically marginal regions were located in the neighbourhood of great powers (as in Central Asia and the Middle East), their inhabitants could supplement their meagre income with wealth coming from outside in the form of subsidies paid by these powers for good behaviour or military services, revenues from participation in international trade, plunder from raids, and the like; and such influx of wealth might suffice for the emergence of embryonic state structures. In the Syrian desert of the sixth century AD, for example, subsidies paid by the Byzantines and the Sasanids for military serivces resulted in the creation of two tribal states known as those of the Ghassanids and the Lakhmids. But whatever the nature of the revenues which stimulated state-building, they had to be invested in agriculture if the states thus formed were to acquire viability, let alone complexity. The Ghassanid and Lakhmid statelets collapsed the moment the imperial subsidies were cut off; and a great many tribal rulers found it simpler to pour their newfound wealth into attempts at conquest of the very lands which had produced that wealth than to invest it in attempts to make the steppe or desert bloom (thus numerous Central Asian conquerors, most famously the Mongols). If the military enterprise was successful, the state would be transferred to the conquered lands; if it failed, it would disintegrate for lack of funds. Either way, statelessness remained the norm in regions with little or no agriculture.

As regards the second presupposition, the fact that institutions take time to spread and even longer to develop on their own meant that millennia might pass between the advent of agriculture in a certain area and the emergence of complex political organization there. Many parts of the pre-industrial world which were perfectly capable of sustaining state structures thus remained stateless too. In Eurasia the discovery of agriculture began about 10,000 BC in the Near East, but complex political organization only emerged about 3000 BC, and it was only in the first centuries AD that state structures finally struck roots in northern Europe. Outside Eurasia sparse populations made for ever slower rates of diffusion. (Three quarters of the world's population live in Eurasia and apparently did even in pre-historic times.) In the Americas agriculture appeared about 6000 BC followed by complex organization about 1000 BC, but the latter stayed put in its Guatemalan-Mexican homeland until the rise, on the western coast of South America, of the anonymous peoples whose legatees were the Incas of Peru. Agriculture reached tropical Africa during the second millennium BC and states emerged during the first millenium AD, but political developments here were slower than in tropical Asia, which was in direct contact with India and China from early on. And Oceania, though likewise equipped with agriculture, remained entirely untouched by political developments in the Old and the New Worlds alike, with the result that here no state structures emerged at all until the arrival of the Europeans (though the Polynesians came close to developing them on their own).

In short, the pre-industrial world was full of primitive peoples, both hunter-gatherers, cultivators and pastoralists, of whom a tiny fraction survived long enough into modern times to be immortalized by anthropologists. In pre-modern times most of them were as blissfully ignorant of the existence of civilization as were civilized people of theirs, but inevitably there were areas where the two came together. When this happened, the primitive peoples were branded as *barbarians*, a term now used by historians to designate peoples who were perceived to be lacking in all those features which add up to civilization and who were aware of this fact, having had sufficient dealings with their neighbours to lose their primitive innocence in both cognitive and other respects.

Barbarians were typically dangerous people because they knew enough about civilization to both covet and despise it, the former because it was rich and the latter because its members were effete 'slaves' who could not practise self-help. Many barbarians were simply raiders but, as mentioned above, the flow of wealth and ideas from a great power to a marginal region was liable to transform its inhabitants into conquerors. Time after time states proved to be so weak that even small numbers of ill-equipped barbarians could overrun them. In the ancient Near East the so-called Gutians overran the Akkadians; in pre-Columbian Mexico the so-called Chichimecs overran the Toltecs; in the Mediterranean of late antiquity the barbarians of western Europe destroyed the western Roman empire, while the Arabs conquered its eastern provinces and destroyed Sasanid Iran; and Huns, Mongols and Turks of various kinds overran parts of China, India, the Middle East, Byzantium and eastern Europe from time to time, destroying a host of states in the process. It was not until firearms were invented that civilization acquired a decisive advantage over its barbarian rivals, who could not produce such weapons themselves (though they soon learnt to import them) and whose mobility could not be combined with, or counteract, the use of heavy artillery. In the early fifteenth century the Ming dynasty of China defeated the Mongol Oirats by means of field artillery, proceeded to rebuild the Great Wall with apertures for cannon and, in the early seventeenth century, defeated the founder of the Manchu kingdom too. But their frontier generals defected: the last great barbarian conquest, that by the Manchus of China in 1644, was not really a conquest at all.

However successful the barbarians may have been in the days before firearms, however, the state as such was always the winner in the long run, for the barbarians conquerors always became civilized themselves (or split in so far as some resisted the process). Their homeland might indeed be incapable of supporting states, in which case those who stayed behind continued the tug of war, as in Central Asia until the Manchus, in Arabia until the discovery of oil, and in parts of North Africa until the arrival of modern armies. But more commonly, the homeland turned out to be endowed with a potential for sustained development so that the changes wrought by exposure to civilization proved cumulative. As the barbarian peoples along the frontiers of great powers began their journey towards civilization, they would trigger comparable developments towards state formation and conquest among their own barbarian neighbours: the Roman empire unwittingly contributed to the Frankish invasion of Roman Gaul, and the Franks in their turn unwittingly contributed to the eruption of the Vikings. In short, destructive though it often was, the encounter between barbarians and civilized peoples was one of the major mechanisms whereby civilization spread. Today, barbarians have ceased to exist altogether, except as a loose term of abuse (in which sense, too, it is amply attested in the past). Every spot on earth today is subject to a state, utterly desolate ones included.

Fragility of state structures

Once invented, the state had thus come to stay. But it is clear from the sometimes astonishing success of barbarian attackers that states were often fragile structures, and this was a point which members of complex societies demonstrated too from time to time: thus a mere handful of Europeans sufficed to cause the instantaneous collapse of the great pre-Columbian civilizations, which is extraordinary even though the invaders came from cultural outer space; and a mere commercial organization, the East India Company, set up thousands of miles away from its prey, proved capable of establishing control over the entire Indian subcontinent for all that the latter was endowed with a long tradition of political organization of its own. The ability of pre-industrial states to generate action, to co-ordinate and to control was limited. This weakness was a factor of major importance in the relationship between them and their own subjects: it determined the nature of this relationship; and once formed, the relationship itself almost always always reinforced it.

The weakness had its roots partly in scarcity and partly in the absence of modern means of transportation and communication. Scarcity meant that rulers rarely disposed of sufficient resources, or even very stable ones. They were chronically short of personnel and other infrastructure, and frequently unable to pay such personnel as they had, with the result that the latter were left to remunerate themselves as best they could at the expense of state and subjects alike. Inadequate resources meant acceptance of behaviour which we now condemn as corrupt, and corruption further reduced the size and regularity of the ruler's income: collecting taxes cost no less than

25 per cent of the total revenues in France under Louis XIV (1643-1715); and in eighteenth-century Egypt it cost some 25 per cent of the land revenues over and *above* the salaries which the tax-collectors were paid.

Being short of personnel, rulers were unable to conduct regular population counts, land-surveys and other forms of inspection required for the regular reassessment of taxes, or to control figures on such matters forwarded by village headmen and other local men; and this too was likely to affect their revenues adversely. They might fix the level of taxation for good, or simply name a certain sum which every province had to meet every year whatever condition might prevail, or farm out the taxes (i.e. sell the rights of the state to the highest bidder, who would then squeeze the population to make a profit). The first two methods had the advantage of ensuring a stable income while the third might even increase it, but all three had a price. If the population fell, the unvaried nature of the taxes might ruin it; and if it grew, the state would fail to benefit from the growth and thus find its resources diminished in relation to the tasks required for the maintenance of the *status quo*, let alone for improvement (as happened in Manchu China). Where taxes were farmed, the state likewise risked the ruin of its agricultural population and moreover renounced direct control (tax-farming was commonly practised before the state had developed its own machinery for the collection of revenues, as in the Roman republic, or after it had begun to collapse, as in the Abbasid caliphate, though by no means under such circumstances alone). The problems of taxation generated a wide variety of solutions, but arbitrariness, oppression and corruption proved to be constant companions of all.

Though we still complain of the tax-burden, the Inland Revenue Service does not normally have to call upon the army to make us pay, nor do we normally engage in prolonged haggling with the tax-collectors, weeping, crying, tearing our clothes or grovelling in the dust to convince them that we have not got a penny left, or calling upon every influential friend we have to ensure that no tax-collector would dare to approach us. Such procedures were however commonplace in most pre-industrial societies. For the peasants, tax-collectors were like swarms of locusts descending to strip them of everything they possessed; for the tax-collectors, peasants were like recalcitrant cattle which had to be milked however much they might protest. The sheer fact that yields were so low accustomed the authorities to take everything they could without destroying agriculture altogether. 'The tax-payers should keep only as much of their cultivated produce as suffices for their subsistence and the cultivation of their lands', a third-century Persian emperor is supposed to have decreed. 'Every care should be taken that there should not remain with the villagers more food supplies than required for one year's consumption, nor more oxen than wanted for [the tillage of] their fields', an eighth-century king of Kashmir is said to have ruled. 'The peasants are the foundation of the state', a seventeenth-century Japanese document declares, 'each man must have the boundaries of his fields clearly marked, and an estimate must be made of the amount needed for his consumption. The rest must be paid as tax'. No wonder that Jesus' disciples were outraged when their master dined with tax-collectors ('publicans') and other sinners.

Primitive means of transportation and communication were an even greater problem than insufficient funds. For one thing, they were a factor in the low degree of economic integration which we have already noted, and they stood in the way of cultural integration too, as we shall see. Very large areas could be conquered, but not amalgamated, or only at the level of the elite. The vast majority of people continued to live in more or less self-sufficient villages with more or less autonomous cultures of their own, a fact which rendered the political unity of pre-industrial states precarious.

For another thing, primitive means of communication and transportation meant that rulers were chronically short of information and unable to react efficiently to such information as they received. They often paid much attention to the problem of communications, building roads, maintaining postal systems based on horses, pigeons or runners, dispatching people whose sole function was to act as 'the king's eyes and ears', and experimenting with smoke signals and other forms of telegraphic communication. The results varied enormously. In the seventeenth century it took thirty days for a courier to travel the 500 miles from Istanbul to Belgrade (an army taking twice as long), and two weeks for a letter from Madrid to reach Milan; but it only took six to seven weeks for a courier to traverse the whole of inner China (i.e. ethnic China without its non-Chinese appendages). In medieval Japan, mounted messengers could cover the roughly 600 miles between Kamakura and Kyoto in five days at a pinch, and the relay runners of Inca Peru could cover the 420 miles between Lima and Cuzco in as little as three. But whatever the result, distance was always a problem. The eighth-century caliph al-Mansur is supposed to have had a magic mirror in which he could see all his enemies wherever they might be; but even if he had actually had such a mirror, he would not have been able to transport himself and his troops any faster than the postal horses could run. The ruler could not be everywhere, though many tried their best, incessantly touring their domains.

Forms of government

This does something to explain why pre-industrial government was typically characterized by total exclusion of the masses. Mass participation in public decision-making was common in simple societies such as bands, tribes and villages: the smaller they were and the less socio-economic differentiation they contained, the more egalitarian they tended to be in political terms. In such communities, every male adult would voice his opinion on public issues, be it in formal meetings or otherwise, and everyone's opinion would carry weight, though the actual decision might well be left to elders and/or a chief. But though procedures of this kind often survived at the level of village and tribe even after a state had been superimposed upon them, popular participation in high politics was extremely rare.

Small size was a precondition for mass participation (or some degree thereof) in high politics too, as is clear from the Greek and Roman city states, the republics of northern India which flourished about the same time, the Italian communes and other examples; but it was by no means a sufficient condition, and numerous very small states, including many limited to a single city, were as authoritarian in their political organization as any empire. Wherever wealth took the form of land and a storable surplus, both of which could be physically seized, a small number of specialists in violence tended to eliminate other participants from the political arena, especially where the military participation ratio was low, or in other words where few adult males were called upon to participate in warfare. By contrast, the means of production (as opposed to the products themselves), could not be physically seized where commercial wealth predominated, nor could the masses be excluded from a say in politics where the military participation ratio was high. But it was only in small polities such as city states deprived of land that commerce could generate more wealth than agriculture, just as it was only in small polities that the military participation ratio had to be high:

though small size was not a sufficient condition, it was certainly a necessary one. In large states, mass participation in government invariably came to an end. (The popular institutions of the Roman city state characteristically failed to survive the Roman expansion.) The nature of wealth and military organization apart, it is a general rule that the larger a group becomes, the more thoroughly the actions of its members have to be co-ordinated if it is not to disintegrate; and under pre-industrial conditions, large-scale co-ordination was impossible unless power was concentrated in the hands of a few. Even if it had been regarded as desirable, popular representation would have been difficult to organize without making decision-making excessively slow and cumbersome, and it would mostly have been positively dangerous too: given that the masses consisted of numerous small communities weakly tied together in economic terms, culturally diverse and thus unlikely to have identical political aspirations, power could not be distributed with any evenness throughout the population without thereby enabling the loosely associated communities to split up. Large states were held together by coercion: power had to be concentrated so that conflicting interests could be suppressed.

Typically, then, pre-industrial states were monarchies in which power was exercised through a small ruling elite. They were monarchies as opposed to oligarchies, partly because the elite could not function without an ultimate arbiter (and was bound to produce one through its competition for power where none existed), and partly because one man elevated above all others was a potent symbol of the community over which he presided: its members often regarded him as a common link with the divine. Monarchs were almost everywhere regarded as the hallmark of civilization, stateless societies being dismissed as barbarian and republics abhorred as positively unnatural in so far as they were known at all: the republicanism of Mediterranean antiquity is distinctly unusual. 'Now make us a king to judge us like all the nations', as the elders of Israel said to Samuel: kings were what all self-respecting people had. In medieval Europe, Iceland was felt to be unreasonable in that it 'would not serve a king even as all other countries in the world'. And when a sixteenth-century Burmese king heard Venice described as a free state without a monarch, he laughed uproariously at what he took to be a joke.

Theoretically, monarchy was almost always absolute. The ruler was seen as endowed with unlimited power, both in the sense that he did not share it with anyone else (as opposed to delegate it to whomsoever he willed) and in that he was not accountable to his subjects for the manner in which he chose to exercise it. Moralists harped on his duty to engage in consultation: kings should take counsel from wise men and ascertain the attitudes of others before taking decisions. Many had formal councils too. But they were free to overrule whatever opinion they received. All kings were expected to uphold 'justice', 'the law', 'ancient custom', 'God's will', 'the natural order' or whatever else the generally accepted way of doing things was called; and this was so however much supernatural sanction they might enjoy: a king who violated the divine order thereby disproved his own claim to divine status, descent or approval. In this sense all kings were all constitutional rulers. But since there were no formal institutions for calling them to account, they could not be made to abide by the constitution except by appeals to their conscience or prudence, or by force. The prospect of having his deeds examined on the Day of Judgement might scare a Christian or Muslim ruler, just as the prospect of a low rebirth might scare a Buddhist one. He would at all events be unwise to antagonize his subjects because, as Machiavelli cautioned, hostile neighbours might take advantage of their discontent, or as Muslim writers put it, God would raise up another king in his stead; indeed, disaffected subjects might prod God into action by actually calling in the hostile neighbours (such as rival rulers or militant tribesmen), or by rebelling on their own. But though there were limits to what the ruler could get sway with in practice, he was not normally subject to formal restraints in respect of the manner in which he arrived at or implemented his decisions.

The fact that he could not easily be held to the constitution does not however mean that his power was absolute in any real sense of the word (if indeed there is such a sense). For one thing, his sphere of competence was usually limited. Rulers rarely enjoyed religious authority, that is the right to settle questions concerning faith or morality. The Chinese emperor did have the authority to regulate aspects of morality (such as the lengths to which filial piety was to go, for example); but those labelled 'caesaropapist' by modern historians, notably the Byzantine emperors, did not actually combine the powers of caesars and popes: they were merely in a position to exercise considerable pressure on the ecclesiastical organization in which religious authority resided. And though early Muslim caliphs did apparently enjoy both political power and religious authority, they were rapidly cut down to size by learned laymen who assumed religious leadership for themselves. The division of labour between political and religious leaders has commonly been both fuzzy and contentious, but a division of one kind or another has nonetheless been the norm. Moreover, rulers were not necessarily empowered to legislate or (given that the very idea of legislation might be absent) to 'find' the law. They might be entitled to regulate matters to do with the state apparatus, taxes, war, crimes and the like, or in other words to promulgate what we would call public law, though their legislative freedom might be circumscribed even here; but for the rest they were commonly expected simply to uphold the ways to which their subjects were committed, be they embodied in customary law or in formal legal systems created by jurists or priests (such as early Roman, Islamic, Hindu or canon law). Since private law was closely entwined with religion and morality, it was more often regulated by bearers of high culture than by wielders of political power.

For another thing, the ruler's power was rarely effective even within such sphere of competence as he did enjoy. Obviously, he could not exercise absolute power in person. If government was so simple that he could manage it on his own with a minimal staff, his kingdom was highly decentralized, meaning that in practice his control was perfunctory; and if he centralized his kingdom, government became so complex that his staff took over most of the decision making. In the late Roman empire, for example, the emperor was so swamped by paperwork that he had no time to read what he signed: every now and again he had to announce that special grants contrary to the law were invalid even if they bore his own signature.

Absolutist rulers had plenty of personal power in the sense of the ability to order whatever they wanted. They might decree that all dogs be killed (as did an eleventh-century caliph in Egypt) or on the contrary that all dogs be protected (as did a seventeenth-century shogun of Japan), and they might indulge in all sorts of other caprices and whims. Their personal power was important in that it gave them *tactical* freedom: they could act as they wished in conducting negotiations and use force whenever they deemed it expedient, be it against individuals or groups; and this put them in a good position to practise divide-and-rule. But though they had much room in which to manoeuvre, they were rarely in a position to exercise much control over either their administrations or their subjects.

The point to note, however, is that even the monarchy as an *impersonal* institution rarely enjoyed power of a kind that could be described as absolute. The fact that news travelled slowly, and troops even more so, invariably meant that considerable power had to be handed over to people on the spot, be they governors despatched from the centre, provincial magnates allied with it, or others. Only they could know what was going on locally and only they could react fast. By the same token, of course, they had considerable freedom to abuse their position, notably by fleecing the local population for private gain or by building up private power-bases with a view to secession or bids for the throne.

Numerous methods were devised for coping with this problem: governors could be rotated at short intervals and/or forbidden to hold office in their native province; local aristocrats might be forced to send hostages to the capital; extensive networks of spies could be maintained; troops could be dispatched when things got out of hand, and so on. But genuine control over provincial affairs simply could not be achieved. 'The mighty dragon is no match for the local snake which knows the ins and outs of the place', as Chinese folk wisdom had it (the dragon being the emperor). The best the ruler could hope for was to secure the co-operation of the local snake, tie him to the monarchic institution and give him a strong interest in the survival of the state, in short to transform him and his likes into a dependable ruling elite loosely or closely supervised by a central staff.

But though the ruler might successfully acquit himself of this task, the political (or for that matter religious) leaders with which he allied himself were not his abject instruments, having autonomous power in their own right; and there were numerous groups endowed with power of their own below them. In principle the ruler might not share his power with anyone else, as opposed to delegate it to whomsoever he willed, but in practice he coexisted with a wide variety of power-holders whom he was lucky even to win over. Ideology might depict him as an autocrat, but ideology was more often than not designed to compensate for a deficient governmental machinery which left both him and his staff unable to translate their policies into action outside the narrow circles in which they moved or to control the society of which they were in charge. The government might issue decrees, but the implementation of these decrees rested with landed magnates, religious authorities, village councils urban notables, guilds, tribal leaders, or kin groups of various kinds, or in other words with self-governing institutions and groups which might be in close or in loose alliance with the state or which might defy it altogether. How many dogs were actually killed in eleventh-century Egypt? How many benefitted from the shogun's protection in seventeenth-century Japan? It stands to reason that there were immense variations in the actual power enjoyed by monarchic institutions (the Japanese shogunate having considerably more than did the Egyptian caliphate). But generally speaking, government was 'self-government at the king's command', as Maitland said with reference to medieval England; and it might be self-government in disregard of the king's command too, not just in medieval Europe, where central government was extremely rudimentary, but also in centralized states such as the early Abbasid caliphate or late imperial China.

The absolutist kings of Europe did enjoy considerable power compared with both their predecessors and many of their non-European counterparts. But they were powerful because they had developed machineries which enabled them to tame their aristocracies, their religious organizations and other self-governing groups, not because of the ideological claims made on their behalf or even because they were exempt from constitutional restraints: the constitutional kings of England were no less powerful. But their power was institutional, not personal, though they still had far too little of the former and far too much of the latter by our standards; and eventually their machineries developed into impersonal states symbolically graced by or wholly devoid of monarchs altogether.

Functions of the state

The deficient nature of the governmental machinery meant that pre-industrial states were unable to take on as many functions as their modern counterparts. Modern states do not just collect taxes, maintain internal security and defend their citizens against outsiders; they also educate their citizens, assign them jobs, hand out money to those unable to earn, regulate economic activities, keep an eye on the environment, both natural and man-made, organize sport and other forms of entertainment, sponsor cultural institutions, maintain a public health service and provide some services for the disabled, the weak and the old. Their activities are countless, and they thoroughly shape the lives of all members of society. By contrast, pre-industrial states engaged in a limited number of activities and lacked the power to shape (or, at times, even to affect) the lives of their subjects. Instead, however, pre-industrial rulers often had religious, moral and symbolic roles which have practically disappeared today.

All rulers endeavoured to defend their territories against outsiders (and usually also to expand them), to maintain internal order, and to promote the 'welfare' of their subjects; by way of payment for these services they collected taxes. Thus far the agenda sounds much the same as it does today, but it was understood in a minimalist rather than a maximalist vein: the state did a little and the subjects did the rest. (Even the *laissez-faire* states of the modern world are maximalist by pre-modern standards.) All rulers had to set up an army for internal and external use as well as an administrative machinery; and some rulers found themselves engaged in organization at grassroot level as a result. (Censuses, registration of land and households, passports, identity-cards and the like are not modern inventions.) All endeavoured to further welfare too, but not after the fashion of their modern successors.

Welfare

As mentioned before, the king was widely regarded as a link between the divine and the human worlds. He might be a god himself, or descended from one, or simply appointed by the deity, but at all events he was expected to use his 'divine effulgence' (as the Persians called it) or his *Heil* (as the Germanic barbarians called it) for the benefit of the community: this was the crucial manner in which he promoted welfare. He was expected to maintain and embody the law in the sense of cosmic, natural and human order, partly by acting as the symbolic head of the community and partly by observing the right ways and setting a good example. If he did so, happiness and prosperity would ensue.

Such ideas are widely attested for primitive societies, but they displayed an amazing tenacity under civilized conditions, being attested for ancient Egypt, China, Japan, South-East Asia (where some kings had no other functions), India, Iran, the Islamic world (in both the concept of the caliphate and that of kingship), as well as the Hellenistic world and Europe. If the king was just, rain would fall; if he was not, famine, flood and other natural calamities would ensue. Natural disasters were thus blamed on the king: they proved that he had misbehaved. Under a good king, 'vices decrease and virtues increase . . . the world becomes prosperous and joyous', ad the Zoroastrians explained; but 'when kings are unjust, even sugar and salt lose their flavour', as the Indians put it. If no king existed, both the natural and the human order would dissolve and chaos would prevail: a country without a king enjoyed 'neither rain nor seed, neither wealth nor wife, neither sacrifices nor festivals', according to the *Ramayana*; people suffered illness, customs ceased to exist and all was nothingness according to Malay literature. It is for this reason that the sixteenth-century Burmese king laughed at the idea of a kingless Venice; and it is for the same reason that the British abolition of the Burmese monarchy in 1886 was a catastrophic shock to the Burmese which the British had not anticipated.

Ritual kingship (as this role is commonly called) might require no action at all: the Japanese emperors performed it for over a thousand years by simply existing, being kept in such ceremonious inactivity that when one of them made a bid for real power he could scarcely even walk. Most rulers, however, combined their ritual role with co-ordinating and warlike functions which tended to transform or eclipse it, while at the same time the development of specialized religious institutions changed their standing vis-à-vis the divine.

Thus the monarch was often required to protect the religious establishment (church, sangha, brahmins, scholars or whatever) and to promote the divine order, not just in the general sense of right-eousness, but also in the specific sense of a religious law and morality elaborated by the establishment in question. Religion and morality being almost invariably public concerns, many states interfered con-siderably in what we now regard as private matters, persecuting heretics, enforcing rules of filial and marital behaviour, punishing or even executing adulterers, and so forth. The monarch might also be expected to dispense justice in person by adjudicating, hearing peti-tions and redressing grievances, including grievances against the state itself, a role in which he was invariably seen as a last resort: he coped with disputes that threatened to disrupt the peace where local arbitration, family courts and other judicial institutions had failed, just as he intervened to protect the social order where negligence of prescribed rights and duties threatened to upset it. He was, so to speak, the general repair-man of a society normally expected to run itself. Differently put, he was the ultimate guarantor of righteous-ness. It was in this vein that the Persian emperor and epitome of justice, Khusraw of the Immortal Soul (531–79), ordered 'that a chain should be set up with bells attached to it, within reach of even a child of seven years, so that any complainants who came to the court would not need to see the chamberlain; they would pull the chain and the bells would ring: the Immortal Soul would hear it and redress their grievances'. In an inscription of 1292 Rama Gamhen, ruler of the Thai kingdom of Sukhotai, likewise boasts that 'he has hung a bell in the opening of the gate over there: if any commoner in the land has a grievance which sickens his belly and gripes his heart, and which he wants to make known to his ruler and lord, it is easy; he goes and strikes the bell which the King has hung there'. Burmese kings, too, made use of grievance bells. Given the number of people with grievances and the distances they had to travel to reach the capital, the practical importance of royal justice must have been limited, but its symbolic significance was clearly considerable. In fact, peasantries all over the world continued to be comforted by the existence of an ultimate guarantor of righteousness long after kings had retired behind impersonal bureaucracies and prosaic courts.

In addition to embodying justice, kings were apt to provide a wide range of welfare services of a more familiar kind in the course of their attempt to display and increase their special qualities. The righteous king would dig canals and irrigation channels, build bridges and rest-houses, found villages and towns, set up schools and other religious buildings, and engage in many other commendable activities, all for the sake of fame in this world and salvation in the next, according to Nizam al-Mulk, an eleventh-century Muslim statesman. In the same vein Indian and Indianized kings would build hospitals and asylums for the poor in conjunction with temples. A great deal of what is now regular state activity was done by the ruler, the elite and whoever else could afford it in display of the merit, glory or piety appropriate to people of high status, not in performance of official duties; or rather, the distinction was likely to be meaningless; the official who engaged in private charity was perceived as discharging public duties too.

In so far as the private and public acts of kings and high officials can be distinguished, institutions of higher education were often maintained by the state, whereas primary schooling was usually left to private initiative or to religious organizations; and the state rarely provided grants and scholarships for such institution of higher learning as it maintained, though there were a few which did. Poor relief, hospitals, the care of orphans and other welfare services in our sense of the word were usually left to private charity and religious institutions too, though most rulers took precautions against famine by maintaining granaries (as did the Pharaoh in response to Joseph's dream), organized relief when it struck, and provided cheap grain at all times to the capital and other major cities by way of averting bread-riots. The Roman state went so far as to provide grain for free to the Roman poor, but this was unusual. The Romans also provided public entertainment in the form of gladiatorial shows and races, but this was unusual too. Most rulers and other public servants, however, sponsored the arts, both for personal satisfaction and for propaganda purposes, but the state as such was not expected to provide support for artists. Many rulers sponsored economic enterprises for their own gain, but the state was not expected to provide credit for private business (though it might provide loans to impoverished peasants). It would probably be fair to say that all or most functions vested in the state today are attested for pre-industrial states too, but never all of them at the same time, hardly ever in the same spirit, and never (apart from the essential ones) on a regular basis: numerous services without which modern society would collapse were mere frills or wholly lacking.

Economic activities

It should be noted that the economic measures of pre-industrial rulers rarely added up to genuine economic policies. Rulers had political aims which impinged on the economic sphere, not economic aims as such. Thus they might take an interest in agriculture because agriculture was the source of their revenues and also because they had to secure adequate supplies of food for their armies, their civil service and their urban populations. Craftsmanship and trade similarly attracted their attention only, if at all, as a source of revenue and a mechanism for the distribution of vital supplies. In short, their interests were of the so-called 'provisioning' kind.

Such interests might involve them in very few or very many economic activities depending on their understanding of their obligation to promote 'welfare'. In addition to founding new villages and otherwise assisting the expansion of cultivated land, they might experiment with new crops, sponsor the diffusion of agricultural manuals, establish granaries, fix prices, create government monopolies (notably on salt and alcohol, but often on other commodities too), regulate guilds, build ports and roads, create uniform currencies, supervise weights and measures, attract (or even kidnap) skilled artisans, place embargoes on the export of vital commodities such as iron, timber, horses or slaves, impose customs duties, and so on. But however varied their activities might be, the interests of the state were uppermost.

Provisioning policies are generally contrasted with the 'mercantilist' policies of seventeenth-century Europe, which do indeed have a modern ring to them; but the difference does not lie in the mere amount of economic activities undertaken, still less in the aim: the key objective of mercantilism, too, was to increase the power of the state. The whiff of modernity in mercantilism lies in the conception of *national* economy to be unified, protected, strengthened and exploited by the state, or in other words an economy coterminous with it. Non-European rulers generally perceived their economies as far-flung phenomena on a par with their cultures and their elites: they might be able to exploit this or that local manifestation of it, but not to fence it off and enclose it for systematic profit-making within a given area. Hence they did not establish national banks or otherwise try to assist the process of capital accumulation within their domains, subsidize industry by tax-exemption or outright grants (though craftsmen were exempted from public duties in late imperial Rome), seek to unify the domestic market by eliminating tariffs and tolls, or to protect this market by state-imposed tariff barriers, the very concept of a favourable balance of trade being unknown to most of them. The fact that the mercantilist rulers did all of these things is symptomatic of the growth, in Europe, of the unusual view of the state as a territorial rather than religious, cultural or dynastic entity.

Self-help groups

In general, then, pre-industrial government was minimal government. The state was expected to provide a protective shell behind which the subjects could get on with their own lives, but not to regulate their activities or to take over their roles except in so far as enemies of the established order had to be squashed and wrong-doers to be restrained. This objective might entail considerable interference (wrong-doing being an elastic category), but even so it always left room for a profusion of autonomous groups. Such groups were essentially self-help groups, and it was they which performed most of the functions now assumed by the state, not because they had been delegated to them, but rather because the state had never taken them over. By far the most important self-help group was the family. The larger a family, the more it was in the nature of a political, economic and charitable corporation. Its members could pool their resources and thus acquire capital to invest in education, business, land and other enterprises, to provide for the old, sick, crippled and demented, and to reap their rewards in the form of government office (once one member of the family had been appointed, office and other rewards would flow to the rest), as well as commercial profit, local standing and clients (that is people seeking their help in return for services of one kind or another). In some cultures, notably China, such family corporations were underpinned by ancestor worship. A man's descendants might stay together to the point that one lineage occupied a whole village; elsewhere, extended families occupied one household; but family solidarity was usually of great importance even where the nuclear family prevailed in terms of residence. The importance of family solidarity was public knowledge: if an official fell, all his relatives and protégés fell with him, being executed along with him or (by way of mercy) merely banished or enslaved.

Large kin groups were not however easily maintained by the poor. The more impoverished a family was, the greater were the chances that its members would disperse, destitute parents being forced to sell their children or even themselves, or to evict them as servants or apprentices, or simply to send them off in the 'wide world' (as fairy tales put it) to make a living on their own. Poor families were small families. Members of small, poor or undistinguished families might attach themselves as clients to a lineage of the above-mentioned kind or to an aristocratic house; and usually there were also clubs, guilds, secret societies, sectarian organizations or other kinds of voluntary societies which provided their members with credit, looked after them when they were ill, paid for their funerals when they died, took care of their widows and orphans and acted as mutual insurance groups in other ways. Mutual help might also be supplied on the basis of quarters, villages or other residential divisions: the strongest self-help groups undoubtedly ensued where kinship, residence and religious affiliation coincided. In most societies there was much charitable activity too, of course; but it could only provide occasional help, not a safety net. At all events, it was usually the kinless who sank to the very bottom of society, ending up as vagrants, criminals, prostitutes and beggars.

Law and order

It should be obvious from what has been said so far that no pre-industrial state was in a position to perform as well as its modern counterparts. In particular, their attempts to maintain internal order met with limited success: all pre-industrial societies had to tolerate a much higher level of violence than we do today.

Thus tax-gathering tended to be a violent affair because scarcity caused the peasants to resist, or more precisely because they *could* resist: unlike modern workers who leave their tools and products behind on clocking off, the peasants were in possession of both their land and their harvest and thus less easy to either tax or evict. At the very least they would hide their assets; at worst they would fight: it was for this reason that tax-collectors were usually accompanied by troops. But everyone was more prone to mutiny and rebellion than we are today, partly because numerous members of society had military power independently of the state and were apt to use it, be it in pursuit of private aims, in protest against the state, to compel it to bargain or to evade it; partly because there were fewer economic ties which had to be protected against disruption; and partly because rulers and subjects long had access to much the same weaponry, though the disparity between their outfits kept increasing.

In addition there were always areas which escaped state control altogether. Densely forested regions, mountainous areas, marshes, moors, deserts and steppes were difficult to negotiate for armies and administrators before the invention of jeeps, aeroplanes and the like, and generally also too sparsely inhabited by people too poor and too warlike to make attempts at direct control worthwhile: most states had barbarians within their boundaries as well as outside them. Depending on where such areas were in relation to the centre they might be left entirely alone or ruled indirectly (i.e. one or more local potentates might be held responsible for the good behaviour of the rest of the population in return for a judicious mixture of subsidies and penal expeditions). 'We do not obey the government in any way other than that we acknowledge it to be the government', as tribesmen of the Kabylian mountains in North Africa told a tenth-century Muslim heretic in search of militant recruits.

In addition to their own fierce inhabitants such areas tended also to accommodate a fair number of outlaws, escaped convicts, runaway slaves and other refugees, who would typically make a living as brigands. Frontier regions between two states, or even between two provinces, also tended to be unruly because there were political or administrative rivalries and confusions over jurisdiction for rebels to exploit, or simply because the central government was very far away.

But even well-governed areas had their share of violence, and policing was always deficient. Every town had its pickpockets, thieves, burglars, swindlers, murderers, assassins and protection racketeers, just as every road had its highwaymen and every sea its pirates. Private war and local feuds, riots and rebellion, marauding soldiers and brigandage, all these and other forms of disorder were commonplace in most societies most of the time.

The authorities reacted to disorder by meting out the most dreadful punishments to such culprits as they caught. People were quartered, bisected, sliced, boiled, skinned, disembowelled and so on, occasionally just hanged, crucified or decapitated, preferably in public; their remains would certainly be publicly displayed as a gruesome warning to passers-by of what lay in store for those who refused to obey. After the suppression of Spartacus' revolt in the Roman republic of the first century BC, the traveller along the Appian Way had 6000 crucified bodies to contemplate. It was the very impotence of the state which made it set such store by exemplary punishment as a deterrent, but of course the subjects had the same brutal attitude to life. 'Thieves are trampled to Death; and though this be a dreadful punishment, yet the Coresians are much addicted to stealing', as a seventeenth-century Dutchman shipwrecked in Korea observed. *Mutatis mutandis*, the same was true of other societies.

Insecurity greatly enhanced the importance of the self-help groups mentioned earlier. Whether they took the form of families, lineages, tribes, quarters, villages, guilds, religious communities or a combination thereof, they were islands of trust and solidarity in an unstable and dangerous world (which is not to say that there might not be rifts or tensions within them). Typically they would keep up a common front by policing themselves, settling their own disputes, marrying in accordance with joint interests, pursuing joint feuds, or even forming or maintaining armies. It is for this reason that people were either friends or allies, as mentioned in the previous chapter, not an undifferentiated mass of citizens who could supply neutral labour. To the state, the existence of such groups was a mixed blessing. They kept people under control, but they also intervened between the state and its subjects, making it difficult to govern directly; they might be heretical, and they were always in danger of growing obstreperous. Some might be proscribed, others accepted, be it with good or bad grace.

A *vicious circle*

We have seen that political organization was a response to certain deficiencies. Now is the time to summarize the various ways in which it acted back on and increased these deficiencies.

Clearly, pre-industrial governments generated mistrust, first because they were brutal (notably in their treatment of peasants and dissenters), and secondly because they were arbitrary. They were arbitrary because they vested unlimited power in whimsical rulers, who, though incapable of controlling the political process, could certainly intervene in unexpected ways and above all bring their power to bear on individuals, whom they would raise to power, demote or execute as they saw fit; 'off with his head' is the standard line of kings in popular tales. Indeed, the very fact that seemingly unlimited power proved impotent when brought to bear on processes rather than individuals encouraged arbitrary victimization. There is a story in the *Arabian Nights* in which the caliph and his vizier find the dismembered body of a young woman in a cask. Shocked, the caliph exclaims that the government ought to prevent such things from happening, an eminently modern sentiment, only to order his vizier to find the murderer at once or else be executed. Contrary to what the modern reader might expect, he does not order him to start a war on crime: the problem being beyond solution, the caliph simply lashed out against the nearest target. In precisely the same way, rulers were apt to respond to economic problems by confiscating private property, sometimes that of their officials and often that of merchants, and to cope with political crises by violation of promises, breach of safe-conduct, imprisonment without trial or trials with predetermined outcome, summary executions, and so forth. The scarcity of information made all wielders of public power, and the monarch above all, dependent on informers who had to be trusted but of whose reliability no-one could ever feel sure, a fact which created ample scope for intrigues, whispered suggestions, carefully planted information and dis-information, all of which caused heads to roll from time to time.

Instability at the top made for predatory rule all along the line, everybody being out to hoard as much gold, accumulate as much land and secure as many advantages as possible before royal favour ran out. The entire machinery of government was thus corrupt, not just because funds were short or because the primacy of loyalties to kith and kin was generally accepted, but also because the unstable and unpredictable nature of government positively encouraged extortion and the accumulation of protective networks. Naturally, we have a vicious circle here, government becoming more brutal and unstable at the top in response to corruption underneath. All in all, pre-industrial governments were nasty things best avoided, as peasants everywhere agreed. 'The two worst places to stand in are behind a horse and in front of an official', as an Indian saying has it; 'happy is he who never has dealings with us', as a pious caliph is supposed to have said. But joining the government might be easier than avoiding it, and those who had the option usually preferred the active pursuit of power, wealth and honour to passive victimization, however great the risks.

In addition to generating mistrust and predatory behaviour where it aimed at co-operation, pre-industrial government was stultifying because it had to suppress rather than mobilize most of the human energy at its disposal. Since the state could neither penetrate nor integrate the society it ruled, it sat on top of a myriad of ethnic, linguistic and religious communities and a myriad of autonomous self-help groups over which it had little control, regulating the surface without getting very far underneath. This being so, it was intensely suspicious of new developments below the surface, especially developments which threatened to endow the masses with a capacity for collective action. This is a point to which I shall revert in the next chapter. Suffice it here to say that since political organization was predicated on the fact that the masses could not be integrated, the masses perforce had to *remain* in a state of non-integration: once you have made a virtue of necessity, you do not want necessity to change. Keeping local communities separate and politically passive was thus a prime objective of pre-industrial government; and as a result, some 90 per cent of human energy in any given polity was written off for all purposes other than taxation and (at times) military service. In the Roman empire of the first century AD, for example, a governor of a province in Asia Minor requested the permission of the emperor Trajan to form a fire-brigade in a town which had been devastated by fire; Trajan refused on the grounds that 'whatever name we give to [such associations], and for whatever purposes they may be founded, they will not fail to form themselves into dangerous assemblies'. Inasmuch as organization amounted to a potential for political action, it was too risky to use the masses even for the extinction of their own fires. But the monarch's fear of losing control over the elite also had the effect of suppressing energy which could have been used to good effect. In nineteenth-century Vietnam, provincial mandarins campaigned for the establishment of granaries in their provinces after the country had been devastated by cholera, but the emperor refused permission because he did not wish provincial officials to acquire more power than they already possessed. Elsewhere, governors were frequently dispatched for tenures so short, and with troops and other personnel so deficient, that however good or bad their intentions were, they could not get anything organized in their provinces beyond the collection of some taxes.

In short, the political organization had a strong tendency to encourage *power stand-off*, that is a situation in which different kinds of power counteract and nullify each other instead of combining for joint effect. Pre-industrial states had considerable power to *prevent* things from happening, but very little to *make* them happen: they were far better at suppressing than at generating energy. This was so because the state tended to sit like a 'capstone' on top of society, keeping its various components in place, but incapable of stimulating further development. Capstone government was the response to the problem of organizing large numbers of people over large areas with inadequate resources: imperial government was capstone government *par excellence* (though non-imperial states frequently exemplified it too). It made emperors specialists in what has been called *extensive* power, that is the ability to organize large numbers over large distances for minimal co-operation. The Mughal emperors of India, for example, are said to have ruled their enormous empire largely by keeping firm control of the main roads and regional trading centres, maintaining no more than minimal order elsewhere. But it did not make emperors good at *intensive* organization, the ability to organize tightly and in depth: no emperor could have devised or kept up the elaborate institutions of public health which the Italian Renaissance states created in response to the plague. Hence the mistrust, the predatory behaviour, the arbitrariness and the constant need to suppress. This was the vicious circle in which not just empires, but practically all pre-industrial states were caught.

It is thus not surprising that states were brittle structures which easily collapsed under internal stress or external pressure. The low degree of integration on the one hand and the minimal services performed by the state on the other meant that there was little to hold them together. The basic ingredients were easily reshuffled, so that states had a tendency to come and go (though some were conspicuously more durable than others). And their machinery was too cumbersome, too overlaid with private interests, too coercive and too mistrusted to work with any degree of speed, precision or efficiency. Evidently, there are enormous variations here too. But it was for such reasons that, until quite late in history, even the most powerful states on earth could be toppled by a handful of spirited barbarians.

4
Politics

Pre-industrial politics were the politics of the elite, or in other words of as little as one or two per cent of the population. It was only in republican societies that the masses stood a chance of gaining political rights (though aristocratic leadership prevailed even when they did); and republics were rare, as has been seen. However, the difference between modern and pre-modern politics did not lie in the number of participants alone.

Semi-private nature

In addition to being the prerogative of a few, politics tended to be dominated by the personal desires, circumstances and connections of those who engaged in them. Theorists might distinguish in the most sophisticated manner between public and private matters, defining the ruler as a mere agent of the community he ruled (or of God or the gods on behalf of the community), charging him with the protection of his subjects as a father is charged with the care of his children or as a shepherd with that of his sheep, and sometimes going so far as to award the community a right to rebel if he failed. Kings were servants hired by the people, as an Indian treatise on statecraft said: one paid them taxes in return for protection. Kings did *not* exist for the satisfaction of their private needs, and they were *not* to treat public revenues as private income. But in practice kings tended to do just that, as did the elite underneath them.

In part this was because hereditary succession encouraged rulers to think of their kingdoms as personal possessions, or more precisely as family property which could be divided among the heirs, included in marriage settlements, pawned (as was most of Denmark in the early fourteenth century), willed away (as was Pergamon by Attalus III to Rome in the second century BC) or sold (as was Rostov, or the political rights over it, by its prince to Ivan III of Muscovy in 1474). This pattern was particularly pronounced in Europe, where it was a feudal legacy: feudal kings were first and foremost rulers of their private domains, whatever else they might be. And here it also made for dynastic politics of a distinctive kind. Kings being rulers of private domains, succession to rulership was identical with that to landed property; and as it happened land could be transmitted by both men *and* women, while at the same time strict monogamy prevailed. Outside Europe, by contrast, succession to rulership was normally distinct from that to private property; women could not usually transmit either land or political rights of any kind, while at the same time polygamy, concubinage or easy divorce ensured that male heirs were plentiful. Hence non-European rulers merely sealed political alliances by their marriages, but their European counterparts were constantly vying for both allies *and* heiresses; and where non-European kings tended to have a surfeit of potential heirs, their European counterparts were forever worrying about their capacity to produce just one, so that the marital affairs of kings were hot political issues; and though succession wars on the death of rulers are attested all over the world, succession wars between reigning monarchs were peculiar to Europe, where dynastic claims to specific territories based on the rules of private succession played a crucial role in international politics until as late as the eighteenth century.

However, heredity encouraged the conflation of public and private matters outside Europe too. Monarchs might see themselves as office-holders, but they still held office by hereditary right with the result that they found it hard to distinguish between dynastic and official interests. Indeed, the very word for 'dynasty' and 'state' might be identical, as it was in Chinese (*kuo*) and came to be in Arabic too (*dawla*). Since the elite was often hereditary too, everyone endowed with political power was inclined to regard his position as private property on a par with everything else inherited from parents and to make use of it accordingly. Both rulers and elite went to war for the sake of personal glory, or to avenge personal slights, and spent public income on private concerns (occasionally vice versa too), while at the same time they made public festivals out of events in their private lives, celebrating royal weddings, births and the like on a magnificent scale to impress everyone with their might.

More particularly, however, the semi-private conception of power was a consequence of absolutism. For one thing, a person endowed with supreme power, be it by heredity or otherwise, cannot easily distinguish between his private and public selves. 'The earth belongs to God, and I am the deputy of God', as the caliph Muawiya (661–80) said; 'l'état c'est moi', as Louis XIV put it in a celebrated statement (the precise meaning of which is however disputed). Since the monarch was the ultimate decision-maker, he impressed his personality on government to an extent impossible where power is divided among impersonal institutions: mad rulers such as the Roman emperor Caligula (12–41) or the Fatimid caliph al-Hakim (996–1021) impressed their madness on it. And inevitably his dispositions reflected his private interests too: forty years after Muawiya's death his numerous kinsmen allegedly owned between half and two thirds of all the land in the caliphate.

For another thing, the concentration of absolute power in a single person conferred a huge advantage on those who had easy access to that person. High politics thus came to be dominated by events in the monarch's antechamber (or indeed bedchamber) on the one hand and by cliques and factions on the other, every member of the court gravitating around those with direct access to the king, exchanging personal services along the line of access. In seventeenth-century France, royal favourites such as Richelieu systematically created their own cliques by appointing friends, relatives and other protégés to administrative posts until they had whole armies of *créatures* working on their behalf.

Personal networks were likely to affect low politics too. Given that there was little or no machinery for the representation of local interests at the centre, or at any rate not below the level of the elite, local groups in need of central support would offer services in return for intercession by recipients who would offer theirs in their turn to people higher up, and so forth, until they reached the court. The particular manner in which factions, cliques and other interest groups operated depended on the socio-political organization with which they had to cope. There might be factions which stretched all the way from village level to the palace, or on the contrary courtly cliques and local factions which did not have anything to do with each other (the local ones having purely local roots) or which interacted despite their different origins. Factions might also operate within one branch of the governmental machinery without spilling over into others, or they might affect both. They might develop ideologies of their own (in which case one would call them 'parties' rather than mere 'factions') or they might remain devoid of ideological differentiation. Whatever the nature of such groups, the sources have an unhelpful tendency only to record the tip of the iceberg, that is the actions of individuals, paying little or no attention to the submerged structure without which their actions are hard to understand. Few individuals were simply individuals, as opposed to representatives of larger networks of various kinds.

Finally, the fact that the wielders of political power were not forced to render account of their activities to outsiders promoted the view that politics consisted of gentlemanly agreements between members of the club. The reduction of public decision-making to private agreements had the advantage of keeping the lines of communication short and ensuring that whatever decisions were taken were agreeable to the individuals involved. By contrast, impersonal rules tend to make decision-making cumbersome and to produce results indifferent or contrary to the private interests of the decision-makers, which is of course their very point. Impersonal rules are however only imposed and observed where the administration is open to inspection by outsiders, be it by means of courts, parliaments or mass media. Pre-industrial rulers were rarely held to be accountable to anyone apart from God; normally, their servants were not held to be responsible to anyone except their superiors either; and mass media did not exist. In short, the political process was thoroughly shielded from the public gaze, leaving everyone free to engage in endless private bargaining behind the scenes.

Warfare

By our standards, the small circle of people admitted to political representation spent an inordinate amount of time and money on warfare. Some cultures were considerably more militant in outlook than others: in China from the twelfth century onwards, military men held a distinctly inferior position. But whatever the nature of the prevailing outlook, warfare everywhere seemed to be a major part of what states were for. In the tenth-century caliphate the maintenance of the army and military installations is estimated to have accounted for about half of the public revenues; in England the state is believed to have spent no less than 75-90 per cent of its revenues on the acqusition and use of military force over the period from 1130 to 1815.

Internal

In most pre-industrial societies military force was required for the maintenance of internal order. The numerous peasant communities of which they consisted were not held together by economic ties, and not on the whole by cultural ones either, cultural ties being weaker at all events; in the last resort they were held together by force. It is true that they might be subjected to administrative control through a bureaucracy, but the bureaucracies of the past were rarely adequate to their task, being understaffed in relation to the size of the population (though often overstaffed in relation to the services they performed), slow-moving, extortionate, and dominated by private interests. Control of the population rested to a greater or lesser extent with local landowners of one kind or another (barons, squires, notables or whatever), who might or might not be office-holders and whose relationship with the centre was at all events liable to be unstable; they might refuse to co-operate, switch allegiance, rebel or harbour those who did. Popular revolts were a danger too.

This being so, the exercise of brute force was regularly required to keep the state together. Today we are no longer in the habit of engaging in armed revolt, and most of us would be deeply shocked to have the army sent against us: the maintenance of modern European states rests on economic interdependence and bureaucratic control, assisted by cultural homogeneity and judicious use of the police (some notorious trouble-spots apart). But in pre-industrial times the army was as much an instrument for the maintenance of internal order as for defence against outsiders.

Indeed, the very distinction between internal and external warfare might be tenuous. Numerous states in history have consisted of a core area and a periphery, the former being subject to both military and administrative control, the latter to military control alone, so that regular displays of military superiority were required to keep the periphery within the fold (in the sense that it continued to pay tribute or taxes, place military contingents, render labour service or whatever). Few pre-industrial states had fixed borders, as opposed to vague frontier areas under the sway of local magnates, tribal groups, bandits or other unruly elements. Punitive expeditions against such areas were often hard to distinguish from actual wars of conquest.

External

Basically, pre-industrial states were expansionist because land was the source of all or most of their wealth: the conquest of tax-yielding agricultural land was by far the simplest method of increasing revenues, and it might also be the only method whereby the ruler could replenish his stock of land with which to reward members of the elite. Internally, too, there might be competition for land and peasants in the form of aristocratic feuding, as was often the case until office-holding came to represent an alternative avenue to wealth. Political frontiers might also be so fluid as to render the distinction between internal and external meaningless. At all events, agricultural land was the key objective of most conquerors, though labour (in the form of slaves) and other booty (notably precious metals) might also be desired. The fact that there is a limited amount of land on earth encouraged the view that wealth was a fixed quantity which could only be acquired at the expense of someone else: you could not get richer without others getting poorer. Even commercial wealth was held to be a limited good (as in fact it was as long as customers were so few), so the mercantilist states of Europe went to war to capture markets too.

War was however pursued for many other reasons in addition, and economic interests were rarely invoked to justify it. To a military elite, war meant glory (religious or secular, collective or individual), a fact which almost always entered as both a contributory and a legitimating factor. Even a king as recent as Frederick II of Prussia (1740-86) thought it perfectly natural that he should have gone to war against Austria for the sake of 'ambition, advantage, my desire to make a name for myself'. Warfare might also provide an opportunity for royal co-ordination and direction of a collective enterprise which could greatly assist the growth or maintenance of royal power in primitive states (such as those of barbarians) or very decentralized ones (such as that of the Cholas in medieval Ceylon); under such circumstances the booty it bought in would likewise assist the growth of the state apparatus. Elsewhere it kept the troops out of mischief (where standing armies existed), diverted attention from internal problems (where the masses were politically influential), and increased the ruler's legitimacy (as in the Islamic world where the conduct of holy war was one of his cardinal duties). On the whole, it was also less destructive than it is today, partly because the technology of annihilation was less advanced and partly because the marching and fighting took place over a relatively small area while the population tended to be widely dispersed. Still, it might greatly increase the tax burden, disrupt trade, cause unemployment among artisans, provoke famine as the soldiers ate their way through the countryside and decimate the population by slaughter and disease spread by the troops. The more complex a society was, the greater its vulnerability became. Five years of Swedish campaigns in Poland between 1655 and 1660 are estimated to have destroyed 35 per cent of the towns, 10 per cent of the villages and 40 per cent of the population in the central provinces. Successful wars of conquest fought on enemy territory might well pay off, but in purely economic terms it would nonetheless be hazardous to say that war was generally a sound investment.

The fact that pre-industrial states were expansionist is one reason why, or rather one precondition for, the common occurrence of empires in history. Where a plurality of states coexisted and interacted, every polity would attempt to absorb its neighbours and the chances were that sooner or later one of them would prevail. Thus the city states of ancient Sumeria gave way to the empire of Sargon followed by that of the Assyrians, just as those of the classical Mediterranean gave way to the empire of Alexander followed by that of the Romans; the Muslim Middle East began with the establishment of an empire (the caliphate), and though it rapidly disintegrated, another empire was eventually created by the Ottomans; India saw the coming and going of several empires; and in China imperial unity prevailed from the sixth century onwards, occasional periods of splits or outright fragmentation notwithstanding. However, the reasons why some attempts at unification succeeded and others failed are more interesting (and also more elusive) than the simple fact that unification was always being attempted.

Elite-building

The small number of participants in pre-industrial politics, their failure to distinguish between private and public affairs and their endless preoccupation with warfare are apt to convey the impression that pre-industrial politics were about nothing much apart from aristocratic bickering over land and glory. But in fact pre-industrial politics were never lacking in serious issues or objectives, though the objectives pursued were of a kind unfamiliar today.

As mentioned in the previous chapter, one of the foremost tasks of the ruler was to transform diverse holders of political or spiritual power into an imperial or nationwide elite united in its loyalty to the same polity, the same dynasty and the same monarch. The ruling elite had to be everything that the masses were not: where the masses were divided into a myriad of diverse communities, the elite had to be homogeneous and cohesive; and where the masses had a diversity of political interests which mostly had to be suppressed, the various branches of the elite had to have a common interest in serving, representing and perpetuating the state. The masses could not be integrated; the means simply did not exist to turn them into members of the same social, political, economic or cultural world. But a small number of people prised loose from the masses *could* be integrated; it was such people who had to keep the kingdom or empire together. In some societies, religious and military leaders appeared before the arrival of kings (kings emerging from their midst); in others, they emerged under the very noses of rulers, unsolicited by or even in opposition to them. But whether such leadership existed already, emerged belatedly or had to be created from scratch, the ruler had to make sure that he had it on his side. In short, he had to forge an alliance between state, church, educational institutions and wealth.

Students often regard the alliance in question as both unholy and inevitable; but whatever one may feel about its moral status, its creation was by no means preordained: elite-building in pre-industrial times was no easier than is nation-building today; and even if an elite was successfully created, its management was anything but easy.

The ruler needed at least some degree of control over the high culture, in the sense of the prevailing world view with attendant language, literature and organization. (For a more detailed account of high culture the reader must await the next chapter.) Religious leaders controlled the definition of rectitude, frequently including the law and/or access to salvation, a fact which endowed them with considerable influence over lay behaviour; they invariably possessed some degree of organization, often controlled considerable amounts of land and other wealth acquired through gifts from the faithful; and they might have a monopoly on literacy too. In short, they constituted a power structure which the ruler could rarely afford to ignore. Co-operation, on the other hand, held out the promise of organizational support, literate personnel and ideological resources with which to legitimate the state and its incumbents, that is show them to be in conformity with the natural or divine order and representative of the values to which the subjects were committed. In particular, it held out the promise of an elite united in a belief system that tied it to the state.

The monarch's attempt to mobilize the high culture and its representatives for his own purposes resulted now in alliance and now in sharp conflict between him and other persons with a vested interest in it, such as monks, scholars, priests, popes or holy men. The high culture was rarely tailor-made for kings in either institutional or ideological terms, being all too often ambivalent in its attitude to the secular powers of this world and sometimes endowed with the additional disadvantage of hallowing a community much larger than that of which the monarch was in charge, as did Christianity after the fall of the Roman empire and Islam after the disintegration of the caliphate. (It was a good deal more difficult to nationalize Islam than Christianity, as a fifteenth-century sultan of Malacca discovered when he declared the pilgrimage to Mecca to be unnecessary, Malacca itself being 'made into Mecca') But the religious or cultural institution was practically always in favour of co-operation; the disagreement was over the terms.

The ruler also needed some degree of control over the land or its produce so that he could reward the elite (be it religious or political) for its services, preferably on a lavish scale. Obviously, the larger the rewards funnelled through the state, the greater the interest of the recipients in its survival. Besides, just as as mastery of the high culture singled out a gentleman from the uneducated rabble underneath (as will be seen), so massive wealth created a gulf between the excluded commoners and the powerful few, giving the latter a common interest, lifestyle and outlook apt to make them stick together as a group, however much they might quarrel among themselves. Indeed, an elite might underscore its distinction from the masses by wholesale adoption of foreign descent: thus Polish nobles were in the habit of claiming descent from the Sarmatians (a nomadic people of Iranian origin which had reached Poland in the first centuries AD), while eighteenth-century French aristocrats presented themselves as survivors of the Franks, mere commoners being descendants of the Romano-Celts that the Franks had overrun.

Unlike the religious establishment, however, the landed magnates whom the ruler tried to tame might well be opposed to collaboration altogether, some desiring independence and others the throne for themselves. But even when they did not, acceptance of the desirability of collaboration once more left room for much disagreement over the terms, the magnates and sometimes also lesser landowners wanting more autonomy than the monarch wished to concede them. The monarch could not do without them, being dependent on their services for local government: policing, dispute settlement, the maintenance of irrigation systems, the assessment and collection of taxes and other duties might be partly or wholly delegated to them. 'A monarchy divested of its nobility has no refuge under heaven but an army', as a seventeenth-century English theorist put it, forgetting the bureaucracy. But even monarchs who had enough non-aristocratic soldiers *and* bureaucrats to manage without aristocratic assistance soon found that local notabilities of other kinds had to be enrolled: however centralized the polity might be, *some* wielders of local power had to be co-opted to facilitate the execution of governmental policies. The question was merely how such leaders were to be slotted in with the state.

The disagreement usually took the form of a tug-of-war between office-holders representing the interests of the centre and local land-owners of one kind or another. The landowners might be members of hereditary nobilities of military origin, as were those of pre-classical China, pre-Islamic Iran and Europe; they might also be civilian notabilities who supposedly owed their wealth and prestige to education, as were those of classical China and the medieval Muslim world. As far as the ruler was concerned, the main problem was that office-holders commonly had to be recruited from the ranks of the landowners themselves, only men of noble status being acceptable in positions of command (as in Europe) or only local landowners producing a sufficiency of educated bureaucrats (as in China); this clearly made for collusion between the two. Even where office-holders could be recruited outside landowning ranks, their appointment was apt to transform them into nobles of the kind they were meant to counteract.

Conquest, revolution or other upheavals might enable the monarch to dismiss an old nobility, replacing it by or transforming it into a service aristocracy dependent on the crown for its access to land and wealth (as happened in very different ways in Carolingian France, Muscovite Russia, Mughal India and elsewhere). But land and other rewards granted by the state all too easily degenerated into private property, leaving the monarch empty-handed, or it was all too easily squeezed for what it was worth by officials whose tenure was limited to the duration of their office. The monarch might play the lesser nobility against the magnates (but then the lesser nobility might also exploit the rivalry between magnates and crown); he might practise sale of offices, thereby throwing them open to commoners and bringing in revenues at the same time (absolutist France provides the most famous example); he might systematically recruit part or all of his officials from among educated townsmen (as frequently in Europe), or foreigners (greatly appreciated by the Mongols in China), or eunuchs (as in China, the Islamic world, Byzantium and, in the form of celibate churchmen, medieval Europe), or from among servile elements (such as the German *ministeriales* or, more spectacularly, the imported slave governors and other officials of the Muslim world). Given sufficient leverage against the landowners, he might try forcibly to deprive this or that obstreperous person of his land (usually awarding it to another), to limit the number of their armed retainers or slaves, to squeeze r. ore services and taxes out of them, and to cope with the regional revolts that such measures were likely to provoke. But whatever he did, the relationship between office-holders dependent on the centre and landowners thriving on local influence was problematic until modernity enabled the central government to organize local society without the assistance of landowners altogether.

All in all, the creation and maintenance of a ruling elite was thus a hard job, and history is full of monarchs who lost the game: the caliphs of the early Muslims were defeated by religious scholars; the Holy Roman emperors of Germany were defeated by the pope; the kings of Poland lost out to their nobility, and so forth. Many other monarchs stayed in the game, but no solution ever proved entirely stable: it was a problem with much dynamic potential.

Organizing the masses

Pre-industrial politics were enacted by the elite, but they were often *about* the masses. It is true that the latter were generally left alone as long as they refrained from revolt and paid their taxes, but measures had to be taken to ensure that they would do so. Besides, how and to whom were they to pay? Elite-building was impossible without specifying the relationship of both crown and elite with the masses underneath.

Peasants
The key question regarding the peasantry was whether the state should keep them free or on the contrary allow the landowning elite to enserf them. The interests of the monarch generally lay in keeping them free, that is under the direct control of the state for purposes of taxation, corvée and military service (as infantry); serfs, like slaves, were accessible only through their masters, who would collect their

contributions and pass on little or (in the case of slaves) nothing to the public treasury. On the other hand, the freedom of the peasantry sometimes had to be sacrificed in order to buy elite support (as it was in seventeenth-century Russia, eastern Europe and Denmark), and there were also times when the state was simply too weak to prevent the nobility from inserting itself between the peasants and the central administration.

Attempts to protect free peasants against the encroachments of large landowners have been common in history, one of the most striking examples being the Chinese 'equitable distribution of land' system (in force between $c.485-750$), according to which the ownership of all cultivated land was vested in the state: every man and woman had a right to a specified amount of land for their lifetime, but it reverted to the state on their death. This was a particularly drastic method, but the battle against large landowners who enserfed free peasants, taking over their land in return for protection (usually, though not invariably, protection against tax-collectors) is well known from the most diverse places: the late Roman empire, late Byzantium, and Vietnam under the Le dynasty (1428–1789) are among the examples. Subtle means are also attested. Thus the state might offer loans to peasants to prevent them from falling into the clutches of landlords and other money-lenders, as it did at times in China and Korea, or declare all debts to be cancelled, as it did in Solon's Athens, or issue moratoria on debts, as it did from time to time in Tokugawa Japan.

However, the struggles often proved futile, sometimes because the very officials who were supposed to enforce the regulations were among the chief offenders, being landowners themselves, as they were in China, and at other times because the state apparatus as such was dissolving, as in the western half of the late Roman empire and Dark Age Europe. But whether they were free or not, peasants had to be organized for the role expected of them, an activity which might involve disarming them (turning their swords into ploughshares or images of the Buddha), registering their persons and their land, assessing taxes, appointing headmen, issuing passports and identity cards, hunting down fugitives, and so on.

Townsmen

Towns only required special policies where they grew up within a socio-political order which was not designed to cope with them (as in medieval Europe and Japan); under such circumstances they obviously posed the question how they should be fitted in. But most towns grew up with the polity in which they were found, in so far as they did not precede them, meaning that they posed no questions at all, having always been centres of established power rather than subversive elements. However, merchants were a problem in all agrarian civilizations.

Mercantile wealth was accumulated outside the ranks of the ruling elite, from sources other than land, by means other than political service or mastery of the high culture: hence it posed a threat to the established order. The fact that merchants thrived on alternative wealth showed in their behaviour too: they had to be calculating or even mean, whereas aristocrats behaved with ostentatious disregard for money; and they had to consort with people from all walks of life, whereas members of the ruling elite had a vested interest in the maintenance of social distance. To this must be added that spend-thrift aristocrats all too often got themselves indebted to the very people they feared and despised, a fact which greatly increased their desire to condemn them as 'thieves known by other names' (as a famous Indian treatise on statecraft describes them). Merchants were also suspect in that they regularly crossed geographical frontiers, both between states and within them, with the result that they were used as spies: thus the Chola invasion of Ceylon in 1017 was under-taken in response to news of internal strife brought by a merchant; the Mongol invasion of eastern Iran was precipitated by the execu-tion, in 1218, of 450 merchants from Mongol territory by a governor who, probably correctly, took them to be spies dispatched by Chingiz Khan; when the British planned the occupation of lower Burma in 1852 it was a Muslim merchant who informed the governor of Rangoon that the British intended to invade; and so on. Merchants were regularly assumed to be spies even when they were not. Being mobile, moreover, they were in a position to spread heretical ideas, as indeed they sometimes did. (Heretics bent on revolutionary action regularly disguised themselves as merchants in the early Islamic world.) In short, merchants were subversive elements which had to be kept under strict control.

They could not be suppressed inasmuch as nobody, not even the wielders of political power, wished to do without their services; but their influence could be contained through formal rules and common prejudice alike. The early Romans forbade their aristocracy to en-gage in trade; the Chinese excluded traders and their descendants from participation in the civil service examinations until the thirteenth century; in early modern Europe (England excepted), the nobility itself insisted on the doctrine of *dérogeance* according to which noble status was lost by those who engaged in trade; in early modern Japan, *samurai* (bearers of arms) were forbidden to engage in it, while the traders themselves were deemed to be the lowest-ranking group of society, outcasts excepted; and so on. The literary remains of all the great civilizations are replete with derogatory statements about commerce and its practitioners (though Islamic literature contains an unusual number of favourable statements too). The larger the scale of the trade, the less offensive it was deemed to be, especially if its sponsors did not participate in it directly; and the richest merchants might well be admitted to the ranks of the elite, only common traders being rejected as despicable. Mercantile activity might also be highly regulated, the state awarding a monopoly to itself over its most lucrative branches, fixing the number of internal markets, limiting the points of entry allowed to foreign traders or even forbidding private foreign trade altogether (as in China every now and again from the thirteenth century onwards, and in Japan from the sixteenth until the nineteenth).

Horizontal linkages

Pre-industrial rulers devoted considerable attention to preventing the masses from organizing themselves for collective action other than that of which the state approved. So do modern rulers in charge of repressive regimes, now as then with a view to preventing the excluded masses from obstructing government. In pre-industrial times the masses were excluded because they could not be integrated in a single political, cultural or economic world: the wisest course was thus to keep them divided, and any development which threatened to generate the same unity among the masses as that which prevailed among the elite was extremely suspect. At best, 'horizontal linkages' could become sources of influence over officials, thereby helping local people to protect their private interests against the state. At worst, they could generate large-scale dissidence.

Thus the fear of horizontal linkages lay behind the prohibition, by Greek tyrants, of clubs for social and cultural activities. Numerous Roman clubs were likewise suppressed by Caesar, while Augustus enacted that every club must be sanctioned by the Senate or the Emperor: funerary clubs received general permission as long as their members only met once a month! But Trajan was suspicious of all clubs, including fire-brigades, as seen already; and both he and other emperors were extremely suspicious of the Christians. The fact that the early Christians were bent on giving unto Caesar what was Caesar's in no way rendered them politically innocuous, nor was the fact that they refused to worship the Roman emperor the worst of their political sins. What really made them dangerous was their capacity to unite hitherto disparate masses in the name of an alternative vision and thus, whether this was intended or not, create an alternative power structure which the emperors ultimately preferred to have on their side rather than against them. The fear of such linkages is attested for other empires too, and though it was sensible enough, the fact that any type of popular organization was suspect sometimes had the effect of forcing quietists into political action: numerous cult societies of nineteenth-century China merely wished to provide world-views more satisfactory to their rural clientele than official Confucianism; but finding themselves an object of official suspicion, they had a rebellious streak, which reinforced the suspicion, thus making them more rebellious, and so on.

As the Roman adoption of Christianity shows, rulers sometimes tried to cash in on horizontal linkages rather than to suppress them (though they usually tried to suppress them first). A monotheist religion such as Christianity offered the possibility of integration of the masses on a new scale: when the Roman empire became officially Christian, the population at large both felt itself and was perceived to be a member of the political and cultural community created by the elite. This was advantageous, though it also created problems. Subjects who preferred their local traditions to the high culture of the (foreign) elite would opt out as heretics, as did the Syrian and Coptic Monophysites of the late Roman/early Byzantine empire: the obverse of mass integration was mass dissent. But at all events the rulers who adopted the religion of the masses, or who attempted to impose their own on them, clearly did so in the hope that a common outlook would induce the masses to identify with their state or church, not that they would start identifying with each other against it. The fear of horizontal linkages in the form of new cult societies, sects and the like remained.

Popular revolts

In keeping with the fact that politics were enacted within the elite, the vast majority of revolts were started by members of the elite in

pursuit of by now familiar aims: autonomy or better terms: vis-à-vis
the monarch, be it individually or collectively. But from time to time
the masses themselves erupted onto the political scene.

Slaves
All slave-owning societies had to cope with runaway slaves and slave
revolts. Fugitives were extremely common: their prayers would not
be heard, just as those of disobedient wives would not, according to
a saying ascribed to Muhammad. But they were not a danger unless
they banded together in autonomous communities of their own,
usually robbers' nests, which of course amounted to revolt, but
which could often be ignored or dealt with by occasional punitive
expeditions because the communities in question were formed in
remote areas difficult of access. (In the West Indies such slaves were
known as maroons.) Outright rebellion was less common, though
numerous minor instances of sedition are attested for all slave-
owning societies. Major revolts were almost invariably associated
with barrack slavery, where slaves were kept under conditions which
prevented them from living more or less normal lives of their own;
where, further, the majority of the slaves were newly enslaved as
opposed to born into slavery and thus full of memories of their lives
as free men back home; and where, finally, a substantial number of
the slaves were of the same ethnic and cultural background which
made it easy for them to communicate and gave them shared models
of action. Domestic slaves and slaves working in small-scale crafts
and manufacturing, on the other hand, were not just dispersed, but
also for the most part able to live ordinary human lives, meaning that
they were unlikely to do more than run away if they found their
masters unbearable.

Before the nineteenth century (when they picked up the idea from
their masters) rebel slaves seem never to have demanded the abolition of slavery, or at any rate not in so far as they were imported
foreigners. Some wanted to go home to resume their lives (as did
Spartacus). Most wanted to reverse the roles between themselves and
their masters, reducing the former to slaves and assigning freedom,
wealth and high status to themselves. Either way, they required
political organization to make a bid for freedom. Unlike runaways,
they would organize themselves right in the middle of the slave-
owning society, meaning that they had to be suppressed at all costs.
All duly were, with the exception of two: the Israelites of Egypt,
who were both runaways and rebels, managed to escape and even-

tually reconquer their own homeland (a story of much inspiration to Christian slaves); and the slaves of Haiti, who rebelled under Toussaint L'Ouverture, successfully fought what eventually became the war of independence for Haiti (1791–1804).

Peasants

Peasant protests were a much larger and more varied phenomenon. Peasants did not necessarily have to rebel to make their wishes heard: in many societies there were mechanisms enabling them to present petitions, which they used to make concrete requests such as the abolition of new-fangled duties, remission of taxes for a year, a moratorium on debts, the dismissal of an unpopular governor or other redress against extortion. 'The labour quota of our village . . . has been raised from six to seventeen men, and this is causing the greatest difficulty to peasants. Every year some must sell their daughters just to keep from losing their land . . . . Only if you hear this appeal and order reductions will we be able to live as peasants': thus a Japanese headman to the *daimyo* (overlord) of Nihonmatsu in 1625. 'The Mughals came to our village, damaged meadow land and gave the remaining grass to their cattle. They cut down unripe crops and took them away . . . What is more, the . . . *jagirdar* [official to whom taxes have been assigned in lieu of pay] of this district took away the villagers' cattle and seized even the smallest amount of money. As a result the villagers have despaired and deserted the village . . . For this reason I beg that the amount of tax levied on this village be revised': thus the head of a rural district in central India to the Maratha government in 1692.

But peasant also had their runaways, as the second petition indicates. If they were tied to the soil, they would run away to districts in which they were not registered, to new lands beyond the political border, or to the army, monasteries or cities. 'Town air makes free', as a medieval German saying had it: runaway serfs were emancipated if they managed to stay in a town for a year and a day. In the Middle East after the Arab conquest it was Muslim town air that was expected to make free, flights to the garrison towns of the new rulers being accompanied by adoption of the new faith. Tied or free, they might run away in order to commend themselves to a landlord, enserfing themselves in return for protection against tax-collectors, brigands or barbarian invaders; or they might take to the hills, usually because they had fallen out with the authorities over behaviour condemned by the latter but regarded as proper by themselves (e.g. private vengeance), forming bandit gangs that directed their violence against landlords and officials and thrived on village support, robbing the rich, that is the authorities, and giving to the poor, that is local villagers, after the fashion of Robin Hood. (There is a good account of such bandits in a Turkish setting in Yashar Kemal's novel *Memed, my Hawk*.) Many became legendary heroes because they embodied peasant ideals, though they inevitably made things worse for those who stayed behind in the villages, increasing their tax burden and their vulnerability to official intervention.

Where flight was not an option, peasants might, so to speak, boil over and engage in *jacqueries*, spontaneous outbursts of violence in which tax-collectors and landlords were killed, manors sacked and records burnt. And of course, they might engage in full-scale, planned revolt.

Such revolts were usually (though not invariably) conducted under the aegis of religion because religion was an obvious source of organization above village level. It was also a source of ideas, and it provided supernatural sanction of the entire enterprise. The leaders were often villagers themselves, sometimes local cult personnel. Typically, they were singled out for leadership by dreams, trances, messages from spirits, revelations or other communications with the divine, and their creed was often millenarian (chiliastic), that is wildly utopian. Everything was expected to be turned upside down: the mighty would fall and the lowly would be elevated; the tyrants would disappear along with taxes and the state itself; the lion and the lamb would lie down together, disease and old age would disappear, and so forth; in short Paradise (or some comparable state of original bliss) would be restored. The sudden change was frequently expected to take place at the hands of a redeemer figure (in which case the movement is labelled 'messianic'). And those who joined were commonly promised invulnerability in battle.

To a modern reader it is hard to understand how people could believe such fantasies, though there are recent examples too: in 1987 British newspapers devoted considerable attention to the rebellious Holy Spirit Movement of northern Uganda led by one Alice 'Lakwena' ('Messiah') who received messages from spirits and promised her followers invulnerability in battle if they used a certain oil. But at all events, messiahs of this kind clearly recruited their followers among people unfamiliar with the realities of power. Having no realistic sense of how to go about improving their position, they were thrown back on the assistance of the supernatural, that is to say their own

imagination. The supernatural guaranteed the success of the outcome; indeed, the outcome was frequently regarded as inexorable,
being the outcome of a revolution in the original sense of the word,
that is to say a revolution of the stars inaugurating a new era: one
merely had to wait, though one ought also to assist. (Marxism is a
secularized version of such millenarian expectations.) Messianic
movements are widely attested for China, India, South-East Asia,
Africa, the Islamic world and Europe until recent times, and they
sometimes gathered enormous numbers of peasants. Where the
peasants had been exposed to foreign conquest, their millenarian
revolts might take a so-called nativist from, the new era being
associated with expulsion of the foreigners and a (usually selective)
restoration of native traditions.

Nativist or otherwise, millenarian revolt was always the reaction
of people without access to the state, such as peasants, tribesmen or
petty townsmen. (Urban millenarianism, however, was often more
sophisticated and less overtly political than its rural counterpart.) It
flourished in all circles deprived of political organization. Generally
speaking, however, it was never successful. One millenarian revolt
(of the nativist variety) succeeded in expelling the Mongols from
China and enthroning a native leader, a former monk, in 1368; but
though the ex-monk was presumably a peasant by origin, the revolt
became increasingly dependent on the co-operation of landowners as
he approached the throne, and though he did enact some revolutionary legislation, little of it was carried out. Most millenarian revolts
were drowned in rivers of blood.

Peasant revolts were commonly egalitarian, or indeed communist.
In the sixth century, a Zoroastrian heretic of pre-Islamic Iran by the
name of Mazdak preached equal distribution (or common ownership) of both land and women. Tenth-century Muslim peasants
converted to messianic Ismailism pooled their resources, instituting
common property and (temporarily at least) wives. In China a rebel
of 874 proclaimed himself 'Heaven-commissioned Great General to
Equalise Inequality', while in 993 two rebels proclaimed that they
'were sick of the inequality which exists between the rich and the
poor and wanted to level it off for the benefit of the people', as
indeed they proceeded to do; twelfth-century rebels declared that
there should be 'no distinction at all between the high and the low or
the rich and the poor', and that 'the law which discriminates between the common and the noble is not good law'; and so on: such
sentiments continued to be voiced in Chinese revolts down to the

Taiping rebellion of the nineteenth century, a millenarian vision of equality partly inspired by Christianity which cost millions of lives.

Unlike imported slaves, native serfs frequently declared lordship and servile statuses to be abolished. Thus seventeenth-century Chinese rebels declared that 'we are all of us equally men; what right had you to call us serfs?' In twelfth-century Korea there were massive revolts by unfree people, some of which explicitly aimed at putting an end to servile statuses: 'if each one kills his master and burns the record of his slave status, thus bringing slavery to an end in our country, then each of us will be able to become a minister or general', a rebel leader by the name of Manjok declared. Revolutionary ideas of this kind are well attested among European peasants too. 'When Adam delved and Eve span, who was then the gentleman?', as the followers of Wat Tyler sang in 1381, demanding the abolition of all unfree tenure (the couplet was also used by rebels in seventeenth-century Germany). 'No king shall reign nor any lord rule on earth, there shall be no serfdom, all interests and taxes shall cease, nor shall any man force another to do anything, because all shall be equal, brothers and sisters', the manifesto of the millenarian (and communist) Taborites of early fifteenth-century Bohemia declared. In 1521 a radical priest promised Castilian villagers that 'by the end of this month there will be no more nobles'; in 1671 Stenka Razin was quartered alive in Moscow for having rebelled with the Cossacks in order to 'remove the traitor boyars and give freedom to the common people'; and so on.

Townsmen

Townsmen did not produce fugitives: on the contrary, people fled to towns, not from them. But they too conducted politics by petitions; and unlike peasants, they were in a position to make good use of rioting, the dense populations of cities being highly combustible. Bread riots in response to food shortages were by far the most common, but riots might be provoked by any grievance of the type found in the petitions, such as unpopular governors or 'innovations', and also by the news of defeat in war: the tenth-century Byzantine reconquest of northern Syria caused much turbulence in Muslim towns. Townsmen too might engage in revolt, be it in defence of their autonomy (after the fashion of the Italian cities against the German emperors), in protest against intolerable fiscal policies, or in response to rapid socio-economic change ill-understood by themselves. There might also be revolts, or at any rate violence of various kinds, by one sector of the urban population against others; tenth-century Baghdad even produced urban Robin Hoods who took from the rich and gave to the poor. But urban revolt as a general phenomenon has not received nearly so much attention as have its servile and rural counterparts so that it is difficult to summarize its many manifestations.

Politics and religion

To a modern student, pre-industrial politics appear to be virtually soaked in religion, both in the sense that rulers devoted much attention to religious questions (including the management of religious personnel) and in the sense that everyone talked endlessly about it, justifying and vilifying all courses of action in religious terms. Most pre-industrial civilizations convey the impression of having been more ideologically orientated than their modern successors (or at any rate their non-Marxist successors), but the impression is particularly strong where the great salvation religions held sway (notably Christianity, Islam and Buddhism, but to a lesser extent also Zoroastrianism and other creeds).

In fact, pre-industrial people were hardly more given to ideology than we are today. Members of (non-Marxist) industrial societies do however tend to invoke different value systems in different contexts where their pre-industrial forebears would invoke one and the same. Thus a modern Englishman will legitimate his actions with reference to democracy in connection with politics, to animal rights in connection with vegetarianism, to the growth of knowledge in the context of science and scholarship, and so on, reserving his religious values (if any) for questions to do with the transcendent. By contrast, a pre-industrial Englishman would have marshalled his religious values in all of these connections and a host of others too. Modern religion typically limits itself to a special aspect of life, but pre-industrial religion was for multiple use.

This difference reflects the fact that the pre-modern world was poor in organization. Modern people are members of an immense variety of associations, both local and nationwide, or indeed international, being organized as voters, artists, scholars, scientists, antivivisectionists, devotees of this sport or that, consumers and so forth in addition to (if they so wish) as believers. But pre-industrial society was less differentiated, less wealthy and far less well equipped with means of communication. Hence there might be little or no organization above the level of household or village apart from that provided by religion. This automatically endowed religion with political importance, as we have seen, but it also meant that religion united under its umbrella numerous activities that would nowadays be pursued under umbrellas of their own. Thus a local cult society might form the nucleus for the formation of vigilante groups, the organization of charity and merry-making, the provision of loans, the settlement of disputes and many other activities over and above attention to the divine. The divine provided both the organization and the ideological language for the activities in question, with the result that those who engaged in them come across as strangely (or admirably) religious to us. Pre-modern religion could be about anything and everything. This is why it appears in every chapter of this book, as well as in a chapter of its own.

The great salvation religions increased the political significance of religion because they addressed themselves to everyone regardless of locality, social position, sex and (in the case of the universalist ones) ethnicity. They created far-flung communities which for the first time included elite and masses alike, establishing communication over both space and time between hitherto isolated groups by means of preaching, writing, pilgrimage and so forth. Ideology thus unified the masses and gave them a common identity which they shared with the wielders of power; by the same token it enabled them to communicate with the centres of power in ideological terms.

Thus rulers found that religion provided them with means of access to local society, including a means of furthering central direction of local ways (in the name of fighting paganism, ignorance, heresy, witchcraft or other). Conversely, their subjects used religion as a means of asserting local authority against the centre (in the name of alternative definitions of the faith, that is heresy). Heresy was used to reject central interference by the above-mentioned Monophysites of Byzantine Egypt and Syria, the Bogomils of Byzantine Bulgaria, numerous tribesmen of Muslim North Africa, and many other heretics in various parts of the world. It could also be used as bids for alternative leadership within the high culture (as it was by Ismailis of the tenth-century Muslim world), or to underscore the isolation of marginal communities where it was neighbours rather than the centre that threatened them with penetration (as in the case of numerous mountain communities of the Muslim Middle East). In short, the adoption of heresy and its converse, the imputation of heresy to others, were always statements about communal membership and leadership, whatever else they might be in addition. Differently put, religion was the major channel of communication between people of different social, cultural, geographical and political backgrounds; hence it was overwhelmingly on this channel that broadcasts were made.

5
Culture

Human beings are distinguished from other animals by their inability to survive without culture, that is information which is not transmitted genetically and which thus has to be learnt afresh by every new generation. (For example, the capacity to reproduce is genetically transmitted, but kinship systems, courtship etiquette and marriage rules are elements of culture; the capacity to utter noises is genetically transmitted, but languages have to be learnt; so do social and political institutions, agriculture, pottery-making, counting, writing and so on.)

The human dependence on culture was taken for granted in the thought experiment we conducted in the first chapter. If we had released bees rather than humans on our island, the bees would have organized themselves in precisely the same fashion as bees of the same species all over the world. If we had released gorillas, the result would probably have been much the same, thought it might have been slightly more unpredictable in the case of chimpanzees. The result would have been the same because the social organization of the animals in question is built into their genes. Their genetic programme might well have been unsuited for the island, in which case they would have risked dying out; but the only, or almost only, way they could have adapted themselves would have been by natural selection. The human animal is of course genetically programmed too. However, its programme for social organization is deficient (and to some extent even counter-productive). The programme does little but instruct its bearer to learn, or in other words to acquire culture with which to supplement (and in some cases even to suppress) such specific instructions as it retains. Without doing so, the species simply could not survive; doing so, it can survive almost anywhere on earth and even, for limited periods, outside it. Culture is thus the species-specific environment of *Homo sapiens*. Living in accordance with nature is an attractive idea, but in the human case it actually means living with culture.

All human societies are thus full of things that have to be learnt, from toilet training to the assessment of taxes. Most of it is learnt in the course of growing up. Parents 'socialize' their children, or in other words induct them into the culture of their particular society, so that they will be able to operate in it and also to pass it on. But the more there is to learn, the more formal instruction will be required. Modern societies would collapse without prolonged schooling for all its members. In pre-industrial societies, however, there was little schooling, and prolonged education was only for a few.

Vocational training

Generally speaking, parents passed on such knowledge and skills as they had to their children. Peasants trained their sons as peasants, fishermen trained theirs as fishermen, and so on. Children learnt by watching and participating rather than by being formally instructed, though there was some of that too. The combination of watching and formal instruction did not always take place in the parental home. Thus, as has been seen, a child might be apprenticed to a craftsman who would feed, discipline and teach him as the father would have done; he might also be sent to the household of his father's lord and learn martial arts from him or his instructors: sending children to live elsewhere (sometimes on a basis of exchange) was common in many cultures, sometimes because it could be used to cement political alliances and at other times because one thereby avoided the inclination to spoil one's children; either way, it helped to integrate the child into society at large.

Initiation into adult roles started early, so that children were often fully trained and ready to marry by the time their modern counterparts leave school. Most occupations, however, required little in the way of special knowledge: agriculture was not a science, crude craftsmanship was not an art, anyone could be a servant, and the heroes of popular tales often shift with enviable ease from one type of work to another as their fortunes rise and fall, being in no need whatever of retraining or further degrees. But in the case of highly skilled occupations such as painting, music, calligraphy, craftsmanship or horsemanship, training from an early age could result in mastery of the kind nowadays rarely displayed outside the ranks of great musicians.

Children went straight to vocational training because there was little in the way of general education for the masses. Today, certain skills and values must be uniformly mastered by all members of society before they move on to their individual careers, and this need for uniformity has transferred elementary education from the home to formal schools: what parents can teach is too varied. But in the past the knowledge which everyone had to master regardless of future occupation was generally identical with that which everyone absorbed through the sheer fact of growing up in the same community: for further training the skills of the parents (or their substitutes) sufficed. All learning over and above that which could be automatically absorbed or imparted by parents and their substitutes was one form or other of high culture, the culture of the elite; and the need of the masses for participation in the high culture was usually slight, though it varied with the nature of the high culture itself.

High culture

High culture is what most people associate with the word 'culture': books one ought to have read, music one ought to like, things one ought to know in order to count as a 'cultured person'; in short, knowledge of a non-vocational nature which, though apparently quite useless (and boring, too, in the opinion of many), enjoys immense respect. Put in less popular terms, high culture is that body of ideas which distinguishes one civilization from another. Its core is a religion, morality or other type of world-view which informs (or is supposed to inform) all activities within that civilization, which shapes (or attempts to shape) all its institutions, and which provides the bulk of the presuppositions in the light of which things are viewed and evaluated within it. Its manifestations are literary and/or artistic works which present these ideas, explore their implications for public and private life, glorify them, criticize them, iron out inconsistencies between them, poke fun at the way in which they work out, or use them for the exploration of sound, colour, space, the natural world, the human mind, or anything else in the world around us.

All pre-industrial societies endowed with states may be presumed to have had one form or other of high culture, but a well-developed high culture presupposes literacy, which frees the exchange of information from the need for face-to-face contact. The Incas are the only civilized people to have had no writing system at all (though several African societies which one might or might not count as complex were also preliterate); but literacy was highly restricted in many other societies, being used only for the recording of matters of public interest such as the receipt of taxes, genealogy, dynastic chronicles, or calendrical calculations. Here as elsewhere, initiation into the high culture served to distinguish those who knew from those who did not, but what follows refers to societies with high cultures of a more developed kind.

Education

In societies with well developed high cultures, education was the prerogative of the few who could afford to invest time and money in a prolonged training unlikely to yield returns for many years. Their education might well start at home, their fathers or (in well-to-do families) specially employed tutors teaching them to read and write and introducing them to whatever subjects were considered fundamental. But even elementary education might well involve teachers outside the home, and higher education invariably did. The teachers involved did not necessarily run formal schools, as opposed to offer instruction privately or in informal circles; but formal schools, both elementary and other, appeared in most complex societies in the course of history.

Typically there was only one kind of higher education, though there might be a bit of specialization at the end. This was partly because the amount of specialist knowledge was limited, but also because the object of higher education was to commit all students to the same beliefs, norms and ideas, not to prepare them for a specific vocation. More precisely, their vocation was to pass on the civilization to which society at large had committed itself; in modern parlance, they were trained to be the *bearers* of that civilization. This was not a task for which much technical knowledge was required, and technical knowledge rarely commanded much respect. It was associated with manual work and thus socially unacceptable; intellectually, it was unenticing except in so far as it was amenable to theory; and morally, it was uninteresting (or worse) because of its usually scant bearing on (or even conflict with) the norms with which the educated were concerned. On all three grounds it was left aside (or even combated): higher education was indeed general education (a fact of central importance to the uncertainty regarding the role of universities in the modern world).

Studies centred on a number of authoritative works from the past, commonly a scripture or other religious composition of a funda-

mental kind (Bible, Koran, Avesta, Vedas, Tripitaka), but sometimes secular works of high authority, or in other words classics
(Homer, the Twelve Tables of the Romans, Confucian writings, the
latter classifiable as scripture too), and sometimes a combination
of both. The works in question were studied in conjunction with
commentaries and other ancillary texts, but the only type of fiction
considered (if any) was poetry.

Whatever the nature of the fundamental works, they were regarded as the embodiment of the ideas and values to which society
had committed itself. To modern students there is something odd, or
even faintly comical, about this: what could seventeenth-century
China, or for that matter Korea, Japan or Vietnam, learn from the
doctrines of a sage who had addressed an altogether different kind
of society some two thousand years before? Why did seventeenth-
century Europe pay so much attention to teachings addressed, some
three thousand years earlier, to a minor tribal society of the region
now known as the Middle East? Why do modern Iranians seek
inspirations in the word of a man who knew practically nothing
about Iran and certainly nothing at all about modernity? The short
answer, of course, is that the teachings in question had been
accepted as the Truth, which remains true however early or late its
discovery may be. The long answer must be left for the chapter on
religion.

Being old, the Truth was usually extant in a language which was
rapidly ceasing to be the vernacular of anyone, or which had died out
as such long ago, but which educated men would nonetheless employ
when addressing one another, both orally and in their writings. Thus
classical Greek and Latin were the learned languages of the Roman
empire; medieval (originally vulgar) Latin that of Christian Europe;
classical Arabic that of the Muslim world; Sanskrit that of Hindu
India; while written Chinese, which had no spoken standard, could
be understood by educated persons throughout the Sinified world.
(In terms of spoken Chinese, the official language was that of the
court, i.e. Mandarin, but this was neither unchanging nor intelligible
to all readers of the script.)

The learned languages enabled educated men to communicate over
space and time. The vernaculars, by contrast, represented the local
divisisions that educated men had overcome, and they were typically
looked down upon as plebeian or provincial tongues suitable only for
informal communication and light entertainment. Most of them had
no written form, and those which acquired it tended to develop into

classical languages in their turn, as did for example vulgar Latin (adopted by the Christians of the western Roman empire with a view to reaching the masses), or Pali and Prakrit (adopted by the Buddhists and Jains of India for the same reason).

Writers modelled their mode of expression on the literary works of the past, not on the spoken language of their contemporaries: 'the language of literature . . . should not depend on that of the populace', as a sixteenth-century Italian said, recommending imitation of Petrarch and Bocaccio. Hence written languages tended to be frozen. Once they had ceased to be regulated by ordinary usage, grammarians, lexicographers and philologists had a monopoly on the formulation of the rules with the result that they tended to become both highly artificial and difficult to learn, let alone to use correctly. Solecisms were the educated man's nightmare: to apply the Arabic word for 'black' normally used of horses to a piece of clothing was a grave mistake suggestive of underlying boorishness; a comparable slip in Latin once exposed a tenth-century Italian of superior education to humiliating mockery by a petty monk of St Gall.

The approach to the authoritative books, and indeed to learning altogether, was conservative. There was much learning by heart, much scholarship that we would characterize as mere regurgitation, and much poetry written in the same frozen style. This follows from the fact that the standards of truth and goodness had been set in the past: the ancients having worked things out, later generations could only assimilate and imitate their insights. The belief that the truth was incarnate in the past also encouraged the view that knowledge was finite: everything had been said; everything could be mastered given sufficient time. (Rigorous training from early childhood produced prodigious results here too.) In practice, the would-be imitators often continued to innovate, but the aim of education was to ensure the preservation of civilized traditions, not to encourage novelty or criticism. People liked to read books (or have them read to them) in order to savour their wisdom and enjoy their memorable formulation of common knowledge rather than to find new information or ideas; and educated men were often veritable store-houses of aphorisms, proverbs, maxims, poetic gems and other sayings with which they adorned their speech and their writings and the manipulation of which gave them endless pleasure.

All in all, the result of higher education was a man sharply distinguished from the masses. He did not speak their language, see things through their eyes or identify himself in terms of their experiences: where they spoke German, he spoke Latin; where they saw big men, he saw senators or biblical figures; and where they evaluated events in village-terms, he applied a wider perspective. His differentiation from the masses might be underscored by formal attribution to him of spiritual powers denied to others, either on the completion of his education (as in Catholic Europe, where consecration endowed churchmen with power over people's souls and a capacity for miracles on Sundays) or as a prerequisite for it (as in Hindu India, where membership of the brahmin caste was necessary for brahmin functions).

Education was an avenue to influence and wealth. The learned man was someone who knew 'what it was all about'. He might be seen as a person endowed with special access to the gods, saints, spirits or other hidden powers assumed to regulate the world, from whom he could obtain rain, fertility, military success, absolution for sins and other benefits for his clients through prayer, sacrifice, meditation and the like. In this respect he played the role of the modern scientist, who likewise manipulates the laws of nature to our advantage. In a more sober vein, he might be regarded as an embodiment of wisdom and virtue from whom one could get advice on the rights and wrongs of things, proper behaviour and right belief.

Either way he and/or the institution to which he belonged were richly rewarded. The wielders of political power needed his services both as private individuals and as guardians of the public order, and the bearers of high culture invariably ended up in alliance with them, though they did not necessarily originate on their side or support them as wholeheartedly as they might wish. Where the core of the high culture was a religion, its exponents worked as priests, administrators of sacred buildings and charitable foundations, and lawyers and judges (in religious law); they might also work as scribes, secretaries and bureaucrats if they were the only educated people available (as in early medieval Europe). Where the education was secular, it was typically associated with government service: it was knowledge of the classics that led to positions in the civil service in imperial China no less than in Victorian England. Educated men of both types might also work as private tutors, teachers and professors.

It should be noted, however, that though there might only be one basic type of higher education, there were sometimes several types of educated men: the religious specialist might coexist with well-educated bureaucrats and other wielders of political power, with professional people such as doctors, jurists and astrologers (futurologists whose forecasting abilities were much appreciated by rulers and private persons alike), and even with some educated laymen. China was unique in the degree to which all types were conflated in the mandarins (who were bearers of the high culture, bureaucrats and governors alike); but even here learning had a number of social incarnations, the mandarins coexisting with Buddhist monks and Taoist practitioners. Where learning had different social incarnations, there was often rivalry between them. In the early Islamic world, for example, the religious specialists were at loggerheads with the secretaries, scribes, doctors and other professional men who thrived at the court and did their best to denounce as impious the secular and typically foreign learning cultivated by the latter.

Some students find it odd that all sorts of learned men could not coexist as they do today, doctors being accepted as authorities in matters of medicine, clerics in matters of religion, and so forth. But in fact there is also rivalry between them today, now as then because not all can enjoy the same general influence and prestige. Besides, the borders between the rival disciplines were not easy to delineate, and cognitive divisions of labour were dangerous: the strength of the overarching world-view rested on the fact that it dominated all aspects of life.

It should also be noted that the educated men, whoever they might be, and a few educated women too, are the people to whom we owe the bulk of our knowledge of the pre-industrial world. The literary works which constitute the vast majority of our sources were almost all composed by and for a tiny fraction of the population; and when this tiny fraction resided in cities, it might say little or nothing about the eighty or ninely per cent who resided in the countryside. Where the literary sources fail us, we are thrown back on documentary evidence and occasional supplementary sources such as archaeology and popular literature, but evidence of this kind may be absent too: all too often our knowledge of the peasantry is very limited indeed.

High culture as veneer

Whatever its nature, the high culture was thinly spread over very large areas. Graeco-Roman civilization stretched from the Rhine to the Euphrates, Latin Christianity from Iceland to Italy, Islamic civilization from Gibraltar to the Indus and eventrally far beyond, Sanskrit culture over all of India with extensions into Indo-China, the Malay world and Indonesia, Confucian culture over the whole of China with extensions into Japan, Korea and Vietnam.

Pre-industrial culture was thus highly international (or, given that modern nations did not exist, trans-local). An educated man could travel over huge distances speaking the same learned language, discussing the same body of ideas and getting the same kind of job all the way. But the trans-local culture did not penetrate very deep: below the elite the masses were divided into a bewildering variety of ethnic, linguistic, religious and cultural communities. A member of the elite might be able to travel from Iceland to Italy speaking Latin all the way, but an Italian peasant might not be able to understand the language spoken outside his native village, and he certainly would not speak Latin. Only 2.5 per cent of the population of Italy spoke Italian (that is, Tuscan) in 1861, at the time of the unification of Italy (the figure had risen to about half by the beginning of the twentieth century); and though France had been politically united for centuries by then, a quarter of its population still did not speak French in 1863.

The high culture owed this peculiar combination of wide expanse and superficiality to the nature of communications in the pre-industrial world, in combination with scarcity and political factors. As regards political factors, it is obvious that conquest could unite large areas in a single culture, as did those of Alexander the Great, the Romans and the Arabs. it is also well known that up-and-coming rulers anxious to put themselves on the map of civilization would begin by importing high culture from their most powerful neighbour. (Obviously, if the neighbour was powerful he must be in possession of good ideas.) State formation with its attendant dissolution or amalgamation of parochial groups created a need for a new body of ideas in terms of which people (rulers included) could make sense of the world under the new conditions. To create such a body of ideas from scratch, or more precisely from the debris of earlier views, was a long and painful task undertaken only by those who simply could not borrow, be it because they were the first in the world to be confronted with it (as were the Sumerians, the ancient Egyptians and their counterparts in America), or because they were too far away from those who had undertaken the task before (as were the Chinese, Indians, Iranians and Greeks between c.800 and 400

BC, though already they were in a position to borrow this or that, and clearly did). With one extraordinary exception, all new arrivals thereafter simply imported pre-fabricated world views for local adaptation and use. The exceptional case is that of the Arabs, who could have been expected to import Christianity in the seventh century AD and who looked all set to do so, only to come up instead with a religion of their own which became the nucleus of a new civilization after their conquest of the Middle East.

However, neither conquest nor importation suffices to explain the huge spread of veneer-like culture. Unification imposed by conquest was usually shortlived; and where it survived, it is odd that regional varieties of the culture, or even quite different versions, did not rapidly appear. Imported world-views could likewise have been expected soon to change beyond recognition under local conditions given that completely different languages and cultures prevailed underneath. Yet they did not.

This brings us to scarcity. The fact that the agricultural surplus was small meant that the customers of traders, craftsmen, professional men, scholars, artists, entertainers and fortune-tellers were few and far between. Hence such men were itinerant. Those of the humbler kind travelled from village to village; those of the more elevated kind travelled from one city, court or centre of learning to the next in search of teachers, colleagues, students and patrons. The bearers of high culture and professional skills thus congregated around the ruling elite, spreading themselves over huge distances and disseminating the same culture in the process.

This culture did not however penetrate very deeply because neither they nor others travelled regularly from one place to another, commuterwise. Contrary to what might be imagined, people travelled a great deal in the pre-industrial world. Kings travelled in the interest of public order, or in search of conquest, or to live off scattered landed estates. Members of the political elite travelled because they liked the company of peers and had the means to travel, because they fought in the same armies, worked in the same institutions and because they were positively encouraged (or even forced) to spend time at the court. Peasants would migrate in search of food (in years of famine) or to escape from oppression; and everyone travelled to visit shrines and holy places, some of them within easy reach and some located very far away (as was Mecca for an Indian Muslim, Jerusalem for a European Christian). Ideas thus spread with great rapidity. But most of this traffic was one-way.

Armies, traders and other travellers might pass through a whole string of villages spreading news of external developments without the villages in question having any direct contact with each other. Only members of the elite were in a position to meet each other regularly, on private visits, at educational institutions, in the army and at the court. In short, where the rural masses might pick up news without interacting even though the distances involved might be slight, the elite exchanged views through constant interaction even though the distances involved might be enormous. Each village could thus remain a world unto itself while the elite developed a common culture over and above them.

The manner in which people moved was of decisive importance because there were no telecommunications, let alone mass media. Of course, books spread ideas without face-to-face contacts, but books were rare as long as they had to be copied by hand, and in Europe they were expensive even after printing had been developed. (In China, by contrast, they sold at prices described by a sixteenth-century Italian Jesuit as 'ridiculously low'.) And the masses were usually illiterate (though literacy rates varied enormously). There were no radios or transistors disseminating news and entertainment in a language which every listener gradually came to adopt at the cost of his local dialect, no cinemas depicting the lives of people in alien social and cultural circumstances, no television pushing news and views at people in their private homes. Nor, of course, were there any telephones allowing for easy communication between those who went on journeys and those who stayed behind; communication by letter was cumbersome, the illiterate masses requiring others to write and read their messages for them and bearers being hard to find. (The postal service, if any, was only or overwhelmingly for government use.) In the absence of regular physical movements among the masses on the one hand and telecommunication on the other, it was only at the very top of society that a uniform culture could develop and survive.

It follows that there was no *national* culture. There was no combination of language, customs, ideas and ideals which was shared by all members of a certain polity and distinct from that of its neighbours. The high culture of the elite might be coextensive with a large political unit, as it was in the Roman empire, the early caliphate, and imperial China (which exported it to its satellites too); it might also be politically fragmented, as it was in Greece, Europe, the medieval Muslim world and India at various times. Either way, it integrated the elite and, willingly or unwillingly, left the masses to their own devices. Each village, district, province or marketing area would have its own spirits, deities or patron saints, holy places, festivals, ancestral customs, weights and measures, dialect, types of clothing (which modern tourist brochures identify as 'national costume'), and so on. Obviously, developments at the top of society had some repercussions on the masses, and the popular sub-cultures might be sufficiently similar to be classified as so many members of a single family. But the degree to which the masses were actually expected to participate in the high culture varied greatly. It is to this point that we may now turn.

High culture and the masses

Paganism

Where pagan religions prevailed, there was generally no sense that elite and masses ought to share the same beliefs and practices at all. Pagan deities (and/or spirits) were simply natural forces in disguise. More precisely, they were representations of all those things that one could not understand or control, but very much wished to control because they mattered greatly to one's life: health, love, luck, child-birth, fertility, disease, death, and so on. You worshipped whichever deities or spirits were most relevant to you: the object of worship was to place the supernatural beings in question under a moral obligation to support you. 'It was from your feet that Chloe was dragged away, and yet you tamely stood by and looked on. She wove garlands for you, she poured you the first drops of her milking, and her pipe still hangs here as an offering . . . ', as Daphnis reproaches the Nymphs in Longus' romance *Daphnis and Chloe* (second or third century AD).

This being so, people evidently could not be expected to worship the same gods: why should a peasant pay attention to a pastoralist deity, or members of one family worship the ancestral spirits of another? At the most, there might be one god so important that everyone paid deference to him over and above their local deities. A 'high god' might be a creator god, or king of the gods, or indeed king on earth (as was Ashur in Assyria); and there might be systema-tic attempts to promote the cult of such deities (or deities of other types associated or identical with the ruler) by way of fostering loyalty to the state. But the existence of such deities in no way implied that other gods ought to be abandoned or that everyone ought to share the same world view.

In pagan Greece the elite abandoned traditional paganism for philosophy, stripping the universe of its human faces, without feeling any urge to disseminate their new visions of the truth to the uneducated masses, who clearly would not have known what to do with these visions anyway: the masses persisted in their own religious cults. The same pattern prevailed in the Roman empire, with the addition of ceremonial worship of the emperor for all loyal subjects of the Roman state. China to some extent also belongs in this category in that it imposed Confucian morality without interfering with such additional cults and philosophies as people might have, except spasmodically (usually because they were perceived as a threat to the established order). Unlike the cult of the Roman emperor, Confucian morality was a world-view in its own right, and concerted attempts were made to disseminate it among the masses too. But even so, it coexisted with Buddhism and Taoism to the point that the three faiths were perceived as identical.

Salvation religions
The great salvation religions had a very different view of things. There was only one truth *and* it had to be shared by everyone on earth. The combination of these two propositions may seem obvious to a modern European (whether he takes the one truth to be religious or not), but there is nothing in the least obvious about it.

Paganism did not deny the unity of truth, but nor did it pay much attention to it. Given that the truth was all the diversity we see around us or (as later pagans were to put it) that there were many avenues to the one and only truth, anyone could choose his own. By about 600 BC attempts to find the single truth behind the diversity were underway in India and Greece, but why should this truth be for everyone? World-views presented in terms of highly abstract concepts were addressed to intellectual elites. Being highly abstract, i.e. shorn of context, they could be exported to elites wherever and whoever they might be, but they simply were not intelligible to the masses.

On the other hand, if the truth reduced to a single God behind it all, why should the adherents of this God wish to share him with anyone else? The Jews and the Iranians both discovered their own god to be the one and only power behind it all (or rather, in the case of Zoroaster's Iranians, the one and only *good* god, an evil one being present too); and both quite naturally assumed him to be their private property: as Yahweh was the God of the Israelites, so Ahura Mazda was the God of the Iranians. Here, then, the truth was for elite and masses alike, but only within the ethnic community in which he had been discovered. He was not for export: if you wanted him, you had to join the community to which he belonged. Much later, in the seventh century AD, the Arabs likewise assumed that the God who enabled them to conquer the world was in league with them, to the exclusion of everyone else on earth. How could he not have been? He patently favoured them above all others. In due course they resigned themselves to the idea that God loved everyone, not just them, which may have been a more sublime proposition, but which was also a less exciting one. A unique God who loves you alone is apt to generate more fervour than one who indiscriminately loves anyone who cares to acknowledge his existence.

In short, the idea that the one and only truth is for everyone, both socially *and* ethnically, is anything but natural: conceptual thought is too abstruse to excite the masses and monotheist Gods are too powerful to be shared with neighbours. It is thus a noteworthy fact that both conceptual and monotheist thought nonetheless generated religions for universal consumption, that is Buddhism, Christianity and (the initial period apart) Islam, plus other systems which proved less successful (such as Manichaeism). Buddhism being a conceptual system, it coexisted with local cults as happily as did Greek philosophy, and popular Buddhism soon became a new form of polytheist religion. Though monotheist Gods are jealous, the old deities crept back here too in the form of angels, devils, demons and saints. Even so, however, all three religions remained committed to the preservation of the original insight among elite and masses alike.

Religious instruction
In societies where these religions prevailed, the masses were thus expected to acquire some familiarity with the high culture, and this required actual instruction. The monotheists (of both the particularist and the universalist kinds) assembled the believers for weekly meetings with attendant sermons (on Fridays among Muslims, Saturdays among the Jews, and Sundays among Christians); and the Zoroastrians, Jews and Protestant Christians eventually all adopted the device of special teaching for boys prior to their formal initiation into adulthood (known by the Protestants as confirmation). So too did the Theravada Buddhists, who would send their sons to spend

some time in a monastery prior to 'becoming men' (in Burma), or prior to marriage (in Thailand), in order to study the faith and learn to read and write. They were fed by the community for the duration, on a par with other monks. In some Mahayana Buddhist countries, too, children were sent to monasteries in order to be educated, though not by way of initiation; but neither Catholic monasteries nor Muslim zawiyas dispensed elementary education, and neither the Catholics nor the Muslims adopted the ancient device of introducing boys to the wisdom of the community before initiating them into manhood.

It is ironic that Buddhism, which was in principle far less committed to communal work than the monotheist religions, proved to be more successful than the latter at the diffusion of literacy: thus nineteenth-century Burma, which was not a highly developed country in political terms, is said to have had a (male) literacy rate of about 80 per cent. By contrast, the Koran schools attended by most Muslim children rarely imparted more than an ability to recite Koranic passages by heart (occasionally all of it), or to read the Koran without being able to read anything else. Despite the proliferation of schools in early twentieth-century Bukhara, only 5 per cent of the population is estimated to have been literate. As for the Christians, missionaries were well aware that literacy might strengthen the faith ('he baptized him and handed him the ABC', as Irish legend says of St Patrick), but of course it might strengthen insubordination too, and in medieval Europe it was more often than not the heretics who handed out ABC's: 'nobody is so stupid that if he joins them he will not become literate within eight days, so that he can be reconverted neither by argument nor by example', as a scandalized monk said with reference to the Cathars. The Reformation greatly speeded up educational efforts on both sides of the fence, as did the introduction of printed books, but even so few European countries could boast a male literacy rate of 80 per cent by the beginning of the nineteenth century.

It is however hard to believe that the literacy of Buddhist peasants was functional, or in other words that they could use it outside the context in which they had learnt it. At all events, craft literacy prevailed in most of the pre-industrial world, that is to say literacy was a skill mastered by the occupants of certain professions, not one which everyone acquired by way of general training. Because it was a specialist skill, there was also much cultivation of calligraphy, the art of writing beautifully and frequently illegibly (to anyone except initiates), as opposed to writing for the conveyance of information in the clearest possible style.

Daily life

Actual instruction was less important than what was absorbed in daily life. The monotheists made assiduous attempts to saturate the lives of the believers through the development of religious law covering all aspects of life and/or ceremonies for both communal events of major importance (such as sowing and harvesting) and the key stages in the individual's life-cycle (birth, puberty, marriage and death); in this respect the Buddhists were somewhat behind. All, however, made use of daily prayer or other forms of ritual service such as alms-giving or sacrifice; all had festivals celebrating the common faith, though only the monotheists ensured that they were celebrated at precisely the same time in all the countries in which the faith held sway; and all developed notions of correct belief (orthodoxy) and practice (orthopraxy), though the monotheists were more assiduous in this respect too than the Buddhists.

Shaping and saturating the believers' lives was more important than actual instruction because it entrenched the religious leaders in local society (the more social relationships they regulated, the more indispensable they became), and because it made the allegiance of the masses unthinking. As far as the bearers of high culture were concerned, both idealism and self-interest dictated that the masses should be deeply committed to the saving truth, and thus also to its bearers; but they evidently had no wish to share their knowledge to the point of losing their privileged position. Specialists are privileged because they have rare skills which others need: if their ranks are swollen, the privileges are diluted; and if the skills diffuse outside their ranks, the privileges cease to be justified, whereupon their organization takes on a parasitical appearance. (Obviously, you would not wish to pay or obey a specialist if you could do everything as well as he could, or thought you could.)

It was basically for such reasons that the ecclesiastical authorities of medieval Europe were wary of lay literacy: lay learning had the deplorable effect of producing endless popular heresies on the theme that everyone could save himself, that the ecclesiastical hierarchy was unnecessary and its wealth illegitimate. But even in post-Reformation Europe there were fears that widespread education might endanger the faith by giving the masses ideas above their station; and the authorities were just as wary of mass learning in countries where mastery of the high culture was the key to a political rather than ecclesiastical organization. In fifteenth-century Korea, for example, the bearers of high culture squashed a remarkable attempt by King Seijong (1418–50) to democratize learning in all its forms. Seijong invented what is supposed to be the simplest and most logical script ever thought up, in twenty-eight letters as opposed to thousands upon thousands of Chinese characters, and sponsored it in a deliberate attempt to raise the educational standard of his subjects. He proceeded to have a mass of books printed in it, some old and some specially commissioned, on history, good government, morality, agriculture, local topography, military strategy, lyrics, phonology and other subjects. (He also improved on the mechanics of printing, sponsored the invention of scientific instruments, installed rain gauges, reformed the fiscal and judicial system, set up granaries and famine relief, put order into Korean musical notation and instruments, and more besides!) But the response of the scholars to the 'vulgar letters' was negative in the extreme: 'if all people should pass the civil service examinations, then low-ranking people will be promoted . . . who will study Chinese philosophy?'. After Seijong's death the new script rapidly degenerated into 'female letters', all self-respecting educated men continuing to use Chinese.

It goes without saying that the attitude of the religious or cultural establishment to the diffusion of learning varied in accordance with both its own nature and that of society at large. In the Muslim world, for example, the religious scholars did not fear lay participation in religious knowledge for the simple reason that they were laymen themselves, not members of a hierarchy sealed off from the lay society: their authority rested on mastery of learning available to anyone; they simply had more of it than the rest. But here as elsewhere knowledge had to be controlled. How could it have been otherwise? No modern trade union would be so silly as to throw the scarcity value of its members to the wind. Muslim scholars were happy to share religious learning with everyone who wanted it, but they were suspicious of different types of learning associated with different exponents (such as doctors and philosophers): obviously, had these types of learning won out, their own knowledge would have been devalued, meaning loss of income and prestige alike.

There might also be opposition to the education of women. According to a thirteenth-century Muslim author, teaching a woman to read and write is like giving poison to a snake, i.e. it adds to the danger of a creature which is dangerous enough already; according to nineteenth-century Chinese villagers it was merely 'like weeding another man's field', or in other words a waste of time since daughters would be married off and belong to her husband's family. But in China, too, there were many who saw ignorance in a woman as positively desirable. (Both China and the Muslim world produced some highly educated women nonetheless.) Educating those destined for a subordinate position, be it by victue of their sex or otherwise, was risky because it meant giving them the tools to seek out such learning as they liked and to make of it whatever they wanted: at the very least censorship might be necessary. Knowledge is power, as those who possessed it knew all too well.

It is not easy to generalize about the extent to which high culture percolated to the masses. Where the educated elite was concentrated in the cities, the countryside was commonly left to its own devices (as in the Islamic world, where the cities however also spawned reformers from time to time). Where it resided in the countryside (as in pre-Islamic Iran, early medieval Europe and most of South-East Asia), its own educational level was often low. Either way, half-studied clerics, mendicants, popular preachers, story-tellers and other entertainers played a major role in the diffusion of official values below the level of the elite, if not necessarily in a form of which the elite approved. Most peasants are likely to have known extremely little about the world view to which they had committed themselves, though their loyalty to it may have been no less unswerving for that. All in all, it is clear that the pre-industrial world was characterized by low degrees of cultural integration. Just as it was the elite which generated long-distance trade over and above autarkic villages, so it was the elite which shared a homogeneous culture over and above the 'little traditions' of the countryside.

6
Society and the Individual

The perception of society

Pre-industrial society was commonly envisaged as a hierarchy (chain of command) in which everyone knew his proper place, enjoyed the appropriate rights and duties and obeyed his superiors, receiving obedience from his inferiors in his turn: all in the last resort obeyed the monarch, through whom human society was slotted in with the divine.

Alternatively, it was envisaged as an organism in which specialized limbs performed the various functions essential for the well-being of the whole, the limbs in question being: scholars or priests or other 'men of the pen'; warriors, be they aristocrats or other types of men of the sword'; peasants; and traders and artisans (sometimes omitted and sometimes counted as separate groups). The ruler and his relatives might be too elevated for inclusion in this scheme, while conversely entertainers, barbers, tanners, prostitutes and other occupants of despised occupations might be excluded as too mean. At all events, classifications of this kind are attested for China (where warriors were omitted from the standard version), India, Iran, Europe and the Islamic world, the classical world being the only major civilization from which they seem to be absent. The three or four functional groups might be mere analytical devices, but sometimes they were actual orders or estates, that is hereditary groups endowed with different obligations and privileges (or 'liberties', as the Europeans put it) in formal or customary law.

Either way, the hierarchical and the organic views were combined in the widespread image of society with a body: the priests were the head, the king and military aristocracy the arms, the peasants the legs or feet, or they sprang from these parts; or the king was the head and the other groups variously distributed. Between them, state and society formed the *body politic* (or simply 'polity'), as English so neatly describes it. Taken literally, the two conceptions do not really fit together: are legs subordinated to arms? Did a lowly man of the

pen rank higher or lower than a middling man of the sword or a
wealthy trader? But both images highlighted the importance of co-
ordination and subordination in social life, and they were not perceived as contradictory. People would illustrate the nature of the
social hierarchy by contrasting neat opposites such as lord and
peasants, elite and masses, rich and poor, elder and younger sons,
and so on, leaving it unclear how the totality was to be ordered on
the (usually false) assumption that anyone could work this out for
himself.

The hierarchical conception of society stemmed from the by now
familiar fact that the ruling elite everywhere had to be sharply
demarcated from the masses. Its various branches usually had to be
ranked in relation to the court, too, so that the top end of the
hierarchy was perfectly real. It seemed real below this level as well
because all social roles were stable, there being little technological or
other change, with the result that they tended to accumulate fixed
rights and duties and to be transmitted by heredity. Indeed, they
might be endowed with fixed rights and duties on a hereditary basis
so as to *induce* stability (this being one of the methods whereby
Diocletian tried to save the Roman empire). The existence of a
highly privileged leadership in a local community in which everyone
was born into a fixed position would inevitably lead to the formation
of a clear-cut pecking order, the relative positions of all local members being perfectly clear however vague they might be in relation to
outsiders. In such a world everyone would indeed see 'a man above
himself whose patronage is necessary to him, and below himself
another man whose co-operation he may claim', as de Tocqueville,
the nineteenth-century French political scientist, said of aristocratic
society (which is not to deny that there might be much competition
for leading positions). In other words, the hierarchy was usually real
at village level too.

The view of society as a hierarchy or organism illustrates the
fundamental fact that the social order was shaped by political rather
than economic relations. It was the overriding need to keep the
loosely integrated parts of the polity together that determined where
people would find themselves in terms of power, prestige and income, be it locally or within the polity at large, not market forces.
Such market as existed was itself dominated by political considerations, as has been seen (people acquired and lost land depending on
their position vis-à-vis the government, promoted their relatives and
gave jobs to their allies, a great deal of commodity movement was

dictated by the needs of the state, etc.). The polity was perceived as a collective enterprise to which everyone had to contribute in accordance with ability, usually on the grounds that the enterprise in question was indispensable for happiness in this world and salvation in the next: where modern classes are defined as the accidental outcome of economic relations, the functional orders by contrast were seen as purposive, or in other words as responses to the intrinsic needs of the collectivity; and where modern classes are perceived as divisive groups generating conflict, the functional orders were seen as so many parts adding up to a harmonious whole. This is not of course to say that they actually did add up to such a whole, or that social relations were more harmonious in the past than they are today; but society was not shaped as an arena for economic competition. The sheer complexity of social organization made it impossible to integrate all socio-economic and political groupings in a single hierarchy, but in principle they should have been, and in Siam (now Thailand) they actually were: from the fifteenth century onwards every member of the Siamese kingdom was awarded 'dignity marks' ranging from five for a slave to 100,000 for the heir apparent (the marks of the monarch himself being beyond enumeration) by virtue of birth into one of the numerous orders of which Siamese society was composed.

Classes

It should thus be clear that pre-industrial societies were not class societies by any definition. Classes may be defined with reference to the different rights of access to the means of production enjoyed by the participants in the productive process, meaning that there are only two classes for practical purposes, namely the owners of the means of production and the actual producers. This was the view of Marx. (Under modern conditions the two classes are the bourgeoisie, alias capitalists or exploiters, versus the proletariat, alias workers or exploited masses.) They may also be defined with reference to the different market values of the labour, skills and capital brought to bear on the productive process by its participants. This was the view of Weber. (Under modern conditions there are held to be six broad occupational categories, namely: professional, managerial, administrative; semi-professional and lower administrative; routine white collar; skilled manual; semi-skilled manual; and unskilled manual.)

There are also numerous intermediate definitions, including some which pay attention to consumption.

Whichever definition is adopted, however, classes are economic groupings. It has been argued, especially by Marxist historians, that classes have always existed even though they have not always been perceived, and it is obviously true that ever since the state was invented there have been those who owned the means of production (formerly land) and others who did not. None the less, the concept of class is unhelpful in a pre-industrial context. States were rarely economic units. Markets were usually local or else international, meaning that classes in Weber's sense could at best be postulated for a handful of pre-industrial societies (such as late traditional China or early modern Europe); and though there were numerous *bits* of classes in Marx's sense (the peasants of a particular village, the landlord of a particular estate), the bits did not add up to real classes because there was little economic interdependence between them. The peasants did not easily develop common aims above the local level, let alone political organization; and though the landlords interacted politically, they were not dependent on one another economically, their crucial ties being with the state rather than the market (except where commercial agriculture prevailed); hence they too fell short of forming a class. Historians often use the word in the loose sense of 'group' or 'stratum', but classes in the technical sense are the outcome of economic, cultural and political integration, as we shall see in chapter 9.

This is not to deny, of course, that the status groups of pre-industrial society tended to be just as sharply differentiated in terms of wealth as they were in terms of power and prestige. But they owed their wealth to their position in the hierarchy, not the other way round, or that at least was the principle: those who had power or authority were rewarded by wealth; those who had neither were poor. To be poor was the opposite of commanding obedience, not the opposite of having money (as in medieval Latin where *pauperes* is the opposite of *potentes*, not of *divites*); it was to be weak, dependent on others and unworthy of respect (*da'if*, as speakers of Arabic would express it).

In practice, of course, nobles and priests might be impoverished while people of low status might acquire too much income for the status ascribed to them, thereby demonstrating that there were sources of affluence other than the military prowess, high cultural learning or noble descent to which the elite owed its privileged position; but this was something which had to be counteracted. By far the most important source of rival wealth was trade, and most agrarian elites accordingly took a dim view of merchants, as has been seen. People who acquired too much wealth for their rank had to be either excluded or co-opted (that is ennobled or otherwise granted formal membership of the elite, on a par with tribal leaders, mountain chiefs, robber barons and others who acquired too much political power). It was only when such methods failed to neutralize the accumulation of commercial wealth that the hierarchical perception lost persuasiveness, as it eventually did in Europe.

An immense amount of historical and sociological literature is devoted to the question how far class struggle can be documented for the past. The interest of this question arises from the Marxist conviction that class struggle is the 'motor' of history, or in other words that it has generated all the complexity and variety that we see around us today and will determine our future too; obviously, if class struggle provides the key to where we come from, what we are and where we are going, then it becomes a matter of great urgency to document its workings in the past. But the Marxist conviction is wrong. The very fact that production is a human invention shows that human history had a motor long before it had production, and thus long before it had classes too in the Marxist sense. The much earlier invention of religion shows the same (unless we are to take it that the invention of agriculture caused history to change its motor, which is somewhat hard to believe).

This being so, the question whether there was class struggle in the past loses its all-absorbing interest. It is obvious that since there were no modern-style classes in the past, there was no modern-style class struggle either. Subservient populations everywhere resented their masters' attempts to dominate and exploit them, and conflict between the above-mentioned 'bits' of classes kept erupting as the peasants or weavers of a particular locality refused to accept the terms dictated by their landlords or employers. Such conflict could be, and often is, loosely referred to as class struggle. But since the social order was based on political rather than economic relations, collective action in pursuit of common economic interest was difficult to organize and even harder to keep up; and the fact that economic relations were subordinate to the political order meant that people might have to compete for political advantages at the expense of what we perceive as their class interests; peasants commonly sided with their landlords against the state, for example, joining them in regional revolts against exorbitant tax-collectors (a pattern well attested for Europe); they might also seek to ally themselves with landlords in an effort to take over the state apparatus (as they often did in China when their revolts gained momentum); and the landlords themselves might pursue their interests as representatives of the state (which needed taxes in order to protect their privileged position) at the expense of their interests as landowners (who wanted to escape taxation in so far as possible), or vice versa.

It was only in city states that something close to modern class struggle appeared. Most city states depended largely or wholly on commercial wealth, meaning that economic relations here came closer than anywhere else in the pre-industrial world to shaping the socio-political order; and the masses had a genuine political presence, partly because they and the elite were cooped up together instead of being dispersed in the countryside, so that mass behaviour was difficult for the elite to ignore, and partly because the elite and no vast expanse of countryside from which to recruit troops, so that either they relied on the urban masses themselves or else they had to recruit mercenaries: the former solution was more conducive than the latter to the acqusition of formal political rights by the masses, but neither allowed for their total exclusion. Here then we have approximations to the modern combination of mass participation and economic inequality which engenders politics *about* this inequality.

But the masses did not normally participate nor were politics normally about the distribution of economic goods; and both the fragmented nature of such class conflict as occurred and the regularity with which it failed to change the lot of the masses show that it was not class struggle which propelled history forwards to the point of bringing pre-industrial society to an end.

Ostentatious inegalitarianism

The hierarchical and/or organic view of society prevailed wherever the market was weakly developed. The social order might in principle be based on merit (acquired through education) rather than heredity, as it was in China and to some extent in the medieval Islamic world, and this allowed for a certain measure of social mobility: mobility tended to blur social divisions. But education was more commonly acquired through rank than rewarded by it, exactly as was wealth. Of course, the degree to which society was affected by market relations varied greatly too. Even so, there is hardly a feature more constant in pre-industrial history than the view of society as a hierarchy or organism in which everyone had his proper place, each place being associated with different rights and duties in formal or customary law, including different penalties for the same offences. Order prevailed when people occupied their proper places, fulfilling their obligations and receiving their rights in return; anarchy prevailed when they did not. Ranking promoted the harmonious cooperation between different parts by showing who should do what in return for what, its absence leading to confusion and insubordination. 'Take but degree away . . . and hark what discord follows', as Shakespeare put it in a famous line: even the heavens themselves observed 'degree, priority and place'.

Pre-industrial societies were thus marked by strong horizontal *and* vertical divisions, being steeply divided in terms of both ethnicity and locality on the one hand *and* rank and status on the other. Rank and status differentiated the elite, or in other words those who had overcome divisions of ethnicity and locality through participation in the high culture; ethnicity and locality (or minority religion) differentiated the rest, those who failed to participate in the high culture being stuck with unprivileged status. Clothing, hairstyle, jewellery, housing, carriage and other aspects of personal appearance were commonly used to indicate either or both. 'Among the nobles, the mere gentlemen have their coats of arms surrounded by helmets, the knights have their spurs and gilded armour . . . among the commoners, the doctors, licentiates and bachelors have their different kinds of hood . . . the advocates their distinctive hats', as a seventeenth-century French lawyer explained with reference to his own country. 'Almost every article of use, as well as ornament, particularly in their dress, indicated the rank of the owner', as a nineteenth-century Englishman reminisced with reference to Burma. Certain types of clothing were formally reserved for literati in China, for senators in Rome, for warriors in Aztec Mexico, and certain types were formally imposed on non-Muslims in the Muslim Middle East; but even where no formal rules existed, people would display who and what they were by the clothes they wore, the mounts they rode, the number of servants in their train and so on, a habit of which the best known residue in current use today is the display of marital status by means of wedding rings. Seating arrangements and rules of precedence at court, in the circus or theatre, in places of worship and on all occasions of public ceremony would likewise reflect the ranks of the participants. Language, too, was an important status-marker, not only in the sense that educated and uneducated persons spoke different languages or dialects but also in the sense that whatever they spoke, they would have available to them a rich variety of honorifics, modes of address and grammatical forms reflecting the age, sex and social position of, as well as the degree of intimacy between, the speaker and the person addressed: not only could you tell at a glance who and what a person was, but you also had to acknowledge in your forms of speech whether he was your superior, inferior or peer. Some languages were considerably more sensitive than others to such differences. European languages abounded in different forms of address (such as 'monseigneur' for princes, 'messire' for knights, 'monsieur' for ordinary nobles, 'maistre' for men of letters, etc.), but were otherwise rather crude instruments in this respect; by contrast, it is impossible to speak Japanese without employing either honorific, polite or blunt forms. In modern Japan people make up for the uninformative nature of modern clothing by exchanging cards which advertise their social position, thus enabling others to select the proper level of speech when addressing them.

Egalitarianism

Generally speaking, the ethos of pre-industrial society was thus anything but egalitarian. Equality meant chaos, conjuring up much the same image of disorder as does the idea of mixing up the different parts of a car engine to us. Nonetheless, an egalitarian streak was almost always present too.

Most cultures were familiar with the idea that mankind had once lived in a primeval state of innocence and bliss, without food production, taxes, violence or kings, without social inequality or sexual discrimination, and without disease or death; one way or the other this golden age or Paradise came to an end, and this was how civilization appeared along with its discontent. A myth to this effect was known in ancient India, from where it passed to the Buddhists who spread it in South-East Asia and China, where it acquired elaborations of its own; a comparable myth circulated in Graeco-Roman antiquity, where it was explored by a variety of thinkers from Hesiod to the Stoics; and yet another myth of this kind is found in the Old Testament, from where it passed to Jews, Christians and Muslims alike. (Curiously, however, the Muslims did not invoke the Fall to explain the origin of the state.) The myth thus defined equality as utopian, that is both highly desirable and impossible to have, and Paradise was not generally assumed to be regainable in this world. But as seen in chapter 4, every now and again people of one kind or another, commonly peasants under semi-educated leadership, expected the present world to come to an end and the next to arrive in the form of millenium of earth, and to such people the myth became a political programme: all aspects of Paradise lost were going to be restored in the here and now.

Belief in one God also fostered (or reflected) egalitarian ideas. 'Since all members of the four castes [here in the sense of functional orders] are children of God, they all belong to the same caste. All human beings have the same father, and children of the same father cannot have different castes', as an Indian text puts it: in principle, human equality was incompatible with social differentiation. The early Christians duly instituted common property, sharing everything except their wives (whom some of them thought they ought to share too); and Muhammad similarly instituted brotherhood among the believers, some of whom briefly shared everything except their wives. Both Christians and Muslims soon got round to the view that equality vis-à-vis God had no bearing on socio-political arrangements in this world, and numerous asseverations of human equality in other parts of the world were meant in a similarly abstract vein. But even so, the idea that society might or ought to be reorganized along egalitarian lines was rarely far below the surface. Intellectuals kept picking at it, and it appealed to peasants familiar with an egalitarian order from their local communities, and usually also from the above-mentioned myth. But though egalitarianism could be practised to a greater or lesser extent within small communities such as villages, city states or sects, and within as opposed to between social strata, large-scale social organization had to be hierarchical. Egalitarianism was either purely moral or else it was heretical and thus (implicitly or explicitly) rebellious too. There was no room for it in the official socio-political creed.

Holism

If society was a body and the functional orders its limbs, individuals were simply cells making up the limbs in question (though the cell imagery was not actually used). Like cells, they were programmed for performance of pre-determined roles and derived their value from performing as expected, not from refusing to conform. Individual interests were subordinated to and defined by collective ones, and an individual who defined his own purpose in life without regard for the collectivity (family, village, religious community and/or polity) to which he belonged was not a romantic hero, but rather a misfit or a cancerous element. Society was holistic rather than individualistic (as sociologists put it): the individual existed for the benefit of the overall group, not the other way round.

The reader is probably familiar with this notion from his reading about aristocratic families who, as everyone knows, subordinated the interests of their individual members to the overriding objective of keeping their aristocratic houses intact; but it prevailed at peasant level too, and for precisely the same reason: they too were born into land-holding corporations. Where children have to derive their livelihood from the same land (or business enterprise) as their parents and to pass it on to their own children in their turn, the long-term interests of the family land (or family firm) must take precedence over the short-term interests of this or that individual member. It is only when children go away to make their living elsewhere that the holistic point of view ceases to prevail at family level. Modern people may identify strongly with the collective enterprise for which they choose to work, be it industrial or professional, but there are limits to how far they will sacrifice their personal interests to it because they cannot pass it on to their children. (They may not even stay with it for long.) Today, only political membership is systematically transmitted on a hereditary basis, and it is only in connection with the nation that modern people can be induced to adopt a holistic view, sacrificing their own interests, or even their lives, to defend it. But in the past, heredity governed the allocation of the means of subsistence too for the vast majority of people.

The high evaluation of conformity went hand in hand with conservatism. Agrarian civilizations did not change very much, a fact which encouraged the use of heredity, which stood in the way of change in its turn. As the same order was transmitted from one generation to the next, it acquired the authoritative status of immemorial custom, usually becoming heavily saturated with religious validation too. Who was the individual to resist divinely ordained ways of doing things endorsed by generation upon generation as far back as anyone could remember?

Thus far the ideal. In practice, of course, pre-industrial individuals did not habitually sacrifice themselves on the altar of collective interest crushed under the heavy weight of the past. On the one hand, nobody is perfect: even the most well-intentioned individual found it hard to exemplify the ideal to which he aspired. On the other hand, the weight of the past was unevenly distributed: generation upon generation as far back as anyone could remember had produced not just conformists, but also rebels raising endless questions of how collective interests could or should be defined. Consequently, many different answers had accumulated in the course of time. All the great salvation religions placed the individual at the centre of their universe, stressing that each person chooses his own damnation or salvation, rejecting the concept of collective responsibility and sometimes dismissing the concept of grace as well along with saintly patronage, intercession and other kinds of moral exemption clauses in order to ram home the message that everyone is personally liable for his own acts. Of course, the great religions had to stress communal interests too, and the early individualism tended to be watered down in the course of time. (Jesus' subversive message that he had come 'to set a man at variance against his father, and the daughter against her mother' evidently ceased to be stressed once Christianity had become a majority religion.) Even so, all complex societies of the second generation were all too familiar with the notion that individual and collective interests might clash; and urbanization, social mobility or social change in general always promoted individualism. People were for ever complaining that their contemporaries had forgotten ancestral virtues and pursued their own opinions and pleasures instead: society was always deemed to be dissolving. None the less, when all is said and done, the fact remains that pre-industrial societies were built on a more holistic model than they are today.

The individual

The holistic outlook produced individuals who were inclined to identify themselves with their social roles rather than to distinguish between their selves and the social slots they happened to fill. They certainly began their training for their adult roles far earlier. Childhood was typically short, or, as some would put it, there was no concept of childhood at all – an unhelpful way of saying that the modern concept of childhood was absent. Obviously, no society has ever failed to see or take account of the differences between children and adults. However, modern society is distinctive in its perception of children as creatures who must be shielded from adult secrets (especially sexual ones) on the grounds that they are innocent, and exempted from adult responsibilities (especially work) on the grounds that they are busy with their education. This, at least, was the concept which prevailed until the arrival of television made the preservation of adult secrets impossible. Childhood is perceived as a long and glorious holiday from adult society, the child being allowed to know nothing and do nothing apart from what his formal education requires. Children are thus luxuries and expensive to rear.

But in pre-industrial societies the infantile holiday was exceedingly short. Then as now, children were commonly perceived as innocent, but there was no premium on keeping them in that state: naturally there were things they could not understand, but this was not to say that the moral failings of the adult world had to be systematically suppressed in their presence. Children learnt the 'facts of life' by watching and hearing just as they learnt anything else, and such education as they received aimed at turning them into morally upright beings rather than at keeping them ignorant of the corrupt and sinful nature of the world in which they had to live their adult lives. Nor could they be exempted from adult responsibility for long. There was little, if any, formal schooling for the majority. Boys would usually start participating in adult work at about the age of seven, girls might begin to acquire domestic tasks even earlier. In short, children were expected rapidly to begin repaying the investment which had gone into their creation: they were sources of labour, not luxuries.

Adult status was conferred by physical maturity, real or presumed, at least as far as boys were concerned: they would don their sacred cord or their *toga virilis* in their early teens in public demonstration of the fact that they were now responsible for their own social and religious acts. Still, they might not be seen as fully adult in either law or custom until they had married (or reached an age where they ought to have done so); and marriage was usually indispensable for social recognition of adulthood in a girl, whatever her legal position.

Marriage

In conformity with the view that the individual existed for the group rather than the other way round, marriage was generally arranged. It was an alliance between two families, lineages or clans rather than between two individuals, the inclinations of the latter being of subordinate importance (though not necessarily ignored altogether). Romantic love was if anything even more romantic than today, a mere glimpse of another person being enough to kindle it, or even a picture or a dream: love at first sight seems to have flourished in direct proportion to the degree of segregation between the sexes. But it was not usually regarded as reasonable or sufficient grounds for marriage (or at any rate not for first marriages), as opposed to a kind of madness, as indeed it was wherever parental plans for the devolution of property and power had to take precedence over passion. Still, people sometimes fell in love with the person for whom they were predestined by social convention; and at all events love was assumed to follow marriage in so far as it had not preceded it. Clearly, it often did, though the emotional regime might be such that the bond between mother and son, or between the parties and their peer groups, was stronger than that between husband and wife.

Child betrothal, child marriage, segregation and chaperonage were common expedients against undesirable love and its even more undesirable consequences. Illegitimate children, or even loss of virginity, were usually regarded as an unspeakable disgrace for the woman and her family, though there were peasant societies in which they were unobjectionable if the woman proceeded to marry the child's father. (Sociologically speaking, the trouble with children of irregular unions was that they lacked both a family unit to care for them and a social position for them to inherit.) If girls were not married off as children, they were usually provided with husbands as soon as they reached physical maturity. Boys, too, could marry soon after puberty where the extended family prevailed, that is where they did not have to be able to support their wives and family immediately; where it did not, they had to wait till they were securely established (meaning that they would typically be much older than their wives). They might be encouraged to practise self-control for the duration; more commonly, they were provided with outlets in the form of slave girls, concubines, prostitutes or high-class courtesans such as the hetaerae of the Greeks, the geishas of the Japanese or the singing-girls of the Muslims.

Such women belonged to what was variously called the 'floating world' or the 'half-world' (*demi-monde*), meaning a world exempt from everyday responsibility: liaisons with them incurred no obligations other than monetary ones. They might be highly educated (fetching enormous sums if they were slaves); they could move about freely where respectable matrons and their daughters had to remain at home; and they could and often did become immensely wealthy, investing their earnings in land, business or new girls whom they trained themselves. Since they were by definition exceptional, nothing they did had any implications for the position of women in general.

The young and the old

Young people passed into their parents' world with great facility because there was no generation gap. Given that society did not change very much, every generation expected to live in much the same world as that of its predecessors, profiting from the same knowledge, using the same skills and coming to grief over the same problems. But there might of course be tensions between the generations of other kinds: the profligate son was proverbial.

There was no youth culture either. Youth culture flourishes in the modern world because modern childhood now extends far beyond the age of physical maturity, a large number of sexually mature persons being denied responsible positions in the adult world on the grounds that their education is still in progress: they cannot work, marry, or settle down. Segregated at school or university and thrown back on their peer groups, they react by forming societies of their own, with their own rules, values, uniforms and leadership, and immediately get massive attention from the consumer industry because they represent a buoyant market. In the pre-industrial world, by contrast, the number of sexually mature persons caught in the educational network was extremely small; and of those who did get caught in it, many were fully admitted to adult roles while they were still students, being expected to marry, administer family land, assume responsibilities vis-à-vis their wider kin, or even public office, while studying as gentlemen of leisure. No youth culture, let alone counter-culture, emerged from such men; and of course there was no consumer industry either. Youth clubs such as the Roman *Iuventus* were designed for boys between the ages of fourteen and seventeen by way of preparation for a career in public service, not by way of dissidence; and though the medieval Muslim organizations cultivating *futuwwa*, the virtues of the young man, were sometimes dissident, they were not closely linked to age. It was only when crises of one kind or another prevented a significant number of sexually mature youths from finding spouses and occupations that something similar to youth culture appeared, be it in the form of chivalry or gangs of adolescents prowling the streets in search of women, booty and heroic exploits.

Then as now, of course, the young were the least conservative and the most adventurous segment of society. 'The fashion of the time insists that no son will take his father's advice, because there is a burning ardour in the hearts of young men which through folly persuades their intellects that their own knowledge is superior to that of their elders', an eleventh-century Persian Polonius explained to his son. Young people are 'foolish' because they lack experience (one became a mature person at forty) and more particularly because they have not invested in the world as it is, so that they have nothing to lose from change and cannot see why others should oppose it; besides, if it were to change at their instigation, they would become its leaders. The more commitments people acquire, the more they thereby invest in the assumption that the world will continue as it is (that the mortage rate will stay stable, that the teaching of history will not be abandoned, that the schools to which children are being sent will not be converted into homes for stray dogs, and so on); and the more successful their investments are, the more conservative they will become. It is the losers, the marginal and the unattached who stand to gain from change, and within all groups it is the young who are the most likely to initiate it.

Heredity often placed very young men in very responsible positions, but there was no systematic attempt to harness the innovative minds of the young because there was no technological change to harness it for. What people aspired to was wisdom, the prerogative of the old. The old were venerated for the experience they had accumulated in the course of their lives, not dismissed as obsolete models, and there was much ceremonious respect for seniority, young people being expected to remain standing and keep silent when elders were present, or at any rate not to sit down or speak without permission, not to look an elder straight in the eye, not to omit polite forms of address, not to adopt the mannerisms of their seniors, and in general not to forget the difference between senior men of wisdom and foolish youth. Among themselves, the young were often full of contempt for 'decrepit old fools', while the old were full of nostalgia for their heady days of youth. But 'though it may be the case that the old men sigh for their youth, yet doubtless also young men hunger after old age... despite the fact that the young believe themselves the wisest of all beings', as the above-mentioned Polonius observed. Cultural norms came down in favour of the old, as they necessarily must wherever ordinary experience plays a greater role than technical or scientific knowledge.

Group pressure

People were made to identify with their social roles through constant reminders that 'boys', 'girls', 'fathers', 'peasants', 'gentlemen', etc., do this and do not do that: boys do not weep, gentlemen keep their word, and so on. In short, they were trained to mould their characters on the basis of pre-defined models, the highest reward being praise as a model boy, a model girl, a model student or whatever other model one might aspire to. Members of modern Western society often dislike such models, regarding them as outmoded and intolerable restrictions on the expression of individuality. Members of pre-industrial societies, however, did not see them as restrictions on their personalities, but rather as *definitions* of the personalities they were expected to adopt. The roles being strongly defined in terms of clothing, ornaments, language and mannerisms, they dominated and indeed constituted the world in which people grew up: it was difficult to think of a self apart from them. The conservative nature of higher education, with its emphasis on imitation of past models and memorization of past wisdom, also made it difficult to see oneself as distinct from the society of which one was part. But above all, conformity was enforced by the immense social pressure exercised by kinsmen and neighbours.

People were constantly being exposed to other people's verdicts on the success or otherwise of their performances. There was little privacy. The poor lived in hovels while the rich were surrounded by relatives and servants; even houses deliberately built to secure privacy against the outside world usually lacked privacy internally, everybody being kept in a state of visibility to at least a few because privacy meant opportunities for illicit relations. Moreover, it was not commonly thought that people should be able to take private holidays from their social roles. A person was the role he played, not a self apart from it. Thus a king was a king whatever he was doing, not just when he was on display (though he might well be on display all the time). In our view even royal persons need privacy to take off their crowns and royal smiles in between performances; but in pre-modern time the crown could not be doffed, and the same was true of other roles.

In short, people were always on stage, and the reactions of the audience mattered intensely to them. Given that most of them lived their entire lives in the communities in which they were born, they could not dismiss gossip as unimportant. The gossips were kinsmen, friends and neighbours, not superficial acquaintances, and they were moreover part of self-help groups without which the victims could not get on. Accordingly, other people's opinions were the very stuff of which life was made.

Emotional economy

The immense importance attached to other people's opinions meant that failure to perform satisfactorily usually evoked feelings of shame rather than of guilt. A man was his reputation: fame was highly desirable. In principle, ultimate judgement on a man's worth might be reserved for God, who alone knew the hearts of men and whose Paradise was far more important than fame in the here and now; in practice, too, inner morality judged by private conscience might be perceived as more important than the verdict passed by external observers: clearly, this made for non-conformity. But external observers usually possessed a social significance so overwhelming that pride in honour and shame at its loss came first in people's emotional repertoires.

A man was shamed by inability to live in accordance with the code appropriate to his rank, be it by exposure of skeletons in his cupboard (e.g. ignoble ancestors), by taking up work incompatible with his station, by unchastity in the women under his control, by improper behaviour on the part of his relatives and, not least, by physical nudity and its psychological counterpart, loss of self-control. Males were generally expected to be calm, unruffled and dignified: cracks in the surface were demeaning; the naked self was not supposed to show through. In short, constant effort went into the maintenance of façades rather than the exploration of interiors.

Consequently, members of pre-industrial societies were not given to introspection. They did not habitually search their selves in contradistinction to what showed on the surface: the surface manifestations *were* their selves, or at least they were supposed to be. They were much given to typecasting of both themselves and others, which is not to say that they failed to appreciate individuality, but rather that they appreciated it in much the same manner as they did originality: there were many ways of playing well-known roles, just as there were many ways of saying old wisdom and using well-worn poetic conventions. ('Horace and Despréaux said it before us; but I say it in my own way', as the seventeenth-century French writer La Bruyère put it in perfect summation of the classicist ideal.) Such introspection as was practised took place under the aegis of religion, battles with the self being what a great deal of spirituality was about; and records of spiritual journeys did attempt the art of self-revelation, whereas ordinary autobiographies and diaries tended to limit themselves to the record of external events, revealing little of the person underneath (in so far as they were written at all). But even those who recorded their spiritual lives tended to be reticent about their individual features, describing themselves in standardized terms: few cared to confess in all the concrete detail volunteered by Saint Augustine.

The fact that they were not given to revelation of their inner selves should not be taken to mean that they were lacking in emotion. However, it does mean that the modern historian may well be unable to get inside them, cracks in the surface being insufficiently numerous to give away what the world was like to them as a subjective experience. Dearth of source material, as well as religious, cultural and linguistic barriers, often stand in the way too. People lived in a violent and inconstant world in which death and disaster lurked in every corner, all too often striking with lightning speed; one might be robbed of parents, siblings, spouse or children overnight at the hands of disease (more parents were lost through death than are parents through divorce today); one might be kidnapped, pressed into service, enslaved, carried off to alien countries, maimed, despoiled or raped at the hands of brigands, pirates, rampaging soldiers or enemy troops, or for that matter government officials, suffering any number of other reversals of fortune in between: the adventures of Voltaire's *Candide* are exaggerated only in that Candide and his friends go through all of them and keep surviving. It stands to reason that the fickleness of the world should have affected people, but we do not really know how. It is supposed to have made them violent and hot-tempered in medieval Europe, resigned, fatalistic and/or given to the cultivation of detachment and inner calm elsewhere, and, once more in Europe (until early modern times), callous and devoid of affection, especially vis-à-vis infants, whom they did not want to love because of the overwhelming likelihood that they would die. No doubt there are examples of such behaviour everywhere, but their value as generalizations are dubious.

As regards children, the best-studied subject to date, it would appear that parents bonded with their children in both Europe and elsewhere on the same scale as they do today (what will future historians make of today's battered children?): though there are occasional callous reactions to the death of infants in pre-modern literature, there are many more of agonized grief. However, the expression of grief might be discouraged, or rather diverted to contexts where it reinforced rather than tore holes in the social fabric: one should not weep excessively for one's own children, but one might cry one's heart out for a holy figure such as Imam Husayn; mature men might be esteemed for their self-control, but both they and others might be allowed or even expected to weep convulsively in response to sermons on the martyrs, the transience of life, death and the world ahead. However, emotional economy is too underresearched a subject to lend itself even to oversimplification.

Outlets

It would hardly have been possible for people to maintain so strong an identification with their social roles if they had not been provided with ways of escaping them from time to time, or even permanently. As has been seen, they were not expected to take private holidays from them; but there were outlets of other kinds.

Thus some societies had what one might call public holidays from the social roles, or in other words festivals in which the normal rules of social interaction were temporarily suspended or turned upside down: commoners would throw dirt at aristocrats, or people would step out of their social roles by dressing up as others or by wearing masks, feeling free to engage in all kinds of frolics because what one does behind a mask is not done by oneself (that is, that responsible self that one presents in public). The intense pleasure derived from such festivals turns on the total domination, in everyday life, of the rules which were suspended, and though some carnivals existed largely for the circumvention of sexual morality, most festivals were sufficiently ritual in nature to confirm rather than undermine the rules involved. (School children may similarly mount school plays parodying their teachers, causing much merriment to everyone involved and at the same time confirming the normal distribution of authority.)

However, some outlets were considerably more dangerous. Humans have a capacity for actual ecstasy (literally 'standing outside'), a momentary dropping-out in which all normal boundaries, restrictions and rules, be they social, emotional, cognitive or other, are not so much suspended or reversed as positively transcended. The great spring festivals of the pagan Mediterranean (associated with deities such as Astarte and Cybele) were not just occasions on which the normal rules ceased to apply, but also moments of ecstatic experience, the participants working themselves into a frenzy by rhythmic shouting and self-inflicted pain until they lost themselves in the divine. The pagan participant in such rites, the warrior going beserk, the mystic seeking union with God, the modern experimenter with mind-bending drugs, all these and many others were and are drawing on the same psychological propensity, though the cultural construction put on it and the social institutions placed at its disposal are very different. And with or without ecstatic experience, numerous people were and still are inclined to step outside by rejecting this world altogether, abandoning all social roles for good and dropping out as hermits, beggars or wanderers in the name of individual salvation.

Such outlets were dangerous because all societies work best if their rules are felt to be as self-evident, inescapable and effortless as the urge to breathe. To query them, see through them or feel above them is to threaten society with chaos even if one continues to live a responsible social life and all the more so, of course, if one does not: every drop-out is a living demonstration that culturally made rules are *not* in the nature of the genetic instruction to breathe; every mystic brushes them aside as matters of secondary importance; and every taker of mindbending drugs places a question mark over the entire cognitive system on which everyday sanity (his own included) rests. All in their own way make a cult of the madman, the drunkard, the fool, the tramp and the beggar, on whom society plainly cannot be based. And all, throughout history, have generated their crop of what we now call Nietzschean supermen, people who pronounce themselves beyond good and evil and who proceed to demonstrate their liberation from humdrum normality by engaging in deliberate violation thereof (in the style of Rodion Raskolnikov, the murderer in Dostoevsky's *Crime and Punishment*). But every society has to come to terms with such phenomena, be it by regulation or repression.

Ecstatic religion was part of fertility rites in some of the earliest civilizations, but the renunciatory ideal first made its appearance in the so-called 'axial age' (the first millennium BC), assuming a wide variety of different forms thereafter: it was by no means always combined with the pursuit of ecstacy, but there was a strong tendency for the two to come together. As might be expected, many societies began by viewing both phenomena with extreme suspicion, but the majority nonetheless came sooner or later to reserve their highest veneration for those who dropped out, temporarily or permanently, to live solitary or monastic lives in search of wisdom, enlightenment, mystic experience or salvation; and where this was so, even those who stayed behind were typically able to cultivate such experience, exploring other realities, seeking mystic union or otherwise transcending the world of everyday reality in religious fraternities of various kinds. Official acceptance of this type of religiosity was usually awarded on various conditions (e.g. that there be no neglect of religious or secular law, no contempt for government or ecclesiastical authorities, no sexual irregularities, no drugs, etc.), so that there were always practitioners who found themselves bracketed with the underworld. But generally speaking, pre-modern societies were much better than modern ones at deriving profit from persons who sought to avoid or transcend them.

The advantages they derived from making room for drop-outs are obvious in the case of monastic institutions, both Christian and Buddhist, which functioned as centres of learning, refuges for misfits, runaways and other unwanted persons (from ex-kings to ex-wives), and dispensers of social and political services of many other kinds. But monasteries apart, one only has to compare the immense value derived by the Christian church from the order of St Francis (1182–1226), a merchant's son who took to a wandering life of mendicant poverty, with the mere nuisance value of the hippie convoys produced by bourgeois drop-outs today to appreciate the extent to which pre-industrial societies could capitalize on human inclinations that modern societies can only suppress. Solitary drop-outs, too, had an important role to play even if they completely stopped interacting with other human beings: they kept the renunciatory ideal alive.

But a man who renounces his worldly ambitions to go and subsist on roots in the desert or the forest, or on alms in the street, or on a pillar, is likely soon to acquire a following of mightily impressed devotees who want him to settle their disputes and compose their feuds (because he is a seeker after the truth with no ambitions of his own, and commonly an outsider too), to cure their diseases, find their lost property, bless themselves and their cattle with numerous offspring, and work sundry miracles as required (because he is in communication with powers above). In short, he comes to function as a holy man or saint.

Contrary to what European students are apt to assume, a saint is not necessarily dead, though it is true that certain types of sainthood can only be achieved by death (martyrdom) and that the saint's powers may well continue to manifest themselves at his shrine, or wherever one invokes him, after he has died. ('Here lies Martin the bishop, of holy memory, whose soul is now in the hand of God; but he is fully there, present and made plain in miracles of every kind', as the tombstone of St Martin of Tours proclaimed.) The cult of dead saints, typically centred on their graves, is attested for many societies. But it was only in Catholic Europe from the twelfth century onwards that all saints *had* to be dead before they could be canonized; and canonization had to be official, which is unusual too. This concept was the outcome of the church's attempt to keep the sacred under control: only the ecclesiastical authorities could authenticate supernatural power, and only those who were no longer around to make use of it were deemed to have possessed it. Generically, however, a saint (a holy man or woman) is a person who has no power to coerce, only to persuade, to whom people can submit without losing face because he or she represents superhuman authority, and to whom they will turn in difficulties of any kind because he or she has supernatural knowledge and power.

Members of cult societies devoted to the pursuit of ecstatic religion often found a comparable role as 'shamans', being asked to use their supernatural powers to heal diseases, expel demons, counter magic, recover lost property, foretell the future, and so on. 'In Transoxania and Turkestan many persons, especially women, claim to have magical powers; and when anyone has a pain or falls ill, they visit him, summon the exorcist, perform dances and similar nonsense and in this manner convince the ignorant and the vulgar', a thirteenth-century Persian historian informs us. But such people did not normally renounce their worldly roles and for this reason they did not usually get involved in dispute settlement, though they might well use their supernatural powers for political purposes in other ways: the Persian historian offered his information by way of background to a revolt by a Bukharan sieve-maker who claimed to be in communication with spirits; and spirit possession was also a common avenue to leadership in popular revolts elsewhere, as seen in chapter 4.

Dispute settlement was however the characteristic function of saints. Holy men and women oiled the socio-political wheels in many a local community where law courts either did not exist or were cumbersome to use or otherwise unpopular. Having renounced the world for the sake of God, they also much appreciated as guides in spiritual and moral matters by urban and rural populations alike, and their popular following might be so great that even kings had to pay attention to their opinions. In fifth-century Syria a famous ascetic by the name of Ephraim the Stylite spent thirty-seven years of his life on pillars of increasing height, devoting most of his time to prayer and meditation, but giving over his afternoons to the multitudes below, settling disputes, curing diseases, dispensing advice and admonitions, consoling the distressed, converting the local bedouin to Christianity and championing the cause of the oppressed; allegedly, he somehow managed to correspond with the emperor, too, along with other persons of consequence in the eastern Roman world. Like many other saints, he certainly acquired considerable political influence.

Ecstasy and/or renunciation also provided one of the few means whereby women could transcend their narrow female roles in that proximity to the divine (demonstrated by ecstatic experience of one kind or another) gave them the wherewithal to work as cult-leaders, exorcists, healers, spiritual advisers, saints and virtuoso mystics: it was not only in Transoxania and Turkestan that women were prominent in such activities. Where monasteries existed, the renunciatory ideal allowed them to work as administrators too.

Saints, both male and female, still exist, though no longer in Europe. There is a good portrait of the nineteenth-century Russian variety in Dostoyevsky's *Brothers Karamazov*.

In short, the renunciatory ideal provided a safety valve by integrating high culture and counter-culture. Wherever it prevailed, it had the odd effect of making society revere its own negation: the lowliest were the highest, kings stooped to listen to the advice of filthy dervishes, devotees drank the water in which they had washed their filthy feet, the maggots which fell from their festering wounds were pearls in the eyes of the believers. Ordinary beggars, tricksters and imposters would duly present themselves as holy men, while holy men would disguise themselves as ordinary beggars in order to humiliate themselves; madmen turned out to be saints and saints turned out to be madmen, in so far as anyone knew where the distinction lay. 'A madman, a fool of God, went naked where other men went clothed', as we are told in a famous poem by a twelfth-century Muslim mystic; a madman who went naked in the streets of nineteenth-century Cairo was carted off to a mental hospital, leaving behind a crowd of desolate female followers and a European observer who greatly approved of his removal. The ideal placed a question mark over the everyday reality in which everyone lived, but at the same time it helped to preserve it.

7
Religion

I should like to round off this part of the book with some general comments on religion. Religion is a distinctive part of culture which generates more bewilderment in modern students than any other aspect of history: some find it difficult to see why it should exist at all, while others take its existence for granted without understanding how it can be related to historical processes, religious truth being in their opinion above worldly change; and all are hampered in their understanding by the fact that religion occupied a very different position in agrarian civilizations from that which it has in the modern West. How and why the role of religion has changed under industrial conditions will be dealt with in the last chapter. Here I shall try to explain why it exists and to dispel some of the most common misconceptions about it.

What is religion?

A religion is a world view, that is a set of ideas which add up to a theoretical construction of the world, or key parts of it. The ideas may be presented in primitive myths or in sophisticated theological systems. Either way, religions differ from ideological, philosophical and moral world views in that they explain the world with reference to supernatural beings rather than abstract principles or impersonal laws. Usually they also have a broader scope, covering all aspects of life here and now as well as the hereafter, whereas ideological, philosophical and moral systems often (though not always) concentrate on specific aspects of this world such as politics, social order or health and ignore or deny the existence of afterlife altogether. But in the present context these differences are immaterial. Religions have been more popular in history than their atheist or non-theist counterparts, presumably because supernatural beings endowed with human feelings are easier to understand, love and obey than abstract concepts such as cosmic order, *karma* or proletarian struggle, which operate like machines without regard for their effect on human beings and which are hard to visualize. But whatever the reasons for the greater appeal of theist world views, the question why people have religions, philosophies, ideologies or moralities is one and the same. In what follows the term 'religion' should be taken to mean any such world view, or all of them, unless the contrary is explicitly stated.

Such world views are however quite distinct from modern science. Modern science also offers a theoretical construction of the world, but it does not engage in any moral evaluation whatsoever, with the result that it never adds up to a prescription: it never tells you what to *do*. By contrast, religions and comparable world views are invariably prescriptive: they identify this as good and that as bad, and tell you to do this as opposed to that if you want to achieve success, righteousness, salvation, or whatever. Religion is not necessarily concerned with otherworldly salvation (this concern being unique to the salvation religions, broadly synonymous with world religions); but whether uniquely concerned with this world or with the next, or jointly with both, it is always concerned with approved behaviour. Arab paganism, a primitive religion, told you to abstain from pork; Islam, a world religion, tells you the same. But science does not tell you to abstain from tobacco: it merely tells you the effects of its use. You may decide to avoid these effects because you are a believer in longevity, but longevity is a value extrinsic to science itself. One can try to *extract* moral values from science (and many have made the attempt), but science goes on regardless. By contrast, values are intrinsic to religions and their secular counterparts: take them away and no systems remain. (Religions also differ from modern science in other ways which do not concern us here.)

Why religion?

The answer to the question why humans have religions, philosophies, moralities or ideologies, or in other words value-loaded systems of thought, lies in the evolution of the human species. There is no agreement as to how precisely the answer should be envisaged, but whatever happened to the hominoids from which we descend, the result is clear enough: as mentioned before, hominids are forced to supplement their deficient genetic programming with culture; differently put, their genetic programming has stopped giving them specific instructions and started to give them general instructions to be inventive instead. What we invent, or in other words culture, is not an unexpected bonus of high intelligence, but on the contrary what our intelligence is for: we could no more survive without it than could beavers without tails or cats without claws. Nor does culture simply mean tool-making, as should be clear already. Religion is part of culture; indeed, in primitive societies it is more or less synonymous with culture. Humans could be said to have religions precisely because they are dependent on culture for their survival.

Among the many functions performed by culture there are two fundamental ones from which religion springs. The first is the drawing of socio-political maps. Unlike other animals, humans are programmed neither for life in a specific type of group nor for a solitary existence. Such instructions as they have clearly make them gregarious, but what they should do with this fact is left for themselves to work out; indeed, the instructions are so open to cultural manipulation that humans can contravene them and live as solitary animals instead.

More commonly, of course, they live social lives, but they have to make up their own definitions of the societies in which they choose to do so. Nature does not tell them where to draw the line between in-group and out-group (should you belong to my group or to another?), or how to distribute social roles within the group to which they belong (should you be in authority and I milk the cows, or the other way round, or should milking be reserved for those in authority?) It does provide some perfunctory clues: thus colour and other visible characteristics can be used for the demarcation of groups, just as sex and age can (and to some extent must) be used for the assignation of social roles within them. But though primitive societies commonly flog such characteristics for all they are worth, there are far too many people of the same colour and far too little difference between women and men, young adults and mature persons, for this to suffice. No human society on earth, however primitive, has managed without additional principles.

The point about these principles is that because they are not given by nature, they have to be *invented;* society has to be based on something *made up.* The invented element may take the form of deities or abstract concepts such as progress or proletarian struggle; but whatever they are, we are here confronted with an irreducible oddity about all human societies: all are strung around figments of the human imagination.

The reader may object to this proposition in two contrary veins. On the one hand, he may accept that human societies are based on invisible entities, but deny that the entities in question are invented; surely God exists; progress is not simply in the mind of the beholder; and besides, many religions have centred on attention to, or outright worship of, ancestors, whose reality cannot be denied.

But the existence of God or progress are matters of belief, and whoever our ancestors may have been, they are no longer around. In all three cases we are up against things which cannot be seen, heard, felt or smelt, but only talked about: without language all three would cease to exist as factors influencing human society. Moreover, there is nothing in these things *on their own* to dictate that they should be of any importance whatever to the way in which we organize ourselves. Cats have ancestors too without making a fuss about them, and whether God exists or not, he does not impinge on the organization of cat society. In short, humans simply *assert* that certain invisible things or processes, to which they themselves give a local habitation and a name, are of great importance for their lives. They behave *as if* the invisible were visible and *as if* the invisible were ordained to have special relations with them. Take away that element of 'as if' and both the invisible entity itself and the society based thereupon dissolve. Without belief in the importance of ancestors, ancestors are forgotten and tribes disappear; without belief in God, he too disappears along with his devotees because it is only in the human mind and behaviour that he is manifest. The same is true of anything else mankind has believed in.

All societies are built around constructs of the human mind which cannot be directly observed, but which, given belief in them, come to be apparent in the manner in which people talk and interact. All, in short, are based on the human ability to construe. Some call this characteristic openness to truth and others a propensity to superstition; typically, we see ourselves as endowed with the former and everyone else as saddled with the latter. But however we choose to describe it, human society would collapse without it.

On the other hand, the reader may accept that the existence of invisible entities is a matter of belief, but deny that they play a role in the drawing of socio-political maps: questions such as whether you are a member of this group or that, or whether you or I should rule or milk the cows, are settled by a combination of material factors such as ecology, population density, the mode of production, brute force or whatever; figments of the human imagination are merely invoked to legitimate such solutions as happen to prevail.

This is a crude version of a view with which I agree. (I shall come back to the relative importance of material or ideological factors later in this chapter.) What concerns me here, however, is the fact that such legitimation should be necessary: no other species seems to need it. Clearly, it is necessary because no social organization devised by humans is 'natural', that is built into their genes. Bees are in no need of cultural justification for their social organization, highly inegalitarian though it is, because the entire organization is given by nature (by the same token, of course, they completely lack the equipment with which to engage in such justification); similarly, humans are not normally in need of cultural justification for the fact that they breathe. But no human society comes as natural as breathing.

Nothing in my genetic equipment tells me that I should milk cows or be forbidden to do so; you may force me to milk them, but if that is all there is to it, I may beat you up or run away the moment you are busy drinking; and though you may be in league with others today, you may fall out with them tomorrow: common interests are highly unstable, as anyone familiar with the phenomenon of intrigue should know. By contrast, if you devise a religion which says that the gods want my kind to milk and your kind to stick together in enjoyment of authority, on the grounds that my kind descend from a cow whereas you and yours descend from a god, then you may hope to create a society which remains stable not only during our lifetime, but also, and crucially, when social roles have to be transferred to the next generation: the religion would both justify and solidify the social order, partly by creating a moral bond between people who might otherwise split up the moment they cease to notice any short-term advantages in sticking together, and partly by justifying the exclusion of the rest from the group in question. Differently put, the religion would mediate between the selfish desires of individuals and the needs of the collectivity, thereby preserving the latter from constant disruption.

In short, no social organization is viable unless ideology makes up for genetic neutrality: whatever solution is adopted, it must present itself as *right* to both the winners and the losers. Obviously, people can be forced to perform roles for so long that they grow to accept them, but they cannot accept them without adopting or devising an an ideological presentation of the roles in question: acceptance involves a moral evaluation. In other words, the invisible entities are indispensable if a society is to hang together. In this sense all societies are indeed based on imagination.

The key entities are supernatural beings and/or natural laws, that is to say phenomena which are infinitely more powerful and enduring than petty human beings and usually, in the case of deities, infinitely wiser and better too. It is their superiority which enables them to legitimate human institutions. The more institutions they can underpin, or differently put, the more they can saturate society, the more stability they will lend to it. This is not to say, of course, that beliefs are unchanging. Many societies have endeavoured to endow their systems with the same appearance of unavoidable reality as that possessed by genetic programming: ideally, everything taught should become 'second nature'. But the very fact that beliefs are *not* given or transmitted by nature means that they respond more rapidly to environmental changes than do genetic features.

The second function of culture from which religion springs is that of providing meaning. Culture has to supply meaning precisely because human life is 'unnatural'. As mentioned already, genetic instructions are not in need of cultural justification: they make sense without there being any need whatsoever to think about them. But culturally imposed rules do not make effortless sense, so a meaning does have to be found for them. (Thus women are notoriously bad at explaining why they want children: no explanation is required because the desire is 'natural'. But women who decide not to have any can always give their reasons: not being 'natural', the decision requires cultural support.)

This is all the more true in that many cultural rules actually go *against* genetic instructions: there is no human society without extensive practice of self-control. Humans invent their own mating systems, which invariably involves cultural regulation of sexual drives; they also regulate aggression, and impose a host of other refinements on what they perceive as 'raw nature'. Going against the genetic grain makes no sense at all. (This should be obvious, but it is also observable in the frustrated behaviour of zoo animals unable to act in accordance with their programmes.) To this must be added that humans are aware of themselves, presumably thanks to their use of language (a precondition for symbolic culture of the type which goes into social organization) and probably reinforced by their practice of self-control. Self-awareness means awareness of death; and death is a source of meaninglessness so profound that it threatens to deprive the entire enterprise of its point. In short, the superhuman beings and laws that petty human beings see as the source of their socio-political organisation must do more than simply provide rules. They must also justify those rules, explain why they are good even though they feel uncomfortable, how they are conducive to happiness, indeed why there is so much unhappiness to overcome and why those who live by the rules rarely seem to be any less unhappy than the rest; and this almost invariably involves explaining why the world exists, what humans are doing in it, how their society relates to it, how and why they should go on, or alternatively how and why they ought to get out of it all again. The more complex a society, the more elaborate its belief system will be, obviously because the more variety there is in the human condition, the more there is to explain.

Religion provides, or forms the nucleus of, the cognitive, moral, social and political world in which the believer lives, however little thought he may give to it. Without it, both the world around him and he himself would lose their familiar identities and collapse into meaninglessness. It is for this reason that people do not change world views as they change clothes, but rather reinterpret them as the world to which it gives meaning changes. Muhammad may have known little about Iran and nothing at all about modernity, but he is nonetheless a crucial element in the identity of modern Iranian Muslims.

Religion and politics

The explanation why religion exists amounts to an explanation of what it is about, and many readers are bound to be surprised by the answer I have offered. Most students (and indeed laymen) of Western origin are of the opinion that religion has nothing to do with anything in this world, and least of all with politics, though it almost invariably gets embroiled in such matters thanks to the nefarious activities of self-seeking priests and politicians. Buddhists, on the other hand, think that religion has nothing to do with gods. What a particular religion has to do with is of course for the believers themselves to decide, but from the point of view of the external observer religion has everything to do with gods and politics alike.

As regards politics, it should be noted that most religions have explicitly put social and political organization on their agenda. Thus polytheist religions usually operated with deities in charge of various aspects of socio-political life, or of whole communities; and the

monotheist Gods of Judaism and Islam are also heavily involved with
the worldly fortunes of their people, as indeed one would expect. (If
everything on earth is created and ruled by a single omnipotent God,
how could politics be an exception?) But even religions which explicitly omit socio-political concerns from their agenda implicitly con-
front such issues, and they usually move on to treating them directly
in the end.

Thus Buddhism, Christianity and Gnostic religions such as Manichaeism all tried to transcend this world rather than to take it over:
all argued that mankind does not belong in it. Similar feelings have
also prevailed from time to time in this-worldly religions such as
Judaism and Islam. Here then we have what our above-mentioned
students take to be 'pure' religion, namely religion that professes
only to concern itself with meaning, not with the drawing of socio-
political maps.

But in fact it is impossible to concern oneself with one to the
exclusion of the other. If you tell people that the world is not worth
having, you will find that they start practising asceticism or dropping
out altogether (assuming that they believe you); and if you induce
people to give up office, renounce the army, leave their land, break
off their education, stop earning money and abandon their wives and
children for a solitary life of meditation in the forest or the desert on
a diet of leaves, locusts, dew or charitable offerings, then you can
scarcely claim to have said nothing at all about socio-political organization; on the contrary, you have been extremely subversive. To
renounce this world is to reject it along with all the institutions it
contains: you cannot renounce it without thereby denying its *authority*, or in other words without threatening to undermine the position
of those to whom the world has been entrusted, whoever they may
be. It is precisely because world-renouncing religions offer ways of
avoiding or transcending unsatisfactory institutions that they seem
persuasive to those who adopt them.

The elementary point to note is that this world happens to be the
one in which we all find ourselves; hence you cannot say *anything*
about the true origin and destiny of human beings without affecting
the world as it is (again assuming that they believe you). Whether
you tell them that they belong here or elsewhere, you must also tell
them what to do here and now. If you tell them they belong elsewhere, you must also tell them how they should go about returning
to their original home; and if you tell them to commit mass suicide
you will either achieve the final solution to all social and political

problems or, more likely, find that only your crazed followers do as they are told, greatly affecting the survivors. The idea that there is such a thing as a 'pure' religion which somehow affects people without affecting the society they constitute is patently nonsensical.

What is more, even if your intent were wholly otherworldly, you would soon be forced to take up socio-political organization yourself. Individual drop-outs may not need much in the way of organization (assuming that the authorities do not put obstacles in their way), but what if lots of people forsake the world? You would have to devise some sort of organization for them. And what about all those who remain behind? You would have to do something for them too, partly out of charity (would you leave them to perdition?) and partly out of self-interest (if you ignored them, your religion would fail to survive, given that those who renounce procreation do not perpetuate mankind). In other words, you would have to devise monastic rules for the renouncers, with some attention to hermits too, plus rules for everyday life to be followed by the rest; and this would involve you deeply in the distribution of social roles and the allocation of authority, or in other words in social and political problems: you do not have to control the state apparatus in order to be confronted with such problems, as students are apt to assume. It goes without saying that if you captured society to the point that your religion was adopted as the official creed, you would have to elaborate rules for the relationship between kings and their subjects too, if you had not done so already. In short, whether you renounce the world or not, the sheer fact that you have a vision of what mankind is about involves you in socio-political affairs.

In other words, religion spawns organization: to propose a new interpretation of the invisible entities is to propose a new way of doing things. There have been times when religion provided most of the organization available in a particular society, including the state itself, as it did in early Sumeria and in Muhammad's Arabia; but even where the state existed independently of the prevailing religion, the religious organization might match or eclipse that of secular government, with the result that religious and political leaders more often than not ended up in the alliance we have encountered already. It is perfectly true that numerous religious leaders have compromised their ideals for the sake of political influence and wealth in the course of history; many have compromised them in the belief that they were furthering them. But whatever they did, the personal ambitions, weaknesses and miscalculations of the actors were simply the mechanics whereby the religious and political establishments got embroiled insofar as they had not been born together. The relationship between the two was sometimes harmonious and sometimes stormy, but a relationship there clearly had to be: given that religious and political leaders were both concerned with the organization and management of people in the here and now, they could not ignore each other for long.

It is, then, a mistake to think that religion has nothing to do with the here and now. They all have everything to do with it: how could they possibly be about anything else? It is in this world that we happen to find ourselves, have ambitions, act, suffer, feel confused and try to find a meaning to it all; whatever our problems may be, they pertain to this world for the simple reason that we have no experience outside it. All religions get adopted, adhered to, loved and defended for the benefits they confer on the believers in their present lives, not for their propositions in the abstract: people drink medicine for the sake of the effects it has upon them, not for the sake of the medicine. A believer who is willing to suffer martyrdom for his convictions does not thereby prove that his beliefs are divorced from this world or that his motives are 'purely religious' but rather that his convictions are immensely meaningful to him, that is, that they solve some burning problem of his. The problem may be cognitive, social, political or other, but a religion which solves a cognitive or spiritual problem is no more 'purely religious' than one which solves a political dilemma. The evolution of the Western world has been such that today one has religion for spiritual problems and secular ideologies for political ones, but this is a historically specific division of labour which should not colour the student's perception of the past. A solution is religious when it is credited to superhuman beings and ideological when it is credited to superhuman laws, in so far as it is worth distinguishing between religions and ideologies at all. (The reader may object to this classification on the ground that it makes Buddhism in its purest form an ideology rather than religion of salvation; but this does have the merit of highlighting a peculiar feature of Buddhism.) The contents of the solution are immaterial. God may tell you to conquer, kill and loot, or in other words to practise holy war. Since we do not approve of war, we may find it monstrous that God should be credited with a desire for it, but this does not mean that holy war is not religious: it merely means that the religion in question is not for us. Personal evaluation and historical analysis should not be mixed up.

Religion as a mask

Given that religion does not owe its involvement with this world to the nefarious activities of ambitious individuals, it should be clear that there has been less cynical manipulation of it than students are inclined to believe. However, this is not to deny that such manipulation occurred. We may examine the phenomenon under the three headings of 'window-dressing', 'impostors' and 'opium for the people'.

Window-dressing

All value-systems are used as window-dressing from time to time. Sheer politeness dictates it. If you are invited out by people you cannot stand, you do not tell them you cannot stand them (social life would be very difficult if this were commonly done); you tell them you are otherwise engaged. In other words, you reformulate your reasons in terms which are both impersonal (it has nothing to do with them) and commonly accepted (everyone knows that prayer, church-going, work or prior appointment take precedence). Most people have sufficient distance between their real and ideal motives to engage in some degree of conscious or semi-conscious shuffling between the two, with the result that the world is full of all the cant, hypocrisy, pious talk and unctuous lipservice which novelists and playwrights are so adept at exposing.

Some people use the term ideology to mean little more than that: ideology in their usage is all the rhetorical fluff that people put into their public speeches, not the value-system implicit in their actions. There is nothing wrong with this usage as long as it is not taken to mean that people's actions are, or can be, governed by 'purely material' interests. Interests can no more be purely material than they can be purely religious. The existence of hypocrisy should not be taken to mean that value-systems are the *opposite* of self-interest; all it proves is that different value-systems, articulating different self-interests, are often in conflict: people respond by paying lipservice to the official one, or to the one which seems most appropriate to the context. If I announce that I am doing something for the sake of the country, whereas in fact I am doing it to promote my business interests, my patriotism is fluff whereas my business activities reflect the values on which I have chosen to act: they define and legitimate my interests as a capitalist as opposed to those I have as a nationalist. The former are not necessarily more (or less) material than the latter, though the context may be such that I cannot publicly admit which ones I have chosen to pursue. It is well known that religion has often been used as 'a mask for the prince's own purpose', as a Renaissance author put it, but this is not to say that the purpose behind the mask was devoid of ideological input: it simply means that the prince's visions were less popular than the religious ones in terms of which he tried to camouflage them.

Impostors

There are however people who are so lacking in commitment to any value system that they can use whatever system presents itself as a means to further their own ambitions without believing in either the system in question or in anything else. Such people are often known as impostors, a somewhat misleading term in that they do not necessarily assume false identity: they merely pretend to believe in something which means little or nothing to them. (If they actively disbelieved it, they could not behave as they do.) A more appropriate term would be opportunists. At all events, they have not been without importance in history. Thus a Chinese cult-leader brough to trial on the collapse, in 1813, of a rebellion in which he had caused the death of some 70,000 people, acknowledged that 'when I thought up the idea of organizing an assembly, I intended it as a way of making money. Later on, the people who believed grew numerous and then, because I wanted to acquire wealth and honour, I started this business [of rebellion]. It is my fate to die. It is not my fate to be a peaceful commoner . . .' Here, then, we would appear to have 'purely material' motives. But this man did not use religion as a mask: unlike Renaissance princes, he had no beliefs worth camouflaging. He used religion as an *instrument* for his ambitions: without his cult society, he would not have been able to translate them into action. In other words, purely material motives may exist in the abstract sense that people want to get rich, powerful and make their mark; but since their ambitions have to be pursued within specific socities with specific institutions and ideas, the ambitions in question must necessarily display themselves in impure form: ideology enters into socio-political organization to such an extent that the material motives of a nineteenth-century Chinese cynic displayed themselves in religious revolt.

It should be stressed, however, that the vast majority of people are must too committed to their own values actively to pretend otherwise. (Keeping them unobtrusive is another matter.) Christians used to suspect Muhammad of insincerity, as if nothing were easier than

to invent a cause in which one does not believe and devote one's life
to getting it accepted. This is obviously an implausible proposition.
It was first proposed by tenth-century Muslim philosophers and
heretics who dismissed all prophets, including Muhammad, as liars
whose real aim was the achievement of political power: like modern
students they saw worldly ambition and religious truth as opposites,
as if one could not get powerful by promoting what one believes to
be correct. (The early Muslims knew better, as they now do again.)
But opportunists such as the above-mentioned Chinese can usually
be seen examining the ideological market, trying out ready-made
causes in the hope of finding one to their taste; they do not normally
invent new ones, still less successful ones, because they lack the
interest and insight into other people's problems to come up with
new and better solutions; and gaining acceptance for entirely new
ways of looking at things requires an effort hard to sustain without
the conviction of being in the right.

Opium for the people
This brings us to the concept of religion as opium for the people.
The expression was coined by Marx, but the idea (as popularly
understood) is old: 'religious doctrines are naught but means to
enslave man to the mighty', as a tenth-century Muslim poet said;
'while men are gazing up to Heaven . . . or fearing Hell . . . they see
not what is their birthright here on Earth', as a member of a radical
Puritan sect in seventeenth-century England put it. In other words,
religion legitimates a certain social and political order and thus keeps
the dispossessed in their place. This is correct, if somewhat unsubtle.
Earlier in this chapter we invented a religion which said that God
wanted my kind to milk cows whereas your kind had to stick
together as a ruling elite: it was the religious validation of the
arrangement that made me accept my position. But the nuances had
better be remembered.

First, it should be stressed that the opium is not necessarily
administered consciously, or in other words those on top are not
necessarily making cynical use of generally accepted values; usually,
they are pushing ideas in which they genuinely believe, the reason
why they believe in them being that they happen to suit their
interests. After all, people usually *do* believe what suits them, not
that which fails to make sense to them.

Secondly, the opium is meant for consumption by the mighty
themselves no less than by the people they enslave: it persuades

them that they are in the right. Most people are keen to do right by the terms of the value system to which they subscribe; indeed, they want to be sure that the value system itself is true. Doubts as to what is right, be it within or between value systems, are paralysing and undermine morale whether you are a member of the elite or otherwise. Thus the Muslim conquest of the Middle East in the seventh century AD greatly undermined the morale of the Christians, and the refutations of Islam they produced were meant for their own consumption as much as, or more than, for that of the Muslims, the purpose of such works being to prove that Christianity was right even though God seemed to have turned against it. Opium proving the superiority of the elite was likewise meant for the elite itself as much as for the masses.

Thirdly, it should be noted that we are all busy selling opium to others and selves alike, consciously or unconsciously, at all times. (In Marx's passage it is in fact the masses who administer opium to themselves.) Since people of necessity see things from their own perspective, much of what they say adds up to comforting ideas or outright propaganda for themselves and the groups to which they belong. What seems obviously right to a bureaucrat does not necessarily seem right to a peasant, yet both may invoke God or democracy in support of their views, or in other words justify their opinions in terms of higher things, and both may feel that they are saying nothing but the plain truth. People in general, not just the elite, believe their own propaganda because they cannot see that this is what it is: the bias is invisible because the angle which produces it is felt as normal, not as a perspective peculiar to a specific group (you cannot see it unless you stand outside it).

In fact, no opinion regarding the right distribution of economic, social, political or moral goods could ever be objective: though one can learn to see things from other people's point of view, one cannot think away one's own experience without thereby depriving oneself of anything to say. University teachers who stress the importance of universities speak from personal experience; but they owe their experience to a position which also gives them a vested interest in the institution they defend, and they cannot acquire the one without the other: insight (or indeed idealism) and self-interest (or indeed cynicism) are necessarily mixed up. However, those who control the educational system, the religious organization and the mass media (if any) clearly stand a better chance of setting the tone than those who do not; though we are all pushing opium, that pushed by the elite tends to win out because they have better access to the means of legitimation.

Fourthly, however, the fact that the opium pushed by the elite tends to win out does not mean that establishment is always united and everyone else drugged. Divisions within the establishment have been common (e.g. between state and church, higher and lower nobility, office-holders and aristocrats); and numerous religions originated outside the establishments of their day, *capturing* power (be it by force or peacefully) because they brought organization to people who had hitherto acted without common aim. Once they were established, moreover, religions could and often did provide ideological ammunition to a host of rival contenders for power and authority, helping to seat and unseat establishments in rapid succession and/or setting up establishments characterized by much internal tension. And all establishments given to mass distribution of religious opium ran the risk of supplying the masses with material which could all too easily be used as dynamite against the suppliers. The establishment never had a monopoly on *thought*, and its very attempt to drug the masses undermined such monopoly as it might have on the distribution and use of knowledge.

Finally, it should be remembered that without general acceptance of one kind of opium or other, all societies would collapse. As has been seen, societies depend for their viability on the existence of value systems which command sufficient consent for a sufficient number of people to live together in accordance with its rules even when coercive attention is withdrawn. Inevitably, some members of society do better out of the resulting organization than others: where in the animal kingdom is that not the case? And clearly there is room for improvement on every system of organization so far tried out by mankind. But without a value system commanding general assent, kings, aristocrats, peasants, capitalists and proletariat would all go extinct without exception: without symbolic culture, hominids would have disappeared from the earth long before the present species had even evolved.

The question of primacy

This leaves us with the final chestnut: should religion and ideology be seen as 'mere superstructure', or on the contrary as something endowed with an autonomous force of its own or even with primacy over material factors?

If you believe that all historical development ultimately has its roots in a single factor, it follows that everything else is mere 'superstructure' which simply reflects the underlying development. Hard-nosed Marxists assert that the ultimate factor behind all development is the mode of production. This has the merit of being neat, but it is also arbitrary: why *should* there only be one operative factor? In fact it is obvious that religion and ideology are not mere reflections of the mode of production, or for that matter of the totality of non-ideological factors.

For one thing, if religion and ideology merely reflected other developments without exerting any influence of their own, it would follow that the history of mankind would have been exactly the same even if no religion or ideology had ever existed. Take away paganism, Judaism, Christianity, Buddhism, Islam and so on, and history would still have been enacted as it was; indeed take away Marx himself and see how nothing changes: the mode of production would have generated the Russian revolution on its own. This is a trifle implausible. Besides, it begs the question why anyone *bothers* to invent religion. The Marxist answer is that religion justifies the position of those who control the means of production, but why should that be necessary? Either the productive forces are irresistible, in which case there is no need to justify them; or else they need to be justified, in which case they are not irresistible. Either religion merely reflects, in which case it is redundant, or else it actually helps, in which case it possesses power of its own: you cannot have it both ways.

For another thing, the materialist view of religion boils down to the proposition that economic, social and political relationships are formed in direct interaction between our natural environment and genetic equipment (including our equipment for tool-making), without the intermediary of symbolic culture which is not itself of any developmental importance.

But on the one hand, what sort of selective pressure could produce an elaborate apparatus for symbolic culture devoid of importance for the animal which possesses it? Why can human beings speak? Language is not required for the capacity to manufacture and use of tools, and non-verbal communication suffices for the transmission of the skills involved. But language *is* required for the presentation of things which cannot be seen, smelled, tasted or heard, as well as for the evaluation of things in terms of good, bad, just or unjustified: language is the vehicle of theoretical and moral constructions. If symbolic culture is simply a kind of television screen displaying the current state of socio-economic and political affairs, how on earth did it get there?

On the other hand, if symbolic culture plays no role in human development, how come that the Marxist theory of history does not apply to other animals? Chimpanzees have social life, power structure, struggles and co-operation over food, a need for defence against predators, and even a certain amount of tool-use. So do many other species (though mostly without the tools). All such societies are explicable along the lines suggested by materialists for human societies: a certain environment and a certain genetic endowment interact *without* the intervention of symbolic culture. But no human-type history has ensued from them.

Marxists might retort that not even chimpanzees have a mode of production; but Neanderthalers did not have a mode of production either, nor did *Homo sapiens* for the first 40,000 (or 90,000) years. Why then did both Neanderthalers and *Homo sapiens* have religion? Indeed, why did the latter proceed to *invent* production? Mankind is the only animal to be equipped with a capacity for symbolic culture and also the only animal to have produced a history. To argue that these two facts are unrelated is absurd.

There is then no question of regarding religion or ideology as mere reflections of other developments (be they economic, social, political or other). Does this mean that ideas have 'primacy' over material factors (a position with which Weber is often, if falsely, associated)?

Of course not. The debate over primacy rests on the false antithesis between 'purely material' and 'purely religious' factors with which the reader is now thoroughly familiar. Materialists place the purely materialist factors in 'the base' and the purely religious ones in 'the superstructure', arguing that the superstructure has little or no autonomous force of its own; idealists agree with the layering, but see the superstructure as a kind of cortex governing the rest. Either way, this is an unhelpful model: the concept of layering should be scrapped along with the debate over primacy itself.

The layering is inspired by the fact that religion professes to be concerned with 'higher things', and to a believer, higher things *must* have primacy over material factors: whatever his view of other people's religions, he cannot see his own as a mere product of material factors without thereby denying its claim to being an eternal truth. To an atheist, on the other hand, it is polemically sound to dismiss all religions without exception as mere superstructure devoid of any autonomous force at all. In other words, the controversy over primacy has served as a covert debate over the possible truth of religion and the ability of humans to choose their own fate: even agnostics tend to feel that there is something 'nobler' about a world in which ideas have autonomous power or primacy than one in which they are products of material factors; conversely, materialists tend to see themselves as tough realists capable of confronting the world as it is. Sentiments of this kind cloud the issue. Religion is no 'nobler' than any other aspect of human society. It has its origins in the human world and offers solutions to human problems, precisely as do 'purely material' phenomena such as the mode of production. Both are the outcome of attempts by humans to order and manipulate the natural world, and both presuppose the existence of symbolic culture: production, whatever its mode, is no less of a human invention than are gods. Given that they are like phenomena, why should they be placed in different layers implying subordination of the one to the other?

In this as in other contexts it is wise to remember that humans are animals. It would not occur to an ethologist studying ants, lions, wolves or giraffes to argue that 'ultimately' it is the animal's need for food which determines the type of society in which it lives, or its need to reproduce, or its mechanisms of defence against predators, or whatever. On the contrary, he will see the society in question as the outcome of a compromise between a variety of fundamental needs and the environment in which it is set. Precisely the same is true of human societies. The human animal needs to eat, reproduce and defend itself against predators (including other members of the same species): as far as nature is concerned, that is all there is to it. For this purpose the human species needs to organize itself, precisely as do other animals; and like any other animal, it seeks to achieve the best compromise between its various needs and the environment in which it finds itself. It merely so happens that it does so by cultural as well as natural means. This endows it with enormous developmental potential, and human societies have acquired a complexity which makes them far more difficult to explain than those of other animals (which are difficult enough as it is). But it nonetheless remains obvious that they represent a compromise between a variety of fundamental needs, both natural *and* cultural ones, in interaction with a natural *and* cultural environment. The addition of culture has not resulted in a *simplification* of evolutionary patterns whereby one factor has acquired overriding importance and the rest been reduced to frills; on the contrary, it has greatly complicated matters, making the achievement and maintenance of the compromise a highly intricate affair: all attempts to explain human history in terms of a single factor are misguided. (The rapidly developing craze for family patterns as the one and only key to everything rests on no better foundations than that for modes of production.)

Once again the reader may object in two contrary veins. The believer may object that I write as an atheist. This is correct. However, historians and social scientists *must* write as atheists: whether or not they are believers, they must suspend all convictions of a non-empirical kind when they work, no religious or ideological beliefs being allowed to impinge on scholarly or scientific research. All invocations of the supernatural are disallowed. This is one of the ground-rules of modern science, but even without going into the nature of scientific thought, it should be clear that all religions must be treated as a man-made phenomenon for the simple reason that there are so many of them. Logic dictates that like phenomena be treated alike. It is impossible to treat all religions as true in the sense of given by supernatural authority because they contradict each other, disagreeing even over the number and nature of the supernatural authorities involved; but it is perfectly possible to treat them all as products of the human mind evolved in response to problems in the here and now.

This is not to say that they are necessarily false. It may well be that the human mind has hit upon the truth in supernatural no less than natural matters, so that this religion or that, or this part of one religion and that part of another, is true in the sense of corresponding to a supernatural reality beyond us. But this is not a scientific question because it is not amenable to empirical proof; it is a matter of belief. Nor is it a historical question because it is irrelevant: ideas generate action when they are believed regardless of whether they are true or not in our opinion. Muslim students are often surprised that Western historians discuss the spread of Islam without adducing its truth as a possible reason for its success; but its truth explains nothing. Even if all modern historians knew Islam to be true, the operative factor is how it appeared to contemporaries: some believed it and others did not (as some still do and others not), and their different reactions to the same truth evidently has to do with the worldly circumstances in which they found themselves. It is such circumstances which determine whether a religion is believed or not, or indeed whether it appears in the first place: after all, it must be this-worldly factors which explain whether a prophet believes his own visions to be of divine, satanic or medical origin.

In short, for historical and scientific purposes, religion is *only* a product of this-worldly factors, the question of its ultimate truth being left to theologians. And as such it is a phenomenon of the same order as the mode of production.

The materialist reader, on the other hand, may object that even materialists commonly concede a certain amount of autonomy to ideological factors without going so far as to abolish the distinction between base and superstructure altogether: thus the base is often taken to generate ideas which act back on it with autonomous force. But the layered model is inadequate however it is modified for the simple reason that human society (as opposed to non-human nature) has no base devoid of ideological factors at all.

The world around us consists partly of nature and partly of culture, nature being everything which functions without the intervention of human consciousness (the universe, the natural world, physiological functions such as breathing), and culture being everything which requires conscious human thought in order to exist (society, religion/ideology, etc.). What materialists call 'the base' is in strict logic all that which is studied by natural scientists; but historians and other social scientists, including Marxist ones, are only concerned with nature in so far as it impinges on and is reflected by culture.

Differently put, the natural sciences are concerned with external phenomena which operate regardless of what they may or may not mean to humans beings, being diametrically opposed in this respect to sciences such as psychoanalysis which are only concerned with internal phenomena and to which the external world is irrelevant except in so far as it has subjective meaning. But the social sciences, including history, are distinguished by the fact that they have a foot in both camps: they are concerned with the external and the internal worlds alike, or more precisely with their interaction.

Thus an earthquake is a natural phenomenon, but it only acquires interest to social scientists when it impinges on human beings by inflicting losses to which they have to react; and how they react will depend on the nature of that tangle of material and ideological factors which we call their society, including their ideas of how earthquakes are caused (divine anger, geological faults). To a social scientist, an earthquake is thus not a purely external, natural or material phenomenon at all. Or again, a war is an external phenomon: you can observe it directly; it is not simply in the mind. But it nonetheless takes human minds to generate it, and the interpretation that humans put on it is crucial for its effect. A war may be seen as having vindicated a military system, which accordingly fails to be changed, or on the contrary as having proved its inadequacy, thereby playing into the hands of reformists; it may generate such humiliation that the outcome is another war, or it may be felt to prove that war is no longer worth it, and so on. Material factors such as the number of dead and the extent of other damage will enter into all of these interpretations, but you cannot study the effects of war by simply measuring such factors, or rather you can only do so if your object of study is the effect on the natural rather than the human world.

All the supposedly materialist phenomena of relevance to social scientists exist externally and internally at the same time: however natural they may be by origin, they cannot become part of the human world without being subject to classification and evaluation, or in other words attempts to identify them in terms of such cognitive and moral schemes as are available. It is thus a mistake to think of ideas, be they religious or other, as sitting on top of material developments, reflecting them and acting back upon them. Ideas are an intrinsic part of such developments: you cannot strip a phenomenon down to base without thereby removing it from the world of human beings altogether. To see society as the outcome of a material base and an ideological superstructure is somewhat like claiming that social sciences consist of the study of natural history with a bit of psychohistory on top, as if culture meant no more than a capacity to speak about and occasionally interfere a bit with nature. In so far as human societies have a 'base', it is constituted by the interaction between natural environment, genetic equipment and symbolic culture from which the history of mankind has ensued: the very oddity of human history lies in the fact that it is enacted within a domain of its own.

Part II
The Departure from the Pattern

8
The Oddity of Europe

Though the identikit presented in this book is not a picture of any one society, it clearly fits some societies better than others. It is largely based on the Old World civilizations from about 600 BC onwards, and it probably has a medieval bias. This should not prevent it from being of general assistance, in so far as it is of any assistance at all; but two sets of societies are so deviant that they are better treated as exceptions to, rather than as variations upon, the picture presented.

The first is that of pre-Columbian America. The indigenous civilizations of the New World need an identikit of their own because they were erected on an extraordinarily slender foundation. For practical purposes all were stone-age cultures. Metals were only used for ornaments, or so at least in Mesoamerica; the Incas made occasional use of bronze for military and productive purposes too, but here as there the art of smelting iron was unknown. Moreover, the region was devoid of draught animals and riding animals, while pack animals were available only in Peru (in the form of llamas). Wheeled transport was absent too, though carts driven by coolies would have been a major advantage; the potter's wheel was similarly absent, the wheel being known only as a toy. Practically all energy had to be supplied by humans unaided by mechanical devices. The tropical lowlands of Mesoamerica from which the Olmecs and the Mayas emerged were largely exploited through shifting slash-and-burn agriculture, a primitive mode of production which, though suitable for the ecology in question, does not normally lend itself to the creation of complex societies. In fact, here as in the Old World, agriculture seems first to have taken off in areas where no forests had to be felled for sowing to be tried out, but where water was nonetheless in abundant supply, that is on raised fields in marshy river basins (by Aztec times in open lakes as well), corresponding to the irrigated river valleys of ancient Iraq, Egypt and India. But though intensive agriculture of this kind undoubtedly constituted the economic basis of early American civilization (and played a major role in the Aztec economy too), the tropical forest (and eventually also the desert) placed a limit on expansion, slash-and-burn agriculture yielding low returns. Finally, though the Olmecs developed a hieroglyphic script which became common property in Mesoamerica, literacy was extremely restricted and the Incas had no script at all, making do with knots as mnemonic aids. The transmission of information was thus overwhelmingly oral. The civilizations of Mesoamerica remained archaic, fragile and haunted until they fell, allaying their fears through endless human sacrifice (itself an archaic feature); and though those of Peru were more secure, all had more in common with the societies of the ancient Near East than with the sixteenth-century Spaniards who overran them.

Europe, too, needs an identikit of its own, at least from the sixteenth century onwards. The European deviation from the pre-industrial pattern is of vital importance for the world today and at the same time a phenomenon which the European student may not perceive as odd at all. Yet odd it clearly is.

Medieval Europe fits the common pattern well enough. Here as elsewhere we have a far-flung ruling elite, partly military and partly religious, a cosmopolitan high culture (Christianity plus what remained of the classics), and a myriad of peasant communities characterized by the familiar absence of economic, political and cultural integration. Medieval Europe was backward in comparison with medieval China, India or the Islamic world, but it was not visibly different in kind. Of course it had its peculiar features, but so did other civilizations, and it is only in retrospect that medieval Europe can be seen to have contained an unusual potential. In fact, post-Reformation Europe fits the pattern too at first sight, the only difference being that by now the backwardness had disappeared. To a historian specializing in the non-European world there is something puzzling about the excitement with which European historians hail the arrival of cities, trade, regular taxation, standing armies, legal codes, bureaucracies, absolutist kings and other commonplace appurtenances of civilized societies as if they were unique and self-evident stepping stones to modernity: to the non-European historian they simply indicate that Europe had finally joined the club. But the excitement is justified. As the institutions of medieval Europe were dismantled, they gave way, not to a sophisticated pre-industrial civilization of the traditional type, but rather to territorial states with vernacular cultures, colonial expansion, capitalist economies and modes of thought, both scientific and other, which we recognize as our own. Europe had not joined the club. As a traditional society it was a failure long before it capped its deviant development by its invention of industry.

Why so? This question underlies a great deal of research on European and non-European history alike, the key problem being the direction in which pre-industrial society in general was going: what was the evolutionary trend? How and why did Europe diverge from it? Indeed, to what extent did it diverge as oppposed to merely take the lead? As might be expected, there are no simple or generally accepted answers to these question, but a considerable amount of work has been done on them in recent years so that provisional answers could be said to be available. I shall devote the rest of this chapter to sketching them out.

The land

Europe is that part of the world which became a cultural unit thanks to the Germanic invasions of the Roman empire. The Roman empire lost its western part to the invaders in the fifth century AD; and all the northern barbarians subsequently pledged their loyalties to the vanquished civilization (that is Christianity and classical culture) in so far as they had not done so already. The result was Christian Europe, a cultural unit stretching from the Mediterranean to Scandinavia.

At first sight, the unit seemed unpromising in ecological terms. 'Since temperateness of climate is destroyed by the excessive cold, the land produces neither wine nor oil', a Sicilian Greek of the first century BC observed with reference to Gaul; 'they cultivate no olives and produce no wine, except to a very slight extent and of very bad quality since the climate is mostly extremely harsh', a third-century Greek from Asia Minor echoed with reference to barbarians along the Danube. In fact, both Gaul and the banks of the Danube were to produce plenty of wine in due course, and a more appropriate contrast would have been between Europe and Egypt. No part of Europe possessed the high fertility of alluvial river valleys such as those of the Nile, Euphrates, Tigris, Indus, Ganges, Yangtze or Mekong. Egypt is assumed to have had a population density of about 725 persons per square mile in the first century BC, but in the sixteenth century AD there were only about ninety-five persons per square mile in Holland, the most densely populated part of Europe.

However, Europe had its compensations. In the first place, it was fed by rain, not by irrigation, meaning that agriculture was far less labour intensive and also far less vulnerable to natural or political disasters than the above-mentioned river valleys. The invention of the heavy plough (possibly in the seventh century AD, the dissemination taking place between the eighth and the eleventh) arguably made the soil of inland Europe the most fertile in the world in relation to labour input, if not in any other terms.

In the second place, the agricultural land was not surrounded by or dotted with desert, tropical forest or (a few exceptions apart) forbidding mountains so that Europe lacked ecological niches for nomadic pastoralists and hunter-gatherers, except in the extreme north; and the Eskimos, Samoyeds and other pastoralists and hunters of the polar circle were not much of a presence, least of all a military one. In this respect Europe was unique: no other part of the world was so uniformly given over to fixed-field agriculture (as opposed to slash-and-burn agriculture or pastoralism), so uniformly amenable to government control and, once the invasions were over, so lacking in internal barbarians. Its complexity of territory nonetheless made it difficult for a single ruler to dominate (though in this respect it is hard to say whether is was unique).

In the third place, it was well protected against external barbarians. Its own supply of northern barbarians being limited, it was vulnerable only on the eastern frontier where it formed the tail-end of the Central Asian steppe. Periodic invasions by Huns, Avars, Magyars, Cumans and Mongols did retard the development of eastern Europe, but they barely affected western Europe; and the Mongol incursion of the thirteenth century was the last. China, India and the Middle East all suffered far more disruption at the hands of barbarian invaders.

Finally, the natural resources of Europe were extremely varied (stretching as it does from the polar circle to the Mediterranean), meaning that it had a great potential for internal commerce, while at the same time an ample coastline and a profusion of navigable rivers endowed it with better and cheaper means of communications than any other part of the world with the possible exception of China. This was a fact of major consequence for traders, rulers, and disseminators of ideas alike. The rivers also gave it a source of inanimate energy far greater than that available in arid regions. All in all, Europe must be described as an exceptionally easy environment to manage and exploit.

The people

Like other stateless peoples, the northern barbarians were organized by kinship, but they did not remain so for long. Tribal particularism is said still to have played a role in tenth-century Germany, but it soon disappeared; and even the Magyar horsemen lost their tribal organization once they were settled in the Hungarian plain. The fifteenth-century Swiss may have been 'cruel and rough people', but unlike their counterparts in the Middle East, the Daylami mountaineers who served as mercenaries in the medieval Muslim world, they were no more tribal in organization than were their employers. 'We have Indians at home – Indians in Cornwall, Indians in Wales, Indians in Ireland', an English pamphleteer lamented in 1652 (with reference to the newly discovered savages of the Americas), while Polish Jesuits lamented the presence of Indians in Lithuania; but the Lithuanians were merely pagans, and though kinship ties played a greater role on the Celtic fringe than anywhere else in Europe, even the Celts fell short of forming proper hill tribes of the type found in India, south-west China, South-East Asia or the Middle East, let alone Amerindia.

To some extent, this is simply to repeat the point that the ecology of Europe did not favour the survival of internal barbarians. Occasional patches of mountainous, marshy, densely forested or arid land notwithstanding, few parts of Europe were so isolated as to enable their inhabitants to retain a socio-political organization radically different from that of mainstream society: constant interaction dictated that even areas which might well have remained tribal under other circumstance adopted non-tribal forms of organization. Thus tribal ties were of no importance in Christian Spain though they had mattered greatly when Spain was under Muslim rule; and the Magyars would undoubtedly have retained their tribal organization far longer than they did if Hungary had remained an outpost of Central Asian rather than European society.

However, given the tribal organization of the barbarian invaders on the one hand and the extreme primitivity of early Europe on the other, the fact that mainstream society itself lost its tribal roots so rapidly is in need of explanation. Why did feudalism rather than tribalism turn out to be the solution to the organization of post-Roman Europe? This is a question to which there is no proper answer yet. It has been plausibly argued that the Christian church did its best to undermine kin groups of any size or depth so as to facilitate the flow of wealth away from the family and into the church; but it is difficult to believe that the church would have made much headway in this respect if other factors had not been at work. European kinship was cognatic, that is traced through both male and female links, which may conceivably have increased its flexibility and by the same token diminished its durability. But more importantly, all the major Germanic peoples had been through extensive migrations by the time the Roman empire collapsed and all proceeded to engage in some five hundred years of chaotic fighting. The migrations must have meant constant reshuffling of tribal groups with accompanying erosion of links between kinship, political power and rights in land; and both the lengthy warfare which preceded the Roman collapse and the chaos which ensued therefrom were more likely to grind away such kinship obligations as remained than to reverse the process. (Constant warfare similarly accelerated the formation of private ties at the expense of tribal ones in Central Asia on the eve of the Mongol conquests. Tribal ties might of course have reasserted themselves in Eurpe, as they did in Mongolia, if the ecology had been impoverished; but it was not.) The systematic use of personal ties characterisitc of feudalism certainly demonstrates that people could no longer enforce their rights by ganging up with their kinsmen: protection, access to land, social status and political power had all become negotiable assets acquired through agreement with whoever could dispense them rather than by birth into a particular family, lineage or tribe.

It is possible that the Germanic invaders brought the so-called European, or more precisely north-west European, marriage pattern with them, though this is not yet certain. However this may be, northwest Europe was or eventually became unique by its practice of delayed marriage for men *and* women: both sexes would postpone marriage until their twenties or even thirties, and a considerable proportion would not marry at all. Delayed marriage for men is common wherever neolocal residence prevails, that is, where the couple sets up home on their own instead of living with the parents of the bride or bridegroom: the husband has to be able to support his wife and children. But this usually means that mature men marry teenaged girls (whose contribution is their dowry), not that both partners postpone marriage until they have accumulated enough wealth between them to set up home. Delayed marriage for men was the Roman pattern, and it was practised in Europe too: it lies behind the endless fun poked at old husbands cuckolded by young wives in medieval *fabliaux*. But for one reason or another women might also, or came to, postpone their marriage on a par with men, at least below the level of the elite, which is where it matters most. The high proportion of celibates in lay European society is likewise unusual. Peasants usually practise universal marriage even when their religion rates celibacy higher than the married state (as do both Buddhism and Christianity) because they rely on children rather than hired hands for their supply of labour.

Whatever the date and origin of the European marriage pattern, it had two consequences of major importance. First, it enabled Europe to escape the so-called Malthusian cycle. Where fertility is uncontrolled, economic advance is nullified by population growth. Increased food supplies enable more children to survive, meaning that still more children will be bred in the next generation, and so on until the population outstrips the resources, whereupon political disorder, famine and epidemics decimate the population on a cataclysmic scale and the cycle starts again. By contrast, the European marriage pattern meant that fertility was controlled. The later a woman marries, the fewer children she will bear. (In early modern Europe women marrying in their late twenties rarely produced more than four children, only half of whom were likely to survive.) And a surprisingly large proportion of women never married at all. The comparatively low reproductive rate made for a balance between population and economic resources which was both favourable and sensitive to economic change, the age at marriage rising and falling in response to the availability of resources. Though Europe did not escape population crises, its numbers rarely multiplied on such a scale that mass extinction was necessary to restore the balance between population and environment, the only Malthusian crisis of major proportions being the Black Death of the fourteenth century.

Secondly, the European marriage pattern made for, or indeed was a manifestation of, individualism. It assumed that children were independent individuals who must leave home to accumulate funds of their own before they can start raising families, as opposed to members of a landholding corporation to which they would offer their labour, from which they would derive their access to land and by which they would be married off as soon as they could procreate, being maintained by it if necessary. Where marriage was delayed, men and women of peasant origin would typically accumulate their funds by working as servants (or so at least from the later Middle Ages onwards). Pre-industrial Europe is unique in that service came to be part of the life-cycle, and the prominence of hired servants in the household is the domestic counterpart to the prominence of feudal retainers in the political sphere: in both cases, recruitment was by contract rather than by kinship.

Since children left home, earned their own money and married late, their choice of spouses tended to escape parental control. Marriage was of the companionate type, based on affection between the spouses rather than family needs; or rather, this type of marriage was surprisingly common. Aristocratic marriages continued to be arranged, and aristocratic brides (and to some extent even grooms) continued to be very young. Yet even at elite level the reconciliation of individual inclination with family needs was perceived as a problem at an early stage, love matches versus arranged marriage being a hotly debated issue in the *Heptameron* attributed to Marguerite de Navarre (1492–1549) and, more famously, in Shakespeare's *Romeo and Juliet*. Whatever the behaviour of the elite, there can be little doubt that geographical mobility and economic independence diminished (without in any way abolishing) the regimentation of behaviour by kinsmen and neighbours among commoners, both in respect of marriage and otherwise.

Though the European marriage pattern has been documented for the whole of north-western Europe at various times, research into individualism has so far concentrated on England, and detailed comparison with non-European societies still has not begun. It is certain that the blunt contrast between European (let alone English) individualism and non-European holism will have to be modified. The historical record of the great civilizations has scarcely been examined from this point of view, and many of the features discussed under the label of 'individualism' in the context of Europe recur under the label of 'loose structure' in anthropological discussions of South-East Asia (especially Thailand). However, though future research is likely to present us with a more nuanced picture, it is unlikely to rebut the contention that the feebleness of European kinship made for an unusual prominence of both individualism and contractual ties.

Once the land and the people had come together, the subsequent development was shaped by the political collapse of Europe on the one hand and the composite nature of European civilization on the other. We may start with the collapse.

Feudalism

Barbarian Europe was the outcome of centuries of chaos, and it continued to be in a state of chaos for another five centuries after the western Roman empire had collapsed, interrupted by a brief restoration of minimal order under Charlemagne (768–814). The state being incapable of protecting property or life, people reacted by placing themselves in servile positions vis-à-vis stronger men, offering to perform whatever services they might require in return for sustenance and protection, or in other words membership of their lords' households or access to land under his control (they were often granted usage of land which they themselves had handed over by way of payment for protection). This process affected everyone from the bottom to the top of society. At the top, however, another factor was at work as well. The ruler would reward his vassals (as retainers performing military service came to be known) with grants of land because there was no money with which to pay either office-holders or soldiers, while at the same time the development of horsemanship meant that the army had to be based on a professional military class rather than conscripted peasants.

So far there is nothing unique about the European development. Peasants commending themselves to powerful landowners on the one hand and grants of land to military or civil governors and soldiers on the other are widely attested in pre-industrial history, both singly and together. The uniqueness of Europe lies in the degree to which the state lost control of the process.

Originally the benefice (or fief, as it eventually came to be known) was revocable or at best granted for life, being supposed to revert to the state on the death of the holder. But it soon became hereditary on the understanding that the vassal's son would continue to perform the same services; and once it was hereditary, the vassal acquired a strong say in the definition of those services too. Moreover, the vassal would grant some of his land to vassals of his own, who would grant some of theirs to others (a process known as sub-infeudation); and vassals soon began to obtain benefices from a plurality of lords, thus accelerating the dispersal of power. By the tenth century,

European feudalism had wholly ceased to be 'prebendal': fiefs were no longer acquired or lost on appointment to or dismissal from a public office or function, the very concept of a public domain having disappeared. The state had dissolved into a welter of overlapping jurisdictions, and all jurisdiction was private, being inherited along with rights in land and conflated with personal ties. This pattern rapidly came to be regarded as normal, so that systematized versions thereof were exported to England and Palestine: despite the opportunities presented by conquest and the centralizing measures which ensued therefrom, neither William the Conqueror nor the Crusaders attempted a return to feudalism in its prebendal form. Nowhere else in the world has such a pattern prevailed (though Japan came close to it in some respects). The result was correspondingly unusual.

State and society

Feudalism amounted to an extreme dispersal of power along vertical lines. No agency had a monopoly on any governmental activity, let alone on the right to use force; taxes had entirely disappeared, the agricultural surplus being siphoned off purely in the form of rent to landlords: even the king was expected to live off his private domains, being simply the top of the social pyramid down which power had been lost.

Yet feudal Europe was not stateless, nor had power been dispersed horizontally, into tribal groups, as it normally is under stateless conditions. A state of a sort existed, but it had little autonomous existence: to a large extent it simply *was* society. Differently put, society was in an extremely strong position vis-à-vis the state even *though* it was no longer tribal. It shared with tribal societies the features of being 'corporate', that is composed of groups through which the individual acquired well-defined rights and duties; of being passionately defensive of liberty or 'liberties', both individual and collective; of being strongly imbued with a sense of reciprocity; and of possessing a leadership of its own as opposed to one imposed by the state. But it owed all of these features to contracts and charters as opposed to kinship on the one hand and to participation in the state as opposed to rejection of it on the other: the barons were representatives of such public power as remained, not tribal leaders sponsoring self-help in opposition thereto; 'liberties' were rights negotiated with authorities, not the freedom which prevails where no such authorities exist; and the sense of reciprocity rested on contractual agreement, not on kinship ties. Differently put, state and society formed a continuum, not an oppressive agency versus subjects who tried to escape it.

Now given the ecological potential of Europe, the feudal solution was too primitive to endure, and the recovery began as soon as the Magyar, Viking and Saracen raids were over. But kings had to recover their power from very local and very humble levels; they had to work for their money because they could not tax; and they had to bargain because their subjects were endowed with well-entrenched rights. Hence the outcome of the recovery was states which were deeply rooted in local society and unusually sensitive to developments within it. In other words, capstone government failed to become a European pattern.

Thus the monarch's inability to tax his subjects (except in emergencies and by their consent) led to the characteristically European conflation of government and estate management. Every king or prince had to nurse his domains, seeing to their productivity, ensuring that they were properly administered, and adding to them by marriage and judicious use of force as best he could. Obviously, this made for a reconstitution of public power along lines very different from those which prevail where immense areas are united by conquest and loosely held together by a single tax-collecting apparatus. Both the king and the magnates whose territories he was in due course to take over governed on an intensive rather than extensive scale, with the result that self-help groups and robber barons were eliminated with a novel thoroughness.

At the same time the quest for revenues and order alike led to the expansion of royal justice, a process whereby the monarch assumed responsibility for dispute settlement throughout his realm (against payment, of course), eventually taking control of the law itself as well. Pioneered by England, this process was to culminate in the formation of judicial machineries coterminous with and controlled by states in place of the normal pre-industrial combination of local courts run by villages, guilds, castes or the like on the one hand and supra-national courts spawned by the religious institution on the other, both of them largely or wholly beyond the monarch's control. (In China, the state did create an empire-wide system of courts, but it was only meant as a last resort, decent people being assumed to submit their disputes to arbitration by lineage heads, gentry, guilds or the like: 'as for those who are troublesome, obstinate and quarrelsome, let them be ruined in the law courts – that is the justice that is due to them', as a Manchu emperor put it.) The monarch's assumption of responsibility for dispute settlement greatly reinforced the territoriality of the European state, contributing to its definition in terms of an area rather than a dynasty or otherwise. It also facilitated adoption of the idea (to which the rediscovery of Roman law accidentally contributed) of law as the command of the sovereign and thus something which could be made, as opposed to law as a regularity inherent in the cosmos, nature or divinity and thus something which could only be found, an idea which in its turn enabled kings to use legislation as an instrument of government and social engineering on a scale to which there are few parallels elsewhere. (The 'legalists' of ancient China did perceive law as an instrument of government, and their views influenced the Confucians; but the instrument consisted of little but punishments.)

It was similarly the weakness of feudal kings which led to the development in Europe of representative institutions. Here as elsewhere, kings were supposed to seek counsel while leading men were supposed to offer it along with other forms of help: the obligation was commonplace, but the feudal dispersal of power endowed it with a novel force. Given that the king was merely the top of the social pyramid, he had to govern in collaboration with that pyramid: he had no state apparatus distinct from it. Differently put, his barons were his state apparatus, not simply local leaders coexisting with it: they constituted his army and were the source of such taxes as he could hope to collect (under the label of 'aid'). But they were not simply his dependants either, and he could not coerce any one of them without the assistance of the rest. Hence he had no choice but to govern by obtaining their agreement. As feudal society stabilized, gatherings of vassals gave way to assemblies of the estates (that is representatives of the functional orders) and parliaments of other kinds in response to royal efforts to broaden the basis of consent: he could not develop his state apparatus on top without drawing in further social groups underneath. The maxim 'what touches all must be approved by all' is of Roman origin, but the use to which it was put in medieval Europe was utterly new, and it enabled kings and subjects to engage in public negotiations in accordance with formal rules, as opposed to private bargaining behind the scene, while at the same time it increased the local anchorage of the state.

Though most parliaments were to wither away in the age of absolutism, many survived, be it at a provincial or (as in England, Sweden, Hungary and Poland) a 'general' level, and none was forgotten. When the French state found itself on the verge of bankruptcy in 1789 it was forced by the nobility to convoke the Estates General again, or in other words to consult its own subjects, an incredible reaction on the part of nobility and state alike from a non-European point of view; and other developments having meanwhile undermined the tradional order, the Estates proceeded to abolish themselves, turning all subjects into citizens and their assembly into a national one, a development that was in due course to be repeated elsewhere.

Cities and trade

Most of the cities which Christian Europe inherited from the Roman empire had either disappeared completely along with commerce or else been reduced to mere administrative centres in the age of invasions (though a limited trade in luxury goods persisted), and northern Europe had never been urbanized at all. But given the regional diversity of Europe, trade was bound to develop once the worst instability was over, and mercantile and manufacturing centres appeared from the eleventh and twelfth centuries onwards. Feudalism located political power in the manors of rural lords whose subjects were serfs, whose income was wholly agrarian and who received it in labour or kind, whereas the cities stood for market forces, non-agrarian income and monetarization. Cities were thus profoundly disruptive of the feudal order.

This was not however obvious to rural lords without prior experience of urban society. In due course they saw all too well that the bourgeoisie had come 'to bring about the ruins of others', as a sixteenth-century Norman noble put it; but at first practically all of them favoured both commerce and urban growth because both were sources of income. The result was unusual in two respects.

First, neither kings nor nobles plundered merchants as a matter of course (which is not to say that they never plundered any). This was partly because much of the trade was in cheap and bulky commodities rather than luxury goods: timber, salt, grain and fish were not worth seizing, though they were well worth taxing. But the fact that commercial goods were not worth seizing does not mean that commercial wealth was not worth confiscating: it frequently was in the Islamic world for example. European rulers, however, increasingly took to humbly borrowing it. Given that Europe was divided into a plurality of states, ill-treated merchants could transfer their services to rival rulers; but so they could (and did) in the Islamic world as well. The crucial point is that Muslim rulers could afford to alienate merchants for short-term windfalls because stable revenues were provided by peasants, whereas European kings had to nurse theirs because they had no right to impose taxes without their subjects' consent. When absolutism finally made its appearance in Europe, mercantile power was far too well organized to allow itself to be fleeced. Generally speaking, European rulers were too dependent on subjects too well endowed with contractual rights to indulge in arbitrary fleecing, arrest and execution of golden geese and inconvenient opponents (as the Magna Carta shows); and since they pacified their domains with novel efficiency, the impulse towards arbitrary victimization was diminished too.

Secondly, kings and nobles alike allowed their cities to administer themselves. Both encouraged urban growth on their domains because cities were a source of income. (Naturally townsmen paid rent to the lord of the land they occupied, as well as other dues.) The lord would provide them with a charter defining their rights and duties, this being the customary way in which collective relationships were ordered; but he would not normally assume responsibility for their administration, or even transfer his residence there, because he had bigger fish to fry in the countryside. In short, medieval cities were juridical entities of their own which were left to govern themselves, not usually in the sense that they made themselves independent of their overlord, though many did that too, but rather in the sense that they ran their own affairs and kept their overlord happy by regular payment.

Like the principle of representation, urban autonomy was a feudal creation, not a legacy from classical antiquity; and it endowed the bourgeoisie with a power impossible to achieve where the landed elite used the agricultural surplus to keep both town and countryside under its own control. Non-European cities were usually administrative centres, and both they and the surrounding countryside were typically administered by governors, that is men dispatched from the capital with full civil and/or military power as miniature replicas of the state itself. In European history the governor scarcely figures at all.

The European reliance on an aristocracy governing its own land and a bourgeoisie governing its own cities is clearly a variant, and a fairly extreme one at that, of the rule which we met in chapter 3 whereby the state did a little and the subjects did the rest. But state and subjects formed part of the same power structure; we do not have the pattern whereby a public agency coexists with a proliferation of private organizations set up in isolation from or opposition to it so that the activities of the one stultify the other. Just as there was no capstone government, so there was no power stand-off: though cities undermined the position of the aristocracy, the state profited greatly from their presence, as did the cities from that of the state.

Composite Civilization

Europe was formed by *barbarian* invaders who adopted a religion of *Hebraic* origin which had long coexisted with *Graeco-Roman* culture, or in other words there were three quite different components to European civilization. This fact was of immense importance for the subsequent evolution.

State system

It is obvious that the relationship between state and society (including cities) would have been quite different if imperial government had been restored; and since the barbarians were spellbound by the idea of recreating the Roman empire, it did in some sense come back, first at the hands of Charlemagne and next at those of the Ottonians. But though the Holy Roman Empire was to survive until 1806, it failed to reverse the feudal fragmentation of power or to benefit from the recovery thereafter, the ultimate outcome of this recovery being a plurality of autonomous states. Far from being stultified by imperial governement, Europe was to be propelled forward by constant competition between its component parts.

The composite nature of European civilization provides part of the explanation of this outcome. The western Roman empire was overrun by a plurality of barbarians who converted to the religion of their subjects, not by a single people endowed with a religion of their own. Far from being united in one barbarian polity and creed, after the fashion of the Arab Middle East, Europe was thus divided among a number of barbarian kings on the one hand and between barbarian kings and a Roman church on the other: political power was not just fragmented, but also embodied in institutions different from that which represented Christianity. This arrangement made the chances of a future unification remote.

The Roman church was the actual legatee of the western Roman empire: the *church* collected taxes (tithes) without consulting the

tax-payers, legislated and disseminated the same high culture wherever it held sway after the fashion of any imperial power. But it had
no army, military muscle being the prerogative of the barbarians. As
the emperor in all respects except one, the pope had no interest in
setting up a rival; on the contrary, a plurality of kings increased his
chances of reducing secular rulers to mere executors of church
directives. But kings were constantly trying to make themselves
masters of their own homes, including that part over which the
church claimed jurisdiction, and they certainly were not going to
unite Europe as mere servants of the pope. Far from reinforcing one
another, the Roman church and barbarian kings were thus competi-
tors; rivalry between them stood in the way of unification.

The political collapse discussed already stood in the way as well.
Conquest on an imperial scale had been possible in the days of
Charlemagne (who united about half of western Europe) because
most of Europe was very primitive in those days: only a modicum of
military and administrative skills was required for Charles to subdue
the backward Saxons. By the same token, of course, his empire was
extremely fragile. But the feudal armies which prevailed after its
collapse were unsuitable as instruments of expansion, being small
and impossible to keep in the field for more than a couple of months,
while at the same time taxes to finance armies of occupation had
ceased to be available. But the longer Europe stayed disunited, the
remoter the chances of unification became because the very feudalism which made expansion impossible promoted the formation of
states which were strongly rooted in local society and increasingly
defined in territorial terms, as has been seen; people with complex
social, political and economic relations are in any case more difficult
to incorporate on a permanent basis than are backward peasants over
whom a military elite can be thinly imposed.

By the time European monarchs had the ability to finance armies
of conquest and occupation, Europe was too highly and too evenly
developed under governments too well-entrenched for empire-
building to be possible: the conquests of Napoleon were more extensive than Charlemagne's, but also more ephemeral; and whereas the
collapse of Charlemagne's empire meant that state building had to
start afresh (this being the usual sequel to imperial collapse elsewhere as well), the fall of Napoleon merely meant another rearrange-
ment of the same political mosaic. The sparsely-inhabited expanses
of Russia enabled Muscovy to expand on an imperial scale, but
western Europeans had to make their empires abroad.

Cultural nationalization

The imperial unity of the church was viable only as long as Europe remained an underdeveloped society consisting of nothing but priests, warriors and peasants (except in Italy). The church could control huge areas because the skills it possessed (literacy, cognitive and moral interpretation, salvatory techniques) were not represented outside it. But the ecological potential of the area ensured that it would not remain underdeveloped for long.

From the twelfth century onwards the urban revival created an ever-growing number of educated laymen on whom monarchs could rely to improve their machinery of government and military defence; and the availability of such skills outside the church made monarchs and laymen alike increasingly resentful of Rome's ability to drain off resources and interfere in politics. In other words, sheer wealth undermined the position of the church, not just (or even mainly) in the sense that the church became richer than the apostolic ideal allowed, but also and more particularly in the sense that it enabled kings to make themselves masters of their own homes while at the same time allowing skilled men to settle in them, the number of teachers, students, colleagues and patrons at home having grown sufficiently large to spare them the necessity of travelling in search of their livelihood. It was in the eyes of such people that Rome suddenly appeared too rich for its own good in terms of both the message it preached and the services that it performed. Sheer wealth, in other words, eventually led to the Reformation whereby the spiritual and material assets of the church were nationalized throughout the northern European world.

Even where the church escaped nationalization, however, it lost out to vernacular culture. The monopoly of Latin on literary culture had always been weak. Unlike Arabic, it was not a genuine sacred language (Jesus had not spoken it, nor had the Bible been composed in it, the Vulgate being a mere translation), and it was not the language of the conquerors, or any one of them, either. Moreover, the sheer primitiveness to which Europe descended prevented the conquest elite from *making* it their own. The illiterate country bumpkins who dominated Europe for a thousand years or so after the fall of Rome had to be entertained and otherwise catered for in their own vernaculars: they knew no better. Had imperial unity been restored in collaboration with the church, the hold of Latin would obviously have been strengthened (as it was during Charlemagne's shortlived 'Carolingian renaissance'); but in practice the bearers of high culture and the wielders of political power once more failed to reinforce one another's position.

The political elite had plenty of respect for Latin, but no command of it, meaning that they generated an immense amount of oral literature in the vernacular; and the larger the number of educated laymen within their kingdoms became, the greater the temptation became actually to write in these languages too, at least as far as poetry and light literature for the entertainment of the elite were concerned. By the sixteenth century Galileo went so far as to publish scientific discoveries in Italian rather than Latin (getting immense publicity as a result). By then the Romance languages were fully equipped with written standards, complete with grammars modelled on Latin, while at the same time the Reformation led to the creation of written standards for the vernaculars of northern Europe as well.

In other words, by the sixteenth century we have the outline of states with fixed territorial identities and (by pre-industrial standards) considerable political, religious and cultural unity. In short we have the trend towards national states that was to be completed by industrialization.

Scientific thought

Just as the imperial unity of the church was doomed, so was the cultural compromise it represented. Christianity and classical culture were two completely different world views which had come together by historical accident and which had fallen into the hands of alien barbarians by yet another turn of fortune. Europe had unwittingly equipped itself with a potential for fundamentalism in three quite different directions, being encouraged by piety to restore original Christianity (as attempted in the Reformation), by learning to revive the original classics (as attempted in the Renaissance), and by politics to rediscover its barbarian roots (as attempted in romantic nationalism). Each revival undermined the compromise, necessitating new thought for the recovery of a coherent world view.

Clearly, had Europe remained underdeveloped, no such revivals might have taken place. Thus the civilization of Buddhist South-East Asia combined a religion (Buddhist) which was in principle incompatible with the high culture (Hindu), and both of which were in their turn quite distinct from the barbarian legacies of their adherents (Burmese, Thai, Khmer); but no return to the foundations upset the synthesis here, South-East Asia remaining a land of monks, warriors and peasants until modern times: there was no 'rise of the bourgeoisie' of the kind which sent Europeans scurrying for the original versions of the creeds and countries to which they adhered.

Given the socio-economic development of Europe, on the other hand, the plural origin of its culture would undoubtedly have made for change regardless of the specific components involved. But the nature of the components matter for the direction of the change, above all for the growth of modern scientific thought.

Classical thought was conceptual and strictly deductive: human reason postulated the operation of regularities in the universe, but empirical testing was disdained on the ground that theory was above the haphazard behaviour which we can actually observe. ('Even the heavens occasionally go astray', as Chinese astronomers said when theory and observation failed to coincide.) Christianity, on the other hand, was monotheist and, once restored to its pristine purity by Calvinists and other Protestants, strictly inductive: the universe is run by a personal and omnipotent God who may behave any way he likes, meaning that no regularities can be postulated (he may choose to raise a miracle any time, a miracle being simply a statistically uncommon form of divine behaviour); human reason can only observe. It was the interaction between these two views which issued in the conviction that the regularities postulated by deductive thought must be systematically tested by empirical observation: if the regularities are the laws by which the omnipotent God chooses to run the universe, they must display themselves in God's daily practice too; more precisely, God was assumed to have delegated the actual running of the universe to regular laws, abstaining from interference in the daily life of his creation however much the believers might try to bribe him with prayers, gifts and the like.

Capitalism

All the factors considered so far come together in the explanation of the rise of capitalism, the economic organization in which the deviant development of Europe first manifested itself in full.

An economy is described as capitalist when the following conditions are met. Everything can be bought and sold, including land and human labour. Everything is a *commodity* as opposed to a means of subsistence. Labour being a commodity, it is distinct from the person who supplies it; it is neutral labour, not political or personal support. Differently put, it is *wage labour*: people are hired, as opposed to born into the productive enterprise, and they are free rather than indentured, enserfed or enslaved. Labour being hired, it is separated from the productive enterprise and from its own product as well: a peasant or traditional craftsman possesses his own land or workshop and owns the crops or pots he produces, but the modern worker (industrial or agricultural) has no access to the means of production except through his employers, that is the *entrepreneurs* who have set up the productive enterprise and hired him, and what he produces belongs to them. He owns nothing *except* the labour which he sells for wages. The relationship between worker, entrepreneur and product is thus a purely economic one. Workers supply labour, not political followings; entrepreneurs supply wages, not protection or homesteads; and the products are destined for the market, not for the households of the producers or their exploiters: the only tie between them is the *cash nexus*. Thus far capitalism is simply modern economy (that is market economy) in general. It is however further distinguished by the fact that the means of production (factories, farms, machinery, sc. capital) are owned by *private* entrepreneurs, or in other words *capitalists*, not by the state, God or the workers themselves.

Many pre-industrial societies had a capitalist sector even though the economy at large was agrarian, but it tended to be heavily dominated by commerce rather than manufacture. Typically it rested on long-distance trade in products obtained through hunting and gathering or agriculture rather than manufacture (e.g. slaves, fish, timber, gums, resins and other forest products on the one hand, grain, oil, wine and such spices as were grown rather than gathered on the other), though there might be a certain amount of trading in manufactured products too; and the commodity production it stimulated tended to concentrate on expensive goods for elite consumption, both at home and abroad, rather than cheap ones for the domestic market, though there might be some production of inexpensive items as well.

Such capitalism is commonly known as pre-modern. Its limits were set by the low purchasing power of the rural masses on the one hand and by the nature of the state, which was rarely designed as an instrument for the furtherance of commercial or manufacturing aims, on the other: both circumstances prevented it from taking over and transforming the economy at large. The exceptions are more apparent than real. Trade did play a dominant role in both the economy and the politics of numerous South-East Asian states (notably those of Malaya and Indonesia); but the goods were gathered rather than manufactured and destined for export to foreign elites rather than internal consumption, while the gatherers were forest dwellers who were both too thinly scattered and too mobile in their impenetrable environment for the state to control them. The suppliers remained external to the state, while the rice-growing peasants of the river-valleys remained external to the commerce: the agrarian economy was in no way transformed. Trade also dominated the economies and politics of mercantile city states such as those of medieval Italy, and here manufacture was of major importance too; but such city states had little or no agrarian economy at all.

More commonly the capitalist sector flourished within an agrarian economy without greatly affecting either the nature or the primacy of the latter, let alone the socio-political relations it engendered. This pattern is well attested for antiquity, the Islamic world, India, China and pre-modern Europe, and the question is how how Europe came to go beyond it. Capitalism of the modern type (dominated by mass manufacture of everyday goods) here made its appearance in the eighteenth century, especially in England, but also elsewhere. It rested on the use of machines and division of labour in mills, as well as the putting-out system (whereby entrepreneurs would supply rural households with raw materials and pay them on receipt of the finished products, typically cloth); and it turned into what we now know as industrial capitalism when steam power was added to the productive process.

The answer to the question takes us back to the factors examined already. Medieval and early modern rulers set the scene for the bourgeoisie, first by allowing it to manage its own cities in accordance with its own wishes and next by clearing their kingdoms of unruly nobles, robber barons and self-help groups, assisted by the wealth and skills of the burghers themselves: this alliance between state and bourgeoisie is distinctly unusual. The growth of urban wealth and skills also assisted the expansion of the state at the cost of ecclesiastical jurisdictions, while at the same time contributing to the emancipation of thought from church control. New modes of thought on the one hand and the happy coincidence between the wishes of equally greedy rulers and bourgeoisie on the other led to the formation of colonial empires and the influx of an immense amount of tributary and commercial wealth capable of investment in manufacture; at the same time the erosion of the political and economic power of the nobility pressurized the latter into commercial exploitation of the land, be it by evicting their tenants or by selling off land to them, either way by drawing rural populations into the commercial network and creating new markets for commodity production, which was transformed by the growth of scientific and technological thought in its turn.

It goes without saying that there are endless controversies over the precise manner in which these and other developments interacted, as well as over the question why England was the first to industrialize. But whichever way the story is told, its protagonists are the peculiar political evolution arising from the feudal collapse, the plural roots of European culture, and the wealth with which the ecology and population control endowed it.

'European dynamism'

Sociologists are apt to speak of 'European dynamism' or 'European restlessness' in a manner suggesting that Europe was born with a magic gift denied to the rest of the world (the gift in question being 'rationality' according to Weber, who even spoke of 'rational restlessness'!). But there was no magic gift, nor was there any particular rationality, all there was being a long formative period: having collapsed politically, Europe devised a primitive organization to suit it only to find that its ecology endowed it with a potential far too great for the solution adopted, so that what ought to have been the end of the formative period turned out only to be the beginning. All formative periods are dynamic precisely because they are formative, or in other words because new patterns of social, political and cultural organization have to be devised; those of antiquity, India, China, Japan or the Islamic world were no less dynamic than the European variety. (On the contrary, that of the Islamic world was a brief outburst of immense inventiveness.) They were not even uniformly shorter.

Europe was inventive in different *areas* from other civilizations, having a peculiar penchant for technology which still has not been explained. By the thirteenth century, it had made such technological progress that Roger Bacon could make his famous prediction that 'machines may be made by which the largest ships, with only one man steering them, will be moved faster than if they were filled with rowers; wagons may be built which will move with incredible speed and without the aid of beasts; flying machines can be constructed in which a man . . . may beat the air with wings like a bird . . .

machines will make it possible to go to the bottom of seas and rivers'; and by the sixteenth century Leonardo was busy sketching such machines on paper, while at the same time the labour-saving and other technical devices of Europe had come to exceed those of non-European civilizations, China included. (China had the lead until then.)

Whatever the ultimate explanation for this penchant may be, the extreme primitivity of barbarian Europe certainly plays a role in it. Outside Europe, the state created sophisticated elites utterly different from the masses in all and every respect; but the unwashed, vermin-infested, badly clothed, badly housed, illiterate and half-studied barons and clerics who held sway in medieval Europe were barely distinguishable from the serfs they ruled: even thirteenth-century crusaders of the most sophisticated variety struck polished Muslim gentlemen as appallingly crude; and by the time the European aristocracy began to acquire proper manners they had lost their monopoly on setting the tone, a bourgeoisie embodying conspicuously different values having appeared. It was the failure of the European elite thoroughly to distance itself from the masses which made technology respectable, not just for military armoury and amusing gadgets, but also for labour-saving and other devices of the most prosaic kind. Differently put, a state without money generated an aristocracy without manners and bearers of high culture without a proper disdain for flywheels and cranks, let alone for the uneducated men who put such things together. A certain amount of technical expertise was tolerable in a Chinese gentleman, the state to which he was wedded taking a strong interest in irrigation systems, canals, agricultural improvement, defensive walls and the like; but technical skills *without* full mastery of the high culture commanded no respect at all. In Europe, by contrast, a man such as Leonardo, who counted as unlettered, was courted and fêted in the highest circles.

That Europe had a particular penchant for technology does not however refute the proposition that its general inventiveness arose from the protracted nature of its formative period. But by the sixteenth century one might have expected this period to come to an end, and in some sense it did: everything thereafter simply spells out implications of the previous development. But the implications were so drastic and the rate of change so immense that in another way Europe could be said never to have come out of its formative period at all. The first thousand years had issued in a system of proto-national states, and competition between these states was the motor of European history thereafter, as has often been observed.

Military competition is absent where a single empire reigns supreme. The Chinese did learn military techniques from the barbarians, and the barbarians did learn from the Chinese in their turn, but the extent to which the latter could modify their techniques was limited: they produced their own horses, thereby forcing the Chinese to learn horsemanship, but they had to import the iron which the Chinese in due course taught them to use for their arrowheads; and when the Chinese took to using firearms, even imports did not enable the barbarians to keep up (as mentioned in chapter 3). The process thus ceased to be cumulative; and there was nothing for the Chinese to learn from the barbarians in non-military respects. Even where a plurality of states exists, however, competition is not necessarily a source of changes other than dynastic ups and downs. In the medieval Islamic and Indian worlds, for example, states were generally too loosely placed on top of society to generate much innovation below; indeed, competition can hardly be said to have displayed its dynamic potential in Europe itself before territorial states had evolved. But once they were there, competition kept propelling them forward.

First or freak?

This brings us to the question whether Europe was a freak or simply the first to complete an evolution begun by all complex societies. Was modernity (in the sense of industrial economy with accompanying social, political and cognitive arrangements) in the making elsewhere? Should Europe be seen as having got there first because it was 'dynamic' and Asia as having lagged behind because it was 'stagnating' (the rest of the world being too backward to figure in the discussion), or should we rather see Europe and Asia, or indeed all complex societies, as travelling in different directions?

The idea of dynamic Europe versus stagnating Asia is both old and well-entrenched, and it underlies much literature to the effect that Europe won the race because comparable developments in Asia were 'blocked' by this or that: both were travelling in the same direction (so it is tacitly assumed), but Europe was less encumbered than its Asian counterparts. It should be clear from what has been said so far that this approach cannot be right.

Given that history is the story of the human accumulation of experience, it does indeed appear to have a unitary direction. As the centuries roll on, stateless societies acquire states under the influence of their neighbours, their neighbours develop better governmental techniques, populations grow, means of communications improve and urbanization increases, making for more trade and manufacture, more individualism, new ideas and greater sophistication: everywhere the earth seems to be 'filling up'. In this very general sense there undoubtedly was an identical trend all over the world.

It is however an altogether different matter to argue that the world outside Europe was moving in the same specific direction as Europe itself, in the sense that elsewhere too there was a development in the direction of nation states, modern science and industrial capitalism. Adherents of the blockage theory implicitly assume that the *general* accumulation of human experience was bound sooner or later to issue in the *specific* package we call modernity, if not by one path, then by another: it merely so happened that the European path led there first. But the historical record suggests that all non-European paths were leading towards modified versions of the same societies, not towards that evolved in Europe. In other words, Europe and Asia would indeed seem to have been travelling in different directions, or more precisely Europe and the different civilizations of Asia were *all* travelling along paths of their own. China was not moving in the European direction, but nor was it moving in that of the Middle East or vice versa; India was not moving closer to the path taken by Japan, and so on: all were developing along the lines laid down in their respective formative periods.

To a modern observer Asian societies may well appear to resemble each other more than they do Europe (particularly of course when the observer is an ignorant European to whom all distant civilizations look the same); but this is merely to say that the modern predominance of the West engenders an illustion trick. If the Chinese way of doing things had come to dominate the world, all non-Chinese societies would likewise have seemed to resemble each other more than China because their countless differences would have appeared much less important than their shared lack of the crucial institutions possessed by the winner. Where in the world is there anything like European cities? But where is there anything like Chinese bureaucracy? Every civilization has its own unique features, and if the Islamic world had won out, all non-Islamic civilizations would have appeared as so many variations on the theme of failure to invent slave soldiers (due to blockages, no doubt).

There is only one respect in which all non-European civilizations genuinely resemble each other more than Europe, and that is in their successful discovery of durable solutions to the problems inherent in pre-industrial organization. Europe failed: had it succeeded, it would have *remained* a pre-industrial society. Human societies aim at stability; all hope to find the social and political organization best suited to the specific cultural and natural environment they inhabit, namely the one that minimizes tension and increases viability to the greatest possible extent. Are we not all trying to find the best solution to our particular problems today? Formative periods are about the invention of basic frameworks. This or that solution is tried out until a viable compromise is found, whereupon tinkering suffices for the accommodation of further change unless it is of a positively cataclysmic kind. What happened in Europe is clearly that the formative period went wrong. The political organization was too primitive and the high culture was too composite to survive once people began to acquire money and to think (people could do plenty of both elsewhere without thereby causing their establishments to totter). Differently put, Europe failed to devise a socio-political and cognitive order in which a united elite kept both the high culture and the society it sanctioned in place and in which drastic change was impossible because all the key members of society had too strong an interest in the order that prevailed.

Adherents of the blockage theory may object with reference to China, arguing that it did indeed travel in the same direction as Europe, or rather that it was the first to take that path, though it was eventually to be overtaken by Europe as its own development came a standstill towards the end of the eighteenth century. By then China had achieved a high agricultural output and developed a large internal market in both agricultural products and manufactured goods for everyday consumption, the whole of China being linked by a dense network of periodic rural markets and market towns; there was some use of machinery and inanimate energy (notably water power), literacy rates were high, and formal barriers to social or geographical mobility no longer existed. All this is apt to convey the impression that a blockage theory is needed to explain the failure of the Chinese economy to take off.

But in fact China is a star example of a successful civilization: the problems inherent in pre-industrial organization had here been solved with such expertise that people could do more thinking and accumulate more wealth than ever before without thereby undermining the prevailing order. China reached the pinnacle of economic development possible under pre-industrial conditions and stopped: no forces pushing it in a different direction are in evidence; no movements towards take-off were blocked.

The durability of the Chinese solution arose from its manner of elite-building. The state recruited its servants through an examination system which, by late traditional times, endowed it with something close to a monopoly on the distribution of prestige (a situation which countless rulers must have dreamed of, but which few achieved): everyone who could afford it competed. In terms of political control, the mighty dragon might not be a match for the local snake who knew the ins and outs of the place, but every local snake wanted the dragon to give him a degree: all educational activities had as their highest aim full mastery of the Confucian culture which tied the educated person to the state. China thus tamed its landowners, not by developing a state apparatus which gradually deprived them of a political role, but on the contrary by transforming them into Confucian degree-holders on such a scale that the state apparatus itself could remain relatively small: many degree-holders, of course, served as actual officials, but many more served as gentry, or in other words as local snakes with a vested interest in the state-sponsored world view to which they owed their prestige.

There was no way in which this alliance could be upset by internal developments. Cities might, and did, grow; but they had never been autonomous enclaves, let alone independent states: they did not hatch urban populations with strong political organizations of their own. Nor were they enclaves of literacy in an otherwise illiterate world, or of social forces with which the state might advantageously ally itself by way of counterbalancing an unruly aristocracy or an all-too-powerful church. Politically, the representatives of trade and commerce were redundant (or, at times, even undesirable). Hence they were not in a position to turn the state into an instrument for their aims, be it directly or indirectly: the agricultural sector was so vast and dominated by landlords so closely tied to official pursuits that the town-dwellers could not transform the latter into spearheads of commercial innovation either. (The isolation policy which gradually came to prevail in late traditional China neatly illustrates the extent to which economic interests remained subordinate to political goals.) The elimination of the barbarian danger on the one hand and the preservation of imperial unity on the other meant there was no inter-state competition (until the European barbarians arrived), while the unitary nature of the high culture meant that urbanization, commercialization and the spread of literacy were in no danger of shattering the traditional world view, as opposed to strengthening its hold by ever wider diffusion among town-dwellers and rural masses alike: capitalists, too, wanted degree-holders in their families. (Confucianism did coexist with both Taoism and Buddhism, but only the latter was a source of real tension; after the ninth-century disestablishment of Buddhism, however, educated men ceased to be officially committed to two rival creeds, whereupon the tension largely disappeared.) Greater productivity and better government did make for population growth, so the market was huge; but it consisted, apart from the elite, of impoverished peasants whose purchasing power could not be raised. Despite its interest in production (occasionally even mass production) of everyday goods, Chinese capitalism was thus pre-modern in terms of its customers and its relationship with the state alike. The abundance of labour enabled landlords to increase their income by demanding higher rents (where tenancy prevailed), as opposed to taking up commercial agriculure themselves; and it deprived manufacturers of an interest in laboursaving devices, labour being cheap in comparison with raw material. Eventually the population pressed so hard against resources that the outcome was a Malthusian crisis. (Some twenty-five million people are estimated to have died in the political disturbances of the 1850s alone.) Where in all this, one wonders, is the dynamic potential supposed to have been blocked? China had succeeded where Europe had failed, and it was the inability of Europe similarly to contain its capitalist sector which eventually caused the Confucian order to collapse.

The only case comparable to Europe is that of Japan. Here too we have a composite culture and a long formative period in which political power was fragmented. Japan started with a solution that was too sophisticated for its developmental level rather than one which was too primitive for its potential, the solution in question being the imperial model provided by seventh-century China. Barbarian Japan was no more capable of reshaping itself along Chinese lines than was barbarian Europe of keeping the Roman empire going in all but name, and the upshot was a long period of constant change culminating, here as there, in the sixteenth century, when Japan was politically united in a proto-nation state and its Buddhist monasteries despoiled (though unlike Catholic ones, they did not owe allegiance to an external power). By then the formative priod of Japan came to an end, precisely as it ought to have done and in some sense did in Europe too.

The crucial difference is that Japan was on its own, not part of a state system. Its only neighbours were Korea and China, the former a peer, but the latter a superpower setting the tone rather than inviting competition; and China set the tone by inventing the policy of isolation. In isolation Japan experienced developments similar to those of Europe, that is taming of the feudal aristocracy, urbanization and agricultural growth. But though some cities had indeed enjoyed chartered autonomy before the political unification of the sixteenth century, they had never had access to far-flung markets after the fashion of their European counterparts, meaning that their position was insecure even before Japan retreated into authoritarian isolation and all the more so thereafter: they did not spawn a comparable bourgeoisie. And the absence of military competition meant that Japan could remain what it was. The drastic effects of the wholly unsuccessful Mongol attempt to invade Japan in the thirteenth century demonstrate that here too membership of a competitive state system would have been a source of constant change; but as it was, Japan enjoyed two centuries of undisturbed tranquility before the West forced it to join the competition.

9
Modernity

The reader may be now find the nature of pre-industrial societies so obvious that he is puzzled by the nature of their modern counterparts instead. At all events, I shall conclude by offering him a thumbnail sketch of modernity; differently put, I shall now think back all the features which we have spent this book thinking away in the hope of thereby clinching the reader's understanding of the past while at the same time restoring him to the world in which he belongs.

From poverty to affluence

Scarcity was a hallmark of pre-industrial society. By contrast, industrialization means wealth to the point that income is used as its defining characteristic: an industrial revolution is deemed to have taken place where real income per head has increased progressively over several decades to levels substantially above those characteristic of pre-industrial economies. A progressive and substantial increase of real income is what all industrializing countries are trying to achieve.

It is important to note that the increase is expected to be perpetual. Wherever the threshold between industrializing and industrial societies may be deemed to lie, constant economic growth is possible as long as inexhaustible supplies of inanimate energy are available and it has so far been regarded as highly desirable too. This may change. The fossil fuels (coal and oil) on which industry has so far depended are running out, leaving a question mark over the future (can nuclear, solar or wave energy make up for the loss?); and the very desirability of perpetual growth has been questioned in the West by exponents of counter-culture, politicians (such as the Greens), academics and others. But whatever the future may hold in this respect, economic growth is still a key objective of all industrial countries.

Though the wealth of the industrial countries continues to grow, the workforce directly engaged in production is contracting. The proportion occupied by agriculture has been falling steadily since the industrial revolution, being now typically between 4 per cent and 10 per cent. The proportion engaged in industrial production has remained stable at around 35 per cent, but that too is falling now under the impact of automation. The rest of the population are engaged in the so-called service industries: government, administration, trade, finance, advertising, transport, education, research, health, recreation and so on.

Some sociologists go so far as to describe contemporary Western society as 'post-industrial' (or 'post-modern' or even 'post-civilized'!) on the grounds that it is no longer devoted primarily to the production of goods, but rather to the expansion of knowledge on the one hand and the provision of personal services on the other: it is a 'knowledge society' because its crucial resource is the theoretical knowledge which lies behind technological advance; and it is a 'personal service society' partly because most people now work in the service sector and more particularly because education, welfare, counselling, and 'caring' have expanded to the point of generating a new middle class (sometimes bracketed with the agents of technological advance under the label 'knowledge class'). However, a society which thrives on the application of knowledge to the production of electronic and other high-technology goods can hardly be described as post-industrial: the knowledge would be economically useless without an industrial base. And though the service sector has indeed come to employ over half of the workforce and spawned a new middle class as well, its expansion has so far taken place overwhelmingly at the cost of the agricultural rather than the industrial sector; to what extent this will change remains to be seen. At all events, what matters here is the simple fact that industry generates a vast amount of new occupations which have the joint effect of making society thickest around the middle rather than the bottom: industrial society is unique in that the majority of its population are middle class in terms of income and prestige alike.

From pre-industrial polity to nation

Pre-industrial society was characterized by low degrees of economic, political and cultural integration. By contrast, a high degree of integration in all three respects is the hallmark of modernity.

Economic integration

Economically, modernity breeds integration by its systematic division of labour. All members of modern society specialize in a single economic activity, offering their labour, skill or capital on the market and receiving monetary payment in return. All are thus dependent on the market (be it free, or more or less so, as in capitalist countries, or wholly regulated by the state, as in socialist ones). People no longer collect their own fuel, grow their own food, make their own clothing, build their own houses or do their own repairs, or rather they only engage in such activities outside their normal working hours, pursuing them as hobbies or as ways of saving money rather than as sources of their livelihood. Even peasants (or farmers, as they are more properly called these days) sell their crops and buy their food in shops instead.

Systematic division of labour goes hand in hand with mass production and mass markets: technology has made it possible to produce very large quantities of goods for distribution among very large numbers of people spread over very large distances; and economically it has become profitable to do so because the masses are not just producers, but also consumers, having completely ceased to be self-sufficient.

All members of modern society are thus abjectly dependent upon one another for their nourishment, clothing, fuel, education, medical attention and a wide array of other services; differently put, all are members of a single economy, the national one, which plays the same role in the life of the modern workforce as did the household in that of the pre-industrial peasantry. Indeed, without a national economy they would not constitute a single workforce at all.

Cultural integration

Culturally, modernity breeds integration by prising loose the masses from their local communities, getting them together in the same factories and the same cities, subjecting them to the same schooling in the same language from early childhood to late adolescence, bombarding them via the same mass media, and putting an end to the isolation of the communities from which they came.

Industry separates production from the household. Manufacture was still a household activity under the putting-out system, but increased reliance on machines transferred the manufacturing process to factories which were located in cities because large numbers of people have to collaborate and co-ordinate their activities in order for an industrial enterprise to succeed. The peasants thus had to leave their villages in order to become workers in the cities. (Under industrial conditions some 70–80 per cent of the population live in cities, though the electronic revolution may now to some extent enable the work force to disperse again.) The result was the formation not only of working class culture, but also of national culture.

Modern industry needs a literate and numerate workforce able to communicate in the same language at all levels and trained in the assimilation of information of all kinds. Once all members of society have come together in a single workforce, moreover, they need a shared value system of a more unitary kind than the traditional high culture superimposed over a multiplicity of local traditions. In short, industry means that the masses have to be integrated culturally. The modern 'guest-worker' phenomenon admittedly shows that unskilled workers can participate in the economic process without sharing any culture whatsoever with the rest of society apart from the conviction that a steady income is desirable and acquired by a steady input of work (a conviction more readily shared by workers of peasant origin than former hunter-gatherers). But at the same time the acute social problems posed by such workers in their host societies demonstrate that there are good reasons why cultural assimilation always ranks high on the agenda of industrializers. 'The proletariat may strangle us unless we teach it the same virtues that have elevated the other classes of society', as a British school union put it in 1884: strangulation was avoided by schooling.

Unlike pre-industrial children, who began their specialist training early and automatically picked up such general knowledge as they needed in the course of growing up, modern children spend years on the same general education before being allowed to specialize: modern society is much too complex for general knowledge to be transmitted by osmosis alone. All children are educated in the virtues of the elite, not just in the sociological sense that those who control the educational apparatus decide what values and skills it ought to impart, but also in the historical sense that mass education disseminates the high culture with associated literary language that used to be restricted to a privileged few. Obviously, it is considerably easier to transform a unitary high culture into mass culture than to create a new one on the basis of a myriad of local local traditions and dialects. It is only where for one reason or another no high culture is available that the latter solution is attempted.

In many countries the functions performed by schools were (and are) assisted by the army, which would take in recruits from a wide variety of ethnic and social groups, teach them the same national language, commit them to the same national policy, and send them out again as acculturated citizens. Both schools and the army had (and have) the additional advantage of keeping the young off the streets without putting them into the workforce, or in other words keeping them occupied without swamping the labour market.

The formation of a single national culture is everywhere assisted by the national press, radio, television and other forms of telecommunication which spread the same language and outlook to all who listen and watch. At the same time improved means of transportation open up traffic between hitherto isolated communities, which are gradually integrated in the national economy too. Local dialects thus disappear along with local costume, cooking and other customs, except in so far as they get picked up by cookery books and tourist brochures destined for national or international circulation. In short, the high culture no longer coexists with, but rather suppresses local diversity, regional accents and other survivals notwithstanding.

Socio-political integration

In social and political terms modernity breeds integration by attaching all individuals directly to a bureaucratic state which processes them mechanically without regard for their social, ethnic or religious background. Privileged and excluded groups give way to persons endowed with identical legal and political rights, though not with the same wealth, or in other words to sharply defined citizens fuzzily divided into classes. Differently put, modernity breeds nation states, that is to say polities composed of free individuals who each bear the same relationship to the government. (Nation states are also identified as polities composed of people who share the same ethnicity, language, history and culture; I shall come back to this definition, and amplify the first, in the next section.) The nation state made its appearance before the arrival of industry, being first proclaimed in the French Revolution; but industry gave it reality to the point that industrialization and nation-building are two sides of the same modernizing process today.

In western Europe, the diverse provinces of which kingdoms were constituted underwent a gradual process of administrative unification from the seventeenth century onwards (largely in response to military pressure), being forced to accept the same bureaucracy, the same law, the same calendar, currency and weights and measures. Local diversity was slowly being eroded.

So was the automomous power of the local nobility. Military change on the one hand and the expansion of the state apparatus on the other meant that European rulers became increasingly able to do without the services of local power-holders, be it for purposes of collecting taxes, getting armies together or maintaining law and order; in so far as aristocrats wished to retain political influence, they had to do so as office-holders, or in other words as appointees of the king rather than as wielders of autonomous power. In this capacity they were still predominant when industrialization began, except in France, where administrative unity had been imposed and the nobility overthrown in the Revolution. But even where they had not been overthrown they had long been under economic threat.

Landed income was increasingly being eclipsed by rival forms of wealth, and industrialization completed this trend. Aristocrats could, and frequently did, join the commercial and industrial worlds themselves, while at the same time successful commoners could, and regularly did, purchase landed estates or noble status for themselves; but the result was that noble status assumed the appearance of arbitrary privilege: it no longer marked off a coherent social group. At the same time the increasing importance of technical knowledge and skills and the ever-growing need for manpower for factories and modern armies transformed ascribed status from a basic principle of social order into an obstacle to successful economic and political performance: the special status of serfs and Jews was as inconvenient as that of aristocrats. Progress required all members of society to be identical legal units for easy administration and placement wherever their skills were needed (a point to which I shall come back in a moment), and all were duly given identical civil status: aristocrats, serfs, Jews and other minorities were transformed into citizens in most parts of Europe in the course of the nineteenth century, and even royalty can be fined for speeding in the twentieth.

It was this erosion of the socio-political hierarchy on the one hand and the emergence of a national economy on the other which led to the perception of society as divided into classes. The class system identifies people with reference to their position in the workforce. This makes sense because everyone is a member of this workforce (be it directly or through the breadwinner of the family), because people's position in the workforce actually matters for their social and political behaviour, and also because no alternative principle of classification survives. Differently put, the concept of class developed in tandem with the creation of a nation, being increasingly adopted by the members of a given nation to envisage a society that could no longer be adequately described in terms of functional orders, estates or aristocrats versus commoners.

The same process encouraged equal distribution of political rights, or in other words the emergence of democracy. Industrialization endows the masses with a political presence because workers congregating in cities, where they learn to read and write and acquire means of mass communication, are considerably harder to ignore than a dispersed and illiterate peasantry sunk in 'the idiocy of rural life' (as Marx called it). Once the peasants are transformed into workers, they invariably organize themselves for collective action. In the cities they become interdependent (wage-rates accepted by workers in one city will affect those of workers in another); and constant interaction endows them with awareness of their shared situation. At the same time their departure from the countryside, the domain of the aristocracy (in the case of Europe), enables them to organize on the basis of class unhindered by loyalties to political superiors. They thus form trade unions or, where trade unions are forbidden, organizations of a consultative nature, with the result that they are able to bring collective power to bear on negotiations with their employers. (It is primarily by granting opportunities for nationwide organization that industry reduces the dilemma of the golden goose to which reference was made in chapter 1.)

Unlike peasants, moreover, workers can strike, and strikes are a powerful weapon because the economy is highly integrated: all aspects of it are affected, and the ultimate weapon, the national strike, brings it to a complete standstill. Strikes may of course be forbidden too. Even where they are, however, large crowds of workers simmering with resentment and threatening to explode into open rebellion in the cities make life too dangerous and disagreeable for the elite to ignore them indefinitely, especially as the dwindling number of peasants means that the army has to be recruited from among the workers themselves. (In many pre-industrial city-states the masses likewise had a political presence without necessarily enjoying any political rights, as has been seen, because elite and masses were cooped up together without the former having access to a large expanse of countryside from which an army could be recruited.) Workers in Bismarck's Germany had considerably more political clout than did peasants in the Germany of Charles V, the authoritarian nature of both regimes notwithstanding.

Given that repressive government is more time-consuming, difficult and expensive than social collaboration, one would thus expect industrialization sooner or later to result in the grant of full political rights not just to the bourgeoisie who have the wealth, but also to the working class. In fact this is what happened in western Europe (where the need for working class co-operation in the First World War greatly accelerated the process), and it has also happened in Japan (thanks to its defeat in the Second World War), but there are good reasons why it has not happened elsewhere.

Leaving aside the fact that Europe happened to possess parliamentary institutions which could be adapted to mass participation in government, Europe also developed industry of its own accord, from scratch and in tandem with the erosion of inconvenient barriers; or more precisely, England did and the rest of western Europe was sufficiently similar to England rapidly to catch on without major upheavals. Everywhere else, however, industry has been imposed upon societies which had not developed in the European direction of their own accord (though Japan turned out to be highly receptive to it). Where industrialization is forced, the structures of society have to undergo violent transformation in order to accommodate the changeling; and the more unsuitable the structures are, the more destructive, painful, disorientating and unwanted the process will be to those who have to live through it. The authorities thus *have* to assume dictatorial powers if they are to succeed: forced industrialization means forced behaviour; attention to the wishes of those affected means that industrialization stops or goes astray, or indeed that the nascent nation state dissolves. The greater the distance an agrarian country has to traverse in order to catch up with the industrial world, the more repression is required; and the more power the state arrogates for itself, the more repressive it will become simply to preserve that power regardless of why it needed it in the first place. Everyone, not just the working class, is excluded from participation in decision-making and sometimes cowed by terror too.

There are of course other reasons why repressive government comes to prevail in a particular place; but the fact remains that where industrialization requires a U-turn, it is more likely to promote universal deprivation (or continued absence) of political rights than their universal acquisition, or so at least until the U-turn is completed. In principle liberalization could set in once the transition is over, particularly where it has been made under a capitalist rather than a communist aegis; but an authoritarian state is not easily dismantled, other factors intervene, and at any rate the number of countries to have completed the transition is still too small for safe bets.

With or without mass participation in government, however, industrial states are characterized by mass political membership: all citizens are directly affiliated to the state, not to intermediate groups; all have rights in it of one kind or another (if not political or civil, then at least social – social rights being those to education, medical care, pension and so on); and their loyalty to it normally overrides the claims of rival political or religious organizations, or so at any rate where nation-building has succeeded. In short, the pre-industrial pattern whereby a far-flung elite and a cosmopolitan culture lord it over a plurality of peasant societies has been replaced by one in which blocks of people ruled by states of their own share the same language, culture and political status. Differences between elites and masses in these repects are greatly attenuated, being typically far weaker than those between the nation and its neighbours. Within each block, all members are tied to nationwide institutions by which they are educated and administered, in which an enormous number of jobs are available, and in which they have economic, social and political entitlements of various kinds. Modern people are wedded to their states to a degree unknown in pre-industrial times, being linguistically incompetent outside them (except in so far as the same language happens to be spoken in several states) and endowed with a host of rights difficult to transfer or unobtainable abroad. To some extent this is changing now that the world is shrinking, but the supremacy of the nation still has not been seriously dented.

Nationalism

Nation-building in Europe bred nationalism, a political ideology which is now of great importance in the non-European world, rival creeds in the form of Marxism, Maoism and fundamentalist Islam notwithstanding.

Nationalism is a doctrine to the effect that political and national borders must coincide: each nation must have its own political house (nations being peoples with a shared ethnicity, language, history and culture). The doctrine assumes nations to exist prior to and independently of state structures. In fact, however, it was the political houses of western Europe (or some of them) that created nations, not the other way round. Europe had always accomodated a plurality of political houses, and its once uniform high culture had long been broken up into vernacular forms. As each state integrated its local

communities in the same economy, exposed them to its own variety
of high culture and eventually granted them identical political rights,
whole peoples came to be differentiated from their neighbours by
language, culture, history and political membership alike: each state,
in other words, came to accommodate a nation. Elsewhere, by contrast, states only integrated the elite, as we have seen; the masses
below them might be divided into 'nations' on the basis of ethnicity,
language, religious allegiance or a combination thereof, but these
divisions were antithetical to political membership and mastery of
the high culture, not, as in Europe, the outcome of participation in
both.

Nationalism condemned this antithesis as intolerable. It did not
however argue that all states must amalgamate their masses, but on
the contrary that the divisions which prevailed among the masses
ought to form the basis of states. It thus validated a European
development, but reversed cause and effect, and this made it immensely explosive: there were plenty of empires to blow up and local
communities to fuse in the name of supposed national identities,
partly in Europe itself and more particularly outside it; in due course
it blew up the colonial empires established by the Europeans themselves.

But whether it validated an existing or a future situation, it played, and still plays, a crucial role in nation-building by instilling a
sense of togetherness among its adherents, incessantly telling them
where their collective future lies with reference to their real or
supposed common past, and thus inducing them to transfer their
loyalties from their local communities or supra-national church to
the nation state. Its aim is the creation of polities in which all
individuals are directly affiliated to the state as identical legal units,
in which all can communicate in the same language (occasionally two
or more) on the basis of a shared body of ideas, and, not least, in
which all are prepared to defend this state of affairs. Where this has
been achieved, a nation state exists, however great the ethnic, cultural and religious diversity it may contain. The nationalist definition
of the nation is prescriptive rather than descriptive: a considerable
amount of diversity can and frequently does persist without being
politically divisive. But the constant harping on the theme of shared
identity on the one hand and the persistent influence of old communal divisions on the other can also do immense damage to minorities
(as it did to the Jews of Germany, the Armenians of the Ottoman
empire and many others besides).

Nationalism is invariably coupled with populism in the sense of admiration for the ways and the will of the masses. Thus national culture is invariably presented as popular culture, though in fact nation-building involves mass dissemination of the high culture of the elite, as has been seen; and national politics are equated with the popular will, though the people may be completely deprived of political rights, as has been seen too. Nationalism thus has both an ethnic and a social aspect to it, being directed against empires in respect of borders and against elites in respect of government: in principle all nations are democracies. Rival creeds such as Marxism, Maoism and fundamentalist Islam lack the ethnic aspect, but venerate the people too. In fact all ideologues do today.

All venerate the people because nation-building is about the reception of the masses. Nations are the outcome of economic, cultural and political integration. Differently put, nation-building amounts to the formation of one huge horizontal linkage: all the masses that formerly had to be kept apart now have to come together in a single world. Ideology 'mobilizes' them (as sociologists put it), taking them out of their autarkic villages and political self-help groups into cities, education and the reach of the modern state. Old community ties are broken, national ones are still embryonic, the rewards are hard to see: industrialization and nation-building are two sides of the same extremely painful process. Ideology plays a key role in keeping people committed to the process, and the more difficult the process, the shriller the ideology is likely to be, total commitment being required. Conversely, where the process is completed the fervour dies down: western European countries still validate their policies with reference to the nation and democracy, but they are only shrill when they are under military threat.

The degree to which nationalism can be said to have existed in the past is a moot point. No pre-industrial polities were nation states, but some clearly approached the model more closely than others, and the historical record is full of sentiments which are often loosely identified as nationalist.

Some of the evidence refers to nativism, the phenomenon which we met in chapter 4 and which one may well count as a primitive species of nationalism: it combined pride in a common past and ethnicity with political action against foreign conquerors, and it was frequently egalitarian. But other evidence refers to ethnic chauvinism of a non-political kind, one ethnic group or 'people' vaunting its superior merits, often its language, over another without thereby claiming a right to a political house of its own. And most of the rest refers to sentiments engendered by ethnic (particularist) religions.

Numerous religions have sanctified a particular people and its political house above all others. In fact, some nativist religions were of this type, but so were others too: the Assyrian god sanctified the Assyrian people (or at any rate their elite) and their monarchy, just as Yahweh sanctified the Jews and their Solomonic polity; Zoroastrianism sanctified the Iranian empire; early Islam sanctified the Arab state, and so on. Clearly there is a nationalist element here, especially in the case of a small and relatively egalitarian people such as the Jews, who were always on the defensive and whose later messianic hopes for the restoration of their polity were easily transmuted into secular nationalism of the modern kind (that is Zionism). But in fact ethnic religion is imperialist, not nationalist, as the Assyrians, Iranians and Arabs demonstrated: one ethnic group being sanctified above all others, it was entitled to dominate others, not simply to coexist with them.

To be sure, modern nationalism has a tendency to develop into imperialism too, with pseudo-science rather than God in the role of sanctifier (as in Gobineau's treatise of 1855 on the natural inequality of the races, or Hitler's Aryan myth). But the fact that pseudo-science has to take the place of God highlights one of the peculiarities of nationalism, for what it basically claims is that ethnic groups must have political autonomy *even though* the truth is universal: all ethnicities have equal value precisely because none has special relations with the divine; and all can have autonomy because the divine has nothing to do with political organization. Once again, it is thus plain that nationalism validates a European situation, Christianity being a universal religion which renders unto Caesar what is Caesar's: the Christian truth was above ethnicity and politics alike, not closely related to either or both as is more commonly the case.

Nationalism being a peculiarly European product, it is not surprising that it is thinly attested in the non-European past. A species of it is documented for Tokugawa Japan, where the political house built by barbarians was also distinct from universal truth (neo-Confucianism imported from China), and there may well be other examples. Generally speaking, however, ethnicity was not used to identify or defend polities in pre-industrial times unless ethnicity was sanctified by religion, in which case the ideology was almost invariably imperialist; and even where the state came to be identified in purely ethnic as distinct from religious or cultural terms, as in Europe and Japan, pre-modern nationalism (or proto-nationalism, as

one might call it) lacked the populist element: it was an elite sentiment destined for elite consumption. It took industrialization for
the nativism of the masses and the proto-nationalism of the elite to
merge.

National politics

Everyday politics in fully industrialized states have a prosaic appearance. Unlike the pre-industrial variety, they are no longer conducted
by the elite alone; and though private interests still proliferate, this
cannot be publicly admitted. Nor are they dedicated to the pursuit of
war and glory, industrialization having magnified the destructive
potential of warfare on a scale so gigantic that it is no longer
regarded as either a normal or desirable activity; such warfare as
continues to be conducted, moreover, is rarely aimed at the acquisition of territory, the incorporation of foreign populations becoming
extremely difficult once states are defined in national terms and the
masses have acquired political importance. The key aim of government these days, apart from internal security and external peace, is
economic growth; and the key issue of normal politics is the distribution of economic goods through taxation, wages, benefits, pensions,
and other kinds of entitlement negotiated by politicians in consultation with civil servants, experts and pressure groups of various
kinds. Class-based ·disagreement is evident, but class struggle is
rarely violent, not necessarily because class relations are harmonious,
but rather because armed revolt has ceased to be an option. The
component parts of national states, be they social or regional, are
generally too tightly integrated in the national economy to have
viability as separate political entities or even to survive brief periods
of disruption (the electricity might be cut off); besides, the immense
military superiority of the state dooms armed revolt to failure, unless
it takes the form of guerilla warfare or terrorist campaigns of attri-
tion. Terrorism apart, the citizens of modern states generally rely on
demonstrations, strikes, vociferous mass media and political lob-
bying, as well as elections (where they have them), to make their
opinions known.

From traditional religion to modern ideology

The mundane appearance of everyday politics in fully industrialized
countries is reinforced by their generally secular nature. Decisions

are legitimated with reference to the nation, democracy or expert
opinion rather than the Buddha, the gods or God. Modern ideologies
of a materialist and wholly this-worldly kind prevail over traditional
world views, theist or otherwise. This takes us to the question raised
in chapter 7: how and why has the role of religion changed under
industrial conditions?

Tradition versus progress
The pre-industrial scenario may be summarized as follows. Society is
tied to a superior being or beings (ancestors, spirits, gods or God),
or principles (such as cosmic order or filial piety) or laws (such as
karma): an enduring truth above mere human beings generates a
socio-political ideal with corresponding institutions. Since the truth
cannot change, the institutions it spawns ought likewise to retain
their original form, only minor changes to meet the needs of the
times being acceptable; and since the truth is whole rather than
partial, it ought to govern all aspects of life. Society was thus
dominated by a tradition, a time-honoured way of doing and
looking at things; and conscious attempts at change were usually
envisaged as restoration: the ideal was a concrete order exemplified in the past, not an unknown future.

By contrast, industrial society has abandoned tradition. Its crucial concept is that of growth or progress, in other words change
assumed to be for the better. Progress was once understood as a
law (as in the Marxist vision in which it inexorably leads to the
elimination of the state from complex society); nowadays, it is only
an ideal, but it is still something bigger and more enduring than
ourselves in that it is meant to be for the common good.

However, an enduring truth to the effect that human society
must always change cannot generate a time-honoured way of doing
and perceiving things; the ideal is not a specific order exemplied in
the past, but on the contrary something new which has never been
tried out before. The supreme truth to which modern society sub-
scribes can only sanctify a *process*, more precisely one of constant
demolition and re-organisation. Society having committed itself to
change, all obstacles to it must be kept out of the way: above all,
religion must be pushed aside.

This is not to say that industrial society is hostile to religion; you
may have as much of it as you like (communist countries being
partial exceptions). But it will not allow you to embroil your religion
in matters of public importance, be they political, social or cognitive.

Religion is not allowed to impinge on such matters because it may not *underpin*: wherever an ultimate truth underpins a phenomenon, it creates a sacred cow, a holy institution, a dogma, something that cannot be changed. Dogmas would mean the end of modern science and scholarship. Both have expanding frontiers, and neither could go on expanding if religious truths were allowed to interfere with them or alternatively if scientific or scholarly theories were allowed to become religious truths. If God's view of things as presented in the Bible had been allowed to shape scientific and scholarly research, a host of scientists and scholars would have had to be executed as heretics; and if the law of gravity been allowed to acquire sacred status, Einstein too would have had to be burnt at the stake. Modern science and scholarship are cumulative, meaning that one insight is assumed to lead to another which will lead to a third, outmoding the first in the process. Nothing is sacred; everything is preliminary. Neither science nor scholarship today ever leads to the discovery of that final truth which will enable us all to rest, satisfying ourselves with the transmission of the truth to future generations.

Science and scholarship are allowed to have ever-expanding frontiers because they given us more and more control over the natural and social world in which we find ourselves: without Darwin or Mendel, no modern genetics; without Newton and a host of modern physicists, no space-ships or landings on the moon; without sociologists, no understanding of the human costs. Though the costs are heavy, the advantages have so far been perceived as greater, but this should not be taken for granted. Modern students tend to find traditionalism repugnant and the desirability of change self-evident, but there is nothing in the least self-evident about a preference for the unseen, unknown and unknowable goods delivered by the future: it merely so happens that the goods delivered so far have proved extremely powerful. Growth is an embattled concept, and it is by no means impossible that the world will abandon it, settling down to enjoy such gains as it has made: just as many people find economic growth at the cost of environmental pollution unacceptable, so many reject scientific growth at the cost of embryological engineering or animal experiments; and the majority may conceivably reject the desirability of growth altogether one day for the sake of a more meaningful universe. If so, traditional religion of one kind or another will come back with all his implies for cognitive, social and political organization. But whether it will happen or not, it has not happened yet; and as long as cognitive and economic growth remain supreme values, neither God nor traditional morality can be allowed to shape the quest for knowledge and wealth.

This is not to say, of course, that the modern world is free of value-loaded systems of thought. Quite the contrary. But traditional value systems such as Christianity are relegated to what Muslims call the harem, that is the private quarters of a certain dwelling, where they gradually wither away for lack of anything to do. It is fashionable to argue that science cannot have caused the decline of religion in the modern West because people do not generally know or understand what science has to say; but this argument is misguided. When ever was a *religion* generally known or understood by its adherents? Science and scholarship have indeed caused religion to decline in the West, not so much because their conclusions run counter to the Bible or Christian dogma, but rather because they have made God severely under-employed: any member of modern society endowed with minimal intelligence is aware of the fact that scientists successfully explain and manipulate the natural world without reference to the will of God, while all sorts of other people explain and administer human societies with equal disregard for the theory that God accounts for the way in which they work. God may still be perceived as the ultimate reality behind it all, as indeed he often is; but his power over the observable universe matches that of Elizabeth II over England: he has been reduced to a purely ceremonial role (in so far as he has not been dethroned altogether).

His power in heaven is mostly left unchallenged (though Marxists are bent on dethroning him there too): he remains in charge of otherworldly salvation. Religion thus becomes 'purely religious', as some would put it, or in other words that it becomes a highly specialized activity as opposed to the multi-purpose phenomenon that it was in pre-industrial times; and as such it is threatened with irrelevance. It is true that privatization can intensify individual religiosity, but the individual's choice of religion becomes like his choice of shampoo: nobody cares what sort he prefers, except the manufacturers (the sale of religion being big business in USA). Whatever religion he chooses, he cannot bring it to bear on public life because schools, courts, hospitals and governmental institutions are shaped by principles of different kinds (though a few may be run by the religious community to which he belongs); he may subscribe to any belief he likes and seek any type of spiritual solace, but he has got to keep his views to himself.

An omnipotent God who rules the heavens without any real power on earth is not, however, a very persuasive force: you communicate with him on Sundays and forget him for the rest of the week, eventually forgetting him on Sundays too, because he does not provide you with rules of behaviour or shape the world in which your life is enacted. What modern priests identify as their main problem is precisely that of making religion 'relevant' again, that is bringing it to bear on the way in which life is actually lived. But a Christian who brings his Christian views on divorce, homosexuality, abortion or the like to bear on public morality in the modern West looks outmoded to most people because he is trying to introduce absolute values to a domain which has ceased to obey them; and if he sacrifices these views on the altar of progress, his Christianity disappears in all but name. Either way, traditional religion is left without a public role in the industrial world. (Communist countries are to some extent an exception in that official disbelief in religion here offers it a role as an ideology of opposition.) Science may not have killed God in the capitalist west: most people undoubtedly still believe in him, a great many scientists included. But they do not often believe in what he says, or only in a vein so metaphorical that little of the message is left; and as a blueprint for a social, political and cultural order, the message is probably beyond restoration. (If religion were to come back as a public force in western Europe, it would not necessarily be in the form of Christianity.)

As regards new ideologies and cults, on the other hand, these proliferate and flourish in so far as they take progress for granted, be it that they want to shape its course, modify its costs, slow it down, or supplement it with other values: thus liberalism, conservatism, socialism, environmentalism, anti-abortionism, anti-vivisectionism, health faddism, food faddism, and many other 'isms'. Such ideologies tend to be construed around, and remain devoted to, a single issue; all-embracing world views do indeed appear from time to time, but they remain exotic growths of purely private importance (except in so far as they generate crime) because no overarching ideology can govern a public world in which all activities must have their own rules and rationales.

Marxism, Maoism and fundamentalist Islam are apparent exceptions to this claim. All three restore religion/ideology to its pre-industrial role of underpinning entire societies, though only the third actually originated in the pre-industrial world. In fact, however, they are not exceptions because they are creeds of modernization unlikely to retain their overarching role once modernization has succeeded: being overarching creeds, they clash, not just with rival religions, but also with their own commitment to growth. Science must have diplomatic immunity from ideology if it is to remain cumulative; but in the Soviet Union of the Stalinist period ideology interfered considerably with scientific thought, several aspects of modern physics being regarded as suspect while at the same time the mistaken theories of the geneticist Lysenko were elevated to the status of dogma: had this situation persisted, Soviet science would have come to an end (in fact, genetics almost did). Economic life must however also be freed from ideological constraints if it is to progress, for though the central truth may itself be about such progress (as in the case of Marxism and Maoism), its prescriptions may not work: alternative methods will thus have to be tried out unless the commitment to growth is to be abandoned. And where both cognitive and economic activities are allowed to follow rules of their own in disregard of the overall creed, political life is apt to follow suit. Sooner or later the overarching truth is thus left as an empty shell, or as a general truth which only retains its meaning in specialized contexts. The reduction of the official creed to this position is well under way in the Soviet Union; it has started in China too; and it will presumably happen in the Muslim world as well, provided that the attempts at modernization succeed and that growth remains a worldwide ideal (neither of which, however, can be taken for gránted). All three creeds are ideologies of transition, their function being to mobilize commitment and energy for a radically different future; but the future for which they strive removes one activity after the other from their domain as they approach it.

Egalitarianism

Just as dogmas would mean the end of modern science and technology, so sacred institutions would mean the end of the society which supports them in the expectation of benefitting from their advance. Modern society must keep itself open to a constant demand for labour, talent and new skills in whatever shape or size they may come (male/female, black/white, Christian/Jewish, privileged/ working-class, able-bodied/handicapped, etc.), at the same time preparing itself for constant demolition of social arrangements in tandem with the decline of well-established occupations (printers go out as computers come in, and so on).

If the social order were to congeal into stable hierarchies and ghettos, the labour market would come to be dominated by ascription rather than talent (women, blacks, Jews, workers, aristocrats and so on being pre-ordained for certain roles by birth), while at the same time society would be too rigid to benefit from technological advance (with the result that it would stop paying for such advances, paying scientists and scholars to underpin the social hierarchy instead). In short, an economy geared to science and technology requires a fluid society with unimpeded social and geographical mobility. Society must be like a pack of cards that can be reshuffled any time, and to some extent it is.

This is why we all find egalitarian ideologies so persuasive today. Much to our regret, our ideologies do not generate egalitarian societies in practice. For one thing, even the most advanced parts of the industrial world are riddled with pre-industrial attitudes and patterns of behaviour (which may well prove too deeply rooted in nature for total eradication by culture): roles are still ascribed on the basis of sex, colour and religion; correct language and other types of behaviour still single out the gentleman from the uncouth masses; head starts conferred by heredity are difficult to eliminate because of the mixture of cultural and genetic factors involved; old-boy networks and other types of patronage are very much in evidence; and so on. For another thing, egalitarianism is probably a utopian ideal in any complex society, whatever its nature. But the inequalities of modern society are not underpinned by a great truth and consequently not stable, sharply demarcated, advertised by conspicuously different froms of dress, housing, language, lifestyle or morality, nor are they warmly endorsed by prevailing sentiment. Ideologically, we are all identical however different we may seem, not, as in pre-industrial societies, different regardless of our fundamental similarities.

What our egalitarian ideologies do succeed in doing is thus to prevent socio-political differentiation from freezing. At the same time, mobility in conjunction with a high standard of living helps to keep the egalitarian ideology alive. In short, industry dictates that we remain socially amorphous, and so in fact we do: classes are notoriously hard to define with any degree of precision. (The only modern society to have combined pre-industrial segregation with an industrial economy, South Africa, has predictably found that the one undermines the other.)

Individualism
Modern society is not just egalitarian, but also individualistic. The individual is generally seen as having a right, or indeed duty, to fulfil

himself above all other considerations; we are no longer identical with our social roles, nor do we automatically accept the rights and duties vested in them.

This is partly because industrial society reduces the number of inherited roles. Since occupational roles are not inherited or enacted at home, children cannot train for theirs from an early age by imitation of their parents. At the same time, however, institutional differentiation means that an individual may occupy very different positions at home, at work, in his church, his club and so on, adopting different moral codes and types of behaviour in each connection. Having very different and indeed incompatible roles to play, he cannot identify fully with any of them: the search for the real self begins.

In addition, modernity drastically reduces the control exercised by kinsmen and neighbours over individual behaviour. Modern states insist on dealing directly with individuals rather than collectivities, and they also take over most of the functions previously performed by self-help groups, thus depriving the latter of their leverage. The individual remains a member of a family, of course, and modern governments generally profess belief in the tenet that the family is 'the foundation of society'. But in actual fact parental control is undermined by the immense power over the national offspring vested by modern governments in educational, medical and welfare institutions on the grounds that 'the interests of the children come first', or in other words that the nation knows better than mere progenitors (a view to which social workers are particularly addicted). Possibly, the indiscriminate dissemination of information and (more importantly) values practised by television undermines parental authority too: the parental view of right and wrong is reduced to one among many. At all events, since the family is no longer a unit of production, as opposed to one of consumption and exchange of services, the economic control enjoyed by parents is also limited, and both geographical and social mobility further reduce their influence. Independent income for wives similarly reduces the control exercised by husbands. Urbanization, mobility and the disappearance of self-help groups mean that neighbours are superficial acquaintances or wholly anonymous persons incapable of exercising pressures of a significant kind. Besides, the privatization of religion means that communal agreement on the nature of right behaviour is limited, the only generally accepted criterion being that individual behaviour may not violate the law, once more defined in national terms. The search for the real self is thus conducted in considerable freedom from external control. The cost of this freedom, of course, is loneliness and a widespread sense of dissolution of identity.

It should be noted, however, that individualism has gone much further in the West (above all America) than in Japan, where group pressure is still strong and role identification more pronounced as a result. Industrialization may have an inherent tendency to promote certain developments, but the actual result clearly depends on the cultural context with which it interacts, and it is only because industrialization has so far been enacted almost entirely within a single civilization that we implicitly assume it to have much the same outcome wherever it takes place. In the long run industrial societies will doubtless prove as diverse as were their pre-industrial forebears, and extreme individualism may turn out to be a dispensable feature.

Fragmentation

All in all, progress generates a world which is fragmented rather than coherent, unstable rather than enduring, and rich in contemporary rather than historical experience. It is fragmented because countless bits of the world conflict with other bits. One and the same God or morality has ceased to preside over all. You may adhere to one set of values as politician, doctor, director or worker, another as a supporter of wildlife and nature, a third as church-goer, and a fourth as spouse and parent. The contrast between pre-modern and modern societies in this respect can easily be exaggerated: conflicting beliefs and norms were commonplace in the pre-industrial world (what else is tragedy about?); and the industrial world is less incoherent than it may seem at first sight once religion is discounted. But even so, it would be hard to deny that the lack of an overarching world view, or more precisely, the unsatisfactory nature of 'growth' in this role, increases the number of dilemmas.

Being fragmented, the industrial world is unstable. More precisely, it is kept fragmented because it *wishes* to be unstable, the expansion of cognitive, technological and economic boundaries being its aim. Rapid change means that past experience rapidly loses intelligiblity and relevance: children grow up in a world appreciably different from that in which their parents had their formative years, radically different from that of their grandparents, and totally unlike that of remoter gnerations. Communication across time is thus impeded. (This is known as the generation gap in so far as communication between parents and children are concerned, but in fact it is an entire culture gap.) But the mass media greatly intensify communication over space. The present is extremely rich in human experience, but it does not lock in with either past or future, the former being irrelevant and the latter unknown. Far from being anchored in a tradition, the modern individual is liable to drift: he has to decide for himself who he is and where he is going. All this is what defenders of traditional societies have in mind when they dwell on the 'moral bankruptcy' of the West.

Bankrupt or creditworthy, the industrial West is the world in which most readers of this book will have grown up. How they should evaluate it is a moral, not a scholarly question: just as science cannot tell you whether or not to forsake tobacco, only the effects of its use, so scholarship cannot tell you whether or not to accept modernity, only the manner in which it works. What matters here is simply the trivial point that it works quite differently from its pre-industrial predecessors. Everyone is aware of this as an abstract proposition, but few can spell it out in concrete terms. The student who has acquired a concrete sense of the differences has learnt all there is to be learnt from this book.

Further Reading

In principle any work on pre-modern history is relevant to this book, but it goes without saying that I cannot produce anything remotely resembling a comprehensive list of what is available; without footnotes I cannot even list what I have used myself. The following works, mostly equipped with further references, should however enable the reader to find his way into all the topics discussed, and many others beside.

Altekar, A. S., *State and Government in Ancient India*, Benares 1949 and subsequent reprints. Cf. Basham, Heestermann, Hocart, Mabbett, Myers.

Anderson, P., *Passages from Antiquity to Feudalism* and *Lineages of the Absolutist State*, London 1974. Powerful analysis of European history by a Marxist. Cf. Mann.

Andreski, S., *Military Organization and Society*, 2nd edn, London 1968.

Ariès, P., *Centuries of Childhood*, London 1973 (French original 1960). A seminal work on the supposedly late arrival in Europe of the concept of childhood and close ties between parents and children; current work goes against it, cf. Herlihy, Pollock (on Europe); Garnsey and Saller (on the Roman world); and forthcoming work by A. Giladi on the Islamic world.

Baechler, J., and J. A. Hall and M. Mann (eds), *Europe and the Rise of Capitalism*, Oxford 1988. Has papers on India, China, Japan and the Islamic world as well as Europe. Cf. Hall, Jones.

Basham, A. L., *The Wonder that Was India. A Survey of the History and Culture of the Indian Sub-continent before the Coming of the Muslims*, London 1954; paperback 1971. A scholarly work, the title notwithstanding. Cf. Altekar, Heestermann.

Bendix, R., *Kings or People. Power and the Mandate to Rule*, Berkeley, Los Angeles and London 1978.

Benn, S. I., and G. F. Gaus (eds), *Public and Private in Social Life*, London and New York 1983.

Berger, P. L., *Facing up to Modernity*, Harmondsworth 1979; id. and B. Berger and H. Kellner, *The Homeless Mind*, Harmondsworth 1974. Cf. Kumar.

—— *The Social Reality of Religion*, London 1969, and (paperback) Harmondsworth 1973; id. and T. Luckmann, *The Social Construction of Reality. A Treatise in the Sociology of Knowledge*, Harmondsworth 1966. Both very readable. Cf. Durkheim, Robertson.

Brown, P., 'The Rise and Function of the Holy Man in Late Antiquity', *Journal of Roman Studies* 1971. On live saints in a complex society. Cf. Gellner.

—— *The Cult of the Saints. Its Rise and Function in Latin Christianity*, Chicago and London 1981. On dead saints.

Cipolla, C. M., *Before the Industrial Revolution. European Society and Economy, 1000–1700*, 2nd edn, London 1976. A classic account by an economic historian, of general interest even though it only deals with Europe.

—— *Public Health and the Medical Profession in the Renaissance*, Cambridge 1976. Brief, highly readable and a good example of intensive power.

—— *Literacy and Development in the West*, Harmondsworth 1969. Cf. Goody, Graff, Rawski.

Claessen, H. J. M., and P. Skalník (eds), *The Early State*, The Hague, Paris and New York 1978. Useful collection of papers on the emergence of states in the most diverse parts of the world.

Cohn, N., *The Pursuit of the Millennium*, London 1957, and (paperback) 1970 and subsequent reprints. Classic account of millenarian movements in Europe, with some attention to Nietzschean supermen too. Cf. Lanternari, Naquin, Worsley.

Davies, N., *The Ancient Kingdoms of Mexico*, Harmondsworth 1982. Cf. Claessen (for the Incas), Hammond.

Durkheim, E., *The Elementary Forms of Religious Life*, London 1976 (French original 1912). One of the classics in the sociology of religion. Cf. Berger, Robertson.

Elvin, M., *The Pattern of the Chinese Past*, London 1973. Cf. also C. Blunden and M. Elvin, *Cultural Atlas of China*, Oxford 1983, a popular and beautifully illustrated introduction to all aspects of Chinese history.

Evers, H.-D. (ed.), *Loosely Structured Social Systems: Thailand in Comparative Perspective*, New Haven 1969. In fact Thailand is only compared with Thailand in this book, but cf. E. Todd, *The Explanation of Ideology. Family Structures and Social Systems*, Oxford 1985, and *The Causes of Progress. Culture, Authority and Change*, Oxford 1987, for a comparative discussion of a somewhat dogmatic kind. Cf. also Macfarlane.

Finley, M. I. *The Ancient Economy*, London 1973, and other works on Greek antiquity by the same author, including his article 'Slavery' in the *International Encyclopaedia of Social Sciences*. Cf. Garnsey, Reid, Wiedemann.

Garnsey, P., and R. Saller, *The Roman Empire. Economy, Society and Culture*, London 1987. A lucid presentation at introductory level.

Gellner, E., *Nations and Nationalism*, Oxford 1983. Highly stimulating. Cf. Kumar.

—— *Plough, Sword and Book. The Structure of Human History*, London 1988. Illuminating analysis which unfortunately appeared too late for me to take much account of it. Not for beginners.

—— *Saints of the Atlas*, London 1969. On holy men in a tribal context; compare Brown on such saints in a complex setting.

—— 'The Savage and the Modern Mind' in R. Horton and R. Finnegan (eds), *Modes of Thought. Essays on Thinking in Western and non-Western Societies*, London 1973; cf. also id., *The Legitimation of Belief*, Cambridge 1974. I have learnt much from these and other works by the same author.

Goode, W. J., *The Family*, 2nd edn, Englewood Cliffs, N. J., 1982. A brief survey of family structures all over the world. Cf. Ariès, Evers, Goody, Herlihy, Laslett, Macfarlane, Mitterauer.

Goody, J., *The Development of the Family and Marriage in Europe*, Cambridge 1983 (on the role of the church). Cf. Herlihy, who disagrees.

—— (ed.), *Literacy in Traditional Societies*, Cambridge 1968; cf. id., *The Domestication of the Savage Mind*, Cambridge 1977. Cf. Cipolla, Graff, Rawski.

Graff, H. J., *Literacy and Social Development in the West: a Reader*, Cambridge 1981. Cf. Cipolla, Goody, Rawski.

Griffeth, R., and G. G. Thomas. *The City-State in Five Cultures*, Santa Barbara and Oxford 1981. The examples dealt with are Sumerian, Greek, Italian, Swiss and German and Hausa.

Grousset, R., *The Empire of the Steppes*, New Brunswick 1970 (French original 1948). The classic, though by now somewhat dated work on the nomadic conquerors from Central Asia.

Hall, J. A., *Powers and Liberties. The Causes and Consequences of the Rise of the West*, Oxford 1985, and (paperback) Harmondsworth 1986. A comparison of Chinese, Indian, Islamic and European civilisation by a sociologist; I owe the term 'capstone government' and other thoughts about the state to this work. Cf. Baechler, Jones, Mann.

Hammond, N., *Ancient Maya Civilization*, Cambridge 1982. Cf. Claessen (for the Incas), Davies.

Heestermann, J. C., *The Inner Conflict of Tradition. Essays in Indian Ritual, Kingship, and Society*, Chicago and London 1985. Cf. Altekar, Basham, Hocart, Mabbett, Myers.

Herlihy, D., *Medieval Households*, Cambridge Mass. and London 1985. Cf. Ariès, Goody, Laslett, Macfarlane, Mitterauer.

Hobsbawm, E. J., *Primitive Rebels*, Manchester 1959, and id., *Bandits*, Harmondsworth 1972. Two highly readable and illuminating accounts of rural forms of protest (including the Robin Hood phenomenon). Cf. Naquin, Shanin, Wolf.

Hocart, A. M., *Kings and Councillors. An Essay in the Comparative Anatomy of Human Society*, ed. R. Needham, Chicago and London 1970 (French original 1930). Interesting work by an anthropologist. Cf. Altekar, Heestermann, Mabbett, Myers.

Hodges, R., *Primitive and Peasant Markets*, Oxford 1988. Cf. Shanin, Weber, Wolf.

Hodgson, M. G. S., *The Venture of Islam*, Chicago 1974.

Hollingsworth, T. H., *Historical Demography*, Cambridge 1969. Cf. MacEvedy.

International Encyclopaedia of Social Sciences, New York and London 1968. A good place to start whenever one encounters concepts in need of definition, analysis or illustration.

Jones, E. L., *The European Miracle. Environments, Economies and Geopolitics in the History of Europe and Asia*, Cambridge 1981. Stimulating analysis of Europe in comparative perspective. Cf. Baechler, Hall.

Kautsky, J. H., *The Politics of Aristocratic Empires*, Chapel Hill 1982. Crude and open to a host of objections, but successfully imparts some fundamental points. Cf. also id., *Political Change in Underdeveloped Countries*, New York 1962; id., *The Political Consequences of Modernization*, New York 1972.

Kumar, K., *Prophecy and Progress. The Sociology of Industrial and Post-Industrial Society*, Harmondsworth 1978. A helpful introduction. Cf. Berger, Gellner.

Lanternari, V., *The Religions of the Oppressed*, London 1963. Helpful survey of nativist movements all over the world, though mostly in recent times; for interpretation, see Worsley.

Laslett, P., and R. Wall, *Household and Family in Past Times*, Cambridge 1972. Mainly concerned with Europe. Cf. Goode, Goody, Herlihy, Mitterauer.

Lewis, I. M., *Ecstatic Religion*, Harmondsworth 1971. Concerned with primitive societies, but illuminating for complex ones as well.

Mabbett, I. W. (ed.), *Pattern of Kingship and Authority in Traditional Asia*, London, Sydney and Dover 1985. Cf. Altekar, Heesterman, Hocart, Myers.

Macfarlane, A., *The Origins of English Individualism. The Family, Property and Social Transition*, Oxford 1978; cf. id., *Marriage and Love in England 1300–1840*, London 1986; id., *The Culture of Capitalism*, Oxford 1987 (a collection of articles on the same subjects). Lucid and stimulating, though somewhat one-sided and highly controversial too. For the comparable 'loose structure' of South-East Asia, see Evett above. Cf. also Goode, Goody, Herlihy, Mitterauer.

Mann, M., 'States, Ancient and Modern', *Archieves Européenne de Sociologie* 1977; id., *The Sources of Social Power. A History of Power from the beginning to A.D. 1760*, vols. i–, Cambridge 1986– (in progress; concentrates on antiquity and Europe); id., *States, War and Capitalism. Studies in Political Sociology*, Oxford 1988. I am indebted to Mann's work in numerous ways. Cf. Anderson, Baechler.

Marx, K., *Pre-capitalist Economic Formations*, ed. E. J. Hobsbawm, London 1964, and other works by the same author. In addition to being the progenitor of Marxism, Marx is one of the founding fathers of sociology, but he does not make easy reading. Cf. M. Weber.

McEvedy, C., and R. Jones, *Atlas of World Population History*, Harmondsworth 1978. Cf. Hollingsworth.

McNeill, W. H., *A World History*, Oxford 1967, and numerous other works by the same author.

Mitterauer, M., and R. Sieder, *The European Family*, Oxford 1982. Cf. Ariès, Goode, Goody, Herlihy, Macfarlane.

Mousnier, R., *Peasant Uprisings in Seventeenth Century France, Russia and China*, London 1971 (French original 1967). Cf. Hobsbawm, Naquin.

—— *Social Hierarchies, 1450 to the Present*, London 1973 (French original 1969); But cf. A. Arriaza, 'Mousnier, Barber and the "Society of Orders". *Past and Present* 1980.

Myers, H. A., *Medieval Kingship*, Chicage 1982. Cf. Altekar, Heestermann, Hocart, Mabbett.

Naquin, S., *Millenarian Rebellion in China. The Eight Trigrams Uprising of 1813*, New Haven and London 1976; cf. ead., *Shantung Rebellion. The Wang Lun Uprising of 1774*, New Haven and London 1981. Splendid accounts of millenarian movements in rural China. Cf. Cohn, Elvin, Hobsbawm, Mousnier, Worsley.

Parkin, F., *Class Inequality and Political Order*, London 1972.

Poggi, G., *The Development of the Modern State*, London 1978. Cf. Strayer.

Pollock, L. A., *Forgotten Children. Parent-Child Relations from 1500–1900*, Cambridge 1983. A good antidote to Ariès (above) and his followers, with a helpful survey of the literature generated by his work.

Powis, J., *Aristocracy*, Oxford and New York 1974. Limited to the European variety, but helpful and stimulating. (I have not however adopted his distinction between aristocracy and nobility.)

Rawski, E. S., *Education and Popular Literacy in Ch'ing China*, Ann Arbor, Michigan, 1979. Interesting study which includes a comparison of literacy in China, Europe and Japan. Cf. Cipolla, Graff, Goody.

Reid, A., and J. Brewster (eds), *Slavery, Bondage and Dependency in Southeast Asia*, New York 1983. Cf. Finley, Wiedemann.

Reischauer, E. O., and J. K. Fairbank, *A History of East Asian Civilization*, London n.d. and Cambridge, Mass., 1960–65.

Robertson, R. (ed.), *Sociology of Religion. Selected Readings*, Harmondsworth 1969. Cf. Berger, Durkheim.

Shanin, T., (ed.), *Peasants and Peasant Societies. Selected Readings*, 2nd edn, Oxford 1987. Cf. Hobsbawm, Hodges, Wolf, E. Weber.

Sjoberg, G., *The Preindustrial City*, Glencoe, Illinois, 1960. A useful introduction to pre-industrial society in general (from chapter 4 onwards), not just the urban variety, though the reader may jib at his use of the term 'feudal' to mean 'pre-industrial of the civilized kind'.

Strayer, J. R., *On the Medieval Origins of the Modern State,*, Princeton 1970. Short and illuminating. Cf. Poggi.

Ullmann, W., *The Individual and Society in the Middle Ages*, Baltimore and London 1967. Actually about the individual and the state.

Weber, E., *Peasants into Frenchmen. The Modernization of Rural France, 1876–1914*, London 1977. Vivid account of nineteenth-century rural autarky. Cf. Hobsbawm, Hodges, Shanin, Wolf.

Weber, M., *Economy and Society*, tr. G. Roth and C. Wittich, New York 1968 (German original 1922), and other works by the same author, one of the founding fathers of sociology. He is not particularly readable, and most of his insights have passed into the secondary literature by now; but some still find him an inexhaustible source of inspiration.

Wesson, R. G., *The Imperial Order*, Berkeley and Los Angeles 1967; cf. id., *State Systems*, New York and London 1978. Makes much the same point about imperial government as Hall (above), but at greater (indeed inordinate) length.

White, L., Jr., *Medieval Technology and Social Change*, Oxford 1962; cf. id., 'What Accelerated Technological Progress in the Western Middle Ages?' in A. C. Crombie (ed.), *Scientific Change*, London 1963.

Wiedemann, T. E. J., *Slavery* (Greece and Rome: New Surveys in the Classics, no. 19), Oxford 1987. Helpful survey with further references. Cf. Finley, Reid.

Wolf, E. R., *Peasants*, Englewood Cliffs 1966 and subsequent reprints. A useful little book on peasants wherever and whenever they are found. Cf. Hobsbawm, Hodges, Shanin, E. Weber.

Worsley, P. M., *The Trumpet Shall Sound. A Study of 'Cargo' Cults in Melanesia*, London 1968. The last chapter offers a lucid analysis of millenarian movements, both nativist and otherwise. Cf. Cohn, Lanternari, Naquin.

Index